Sunset

Oregon

TRAVEL GUIDE

By the Editors of Sunset Books
and Sunset Magazine

Lane Publishing Co. ■ Menlo Park, California

Incoming breaker leaps high as it fans out on cliffs at Cape Kiwanda.

Edited by Cornelia Fogle

Photo Editor: **Barbara J. Braasch**

Design: **Steve Renick**

Maps: **Vernon Koski**

Illustrations: **Susan Jaekel**

Cover: Low tide and morning sun lure beachcombers to Bandon's broad sands and tidepools south of Coquille Point. Photograph by Jeff Gnass.

Thanks...

to the many Oregonians who generously shared their information and suggestions during the preparation of this book. Nearly 200 individuals and officials contributed to or reviewed portions of the manuscript. They represent various state, federal, and county agencies; city and regional chambers of commerce; and private organizations. We especially wish to acknowledge the continuing assistance of Frank Howard, Information Services Manager of the Tourism Division, Oregon Economic Development Department.

We hope Oregonians and visitors alike will discover interesting new facets as they set out to explore Oregon.

Sunset Books
    Editor: David E. Clark
    Managing Editor: Elizabeth L. Hogan

First printing May 1987

CONTENTS

SAVORING OREGON'S SPLENDORS

Enjoy an array of recreational pursuits in this scenic land

Dense green forests, snow-capped mountains, unspoiled ocean beaches, wheat-covered prairies, wilderness lakes and rivers, awesome desertlike plateaus—nature passed out scenery with a lavish hand in Oregon. Few states can match Oregon's natural splendor or recreational spectrum.

Two broad interstate freeways cross the state. The primary north-south route is Interstate Highway 5, a ribbon of concrete stretching from the Columbia River south through the Willamette, Umpqua, and Rogue valleys to the California border. Interstate Highway 84 follows the Columbia east from Portland, approximating the route of the Oregon Trail to Ontario, gateway to Idaho.

U.S. Highway 101 parallels Oregon's scenic coast. East of the Cascades, the main north-south routes are U.S. Highway 197-97 (The Dalles-California Highway) and U.S. Highway 395, which travels from Hermiston across central Oregon to Lakeview and into California. Other major east-west routes crossing the state are U.S. Highway 26, linking Astoria and Vale; U.S. Highway 20, crossing the center of the state eastward from Newport; and the Winnemucca to the Sea Highway, joining the main southern Oregon towns.

What Makes Oregon Special?

Bordered on the west by the Pacific Ocean, Oregon boasts a dramatic 400-mile coastline. The great artery of the Pacific Northwest—the Columbia River—flows for some 300 miles along the state's northern border adjoining Washington. To the east lies Idaho, partially separated from Oregon by mile-deep Hells Canyon, carved over eons by the waters of the Snake River. California and Nevada butt the state's southern border.

Oregon's backbone is a majestic string of snow-capped dormant volcanoes—the Cascade Range—dividing the state into two distinct regions. Most of the state's population lives on the moist, heavily forested western side of the Cascades. East of the mountains, a broad, high plateau stretches eastward to the Blue Mountains and the lonely land of the Great Basin.

Fed by numerous tributary streams draining the coastal and Cascade mountains, the Willamette River meanders through the broad, fertile Willamette Valley. Major southern Oregon waterways are the Rogue and Umpqua, both emptying into the Pacific. East of the Cascades, the Deschutes and John Day rivers drain vast areas of the state, carving deep canyons on their northward course to the mighty Columbia.

Sightseeing highlights

A broad array of intriguing destinations entice Oregon residents and visitors.

Focus of the Willamette Valley is Portland, center of urban activity. Other busy valley towns are Salem, the state capital, and the university towns of Eugene and Corvallis. Along the Columbia, visitors thrill to the many waterfalls of the Columbia Gorge and the massive impoundments behind Bonneville, The Dalles, John Day, and McNary dams.

Dozens of state parks and recreation areas border the coast. Four favorite stops are Fort Clatsop National Mememorial, Mark O. Hatfield Marine Science Center, Cape Perpetua Visitor Center, and Oregon Dunes National Recreation Area.

In southern Oregon, you'll want to tour the Oregon Caves and historic Jacksonville, attend Ashland's Shakespearean Festival, and perhaps experience a boat trip on the Rogue.

Nearly every Oregonian cherishes a favorite little-known lake or trail in the Cascades, but most visitors head for Mount Hood's Timberline Lodge, the Cascade lakes district west of Bend, or Crater Lake National Park. East of the crest, the fascinating world of volcanoes awaits at Lava Lands Visitor Center. Learn about Oregon's fossil country at John Day Fossil Beds National Monument.

Near the state's eastern border, look for remnants of the Oregon Trail, the alpine wilderness of the Wallowa Mountains, old mining towns, the surprising beauty of Steens Mountain, and the impressive canyons of the Snake and Owyhee rivers.

Varied climates & changing seasons

In Oregon you can have it wet and green or high and dry. The folklore about the rain isn't *all* true.

A patchwork of green trees and lush farm lands blankets land west of the Cascades. Rain clouds drop their moisture as they nudge against the coastal and Cascade mountain ranges. Most of the rain falls during the mild winter, from November through early April. Gentle "Oregon mist" soaks the Willamette Valley, but downpours drench the western slopes of the coastal mountains.

East of the Cascades, you experience greater extremes in temperature. Westerly air masses lose most of their moisture over the mountains, so central and eastern Oregon have less rain, more snow, and abundant sunshine. Temperatures are colder in winter and warmer in summer.

Oregon's northern latitude and 11,000-foot variation in elevation—from sea level to Cascade peaks—trigger a progression of delightful seasons. When spring or autumn arrives in Oregon, you know it!

Informal living & a relaxed pace

To most Oregonians and many visitors, Oregon is a special place. But why?

Oregonians live close to their land. Forests and farm lands, the sea, mountains, and desert are never too far away to enrich the spirit. Informal living and a relaxed pace prevail, even in the main urban areas.

Residents take pride in the past—you'll note historical markers along pioneer routes, covered bridges preserved by community effort, century-old houses and churches still in use, and excellent historic museums throughout the state.

Cities are of manageable size: the state's largest city is Portland, with a population of 370,000, followed by Eugene (104,000) and Salem (91,000). Only three additional towns—Corvallis, Medford, and Springfield—top 40,000 in population. Approximately 2.7 million people now live in Oregon, about two-thirds of them in the Willamette Valley.

Cities and towns thrive on a "do it ourselves" spirit, as residents enthusiastically support community cultural organizations and other local activities.

Enjoying Yourself in Oregon

Few states can equal Oregon for scenic attractions and its corresponding recreation opportunities. Follow your interests—whether rockhounding or birdwatching, cycling or beachcombing, Indian culture or fossils and geology, marine biology or covered bridges, Oregon wines or Northwest art and crafts—in Oregon's cities, mountains, desert, or ocean shore. If you prefer, you can relax at a resort or guest ranch, explore back roads, or attend a rodeo or festive local celebration.

Hospitality at resorts, motels, guest ranches

Accommodations and food add to the fun of exploring Oregon. In addition to an excellent range of hotels and motels, travelers discover luxurious coastal and mountain resorts, fishing retreats and a vintage ski lodge, rural inns and guest ranches.

You can rough it in a rustic private cabin, savor bed-and-breakfast hospitality, or enjoy the comfort and convenience of a fine resort complex. For a western-style vacation, stay at one of a half-dozen guest ranches. Or arrange a guided fishing or hunting trip, a white-water river excursion, or a pack trip into a mountain wilderness.

For a copy of *Oregon Traveler's Guide to Accommodations*, contact the state's Tourism Division (see page 9 for address and toll-free phone numbers); or write to the Oregon Lodging Association, 12724 S.E. Stark Street, Portland, OR 97233. Accommodation information is also available from travel and automobile touring clubs and from local tourist offices.

In restaurants you'll sample Oregon's bounty—freshly caught salmon, Dungeness crab, and trout; clams from coastal bays and beaches; locally-grown fruits and vegetables; Oregon-made cheeses and wines. Dining guides available in Oregon bookstores list many fine restaurants, and travelers can inquire to discover other local favorites.

State parks & recreation areas

Oregon's unparalleled system of state parks, roadside rest areas, and scenic waysides serve travelers well.

State parks are usually open for day use throughout the year, weather permitting; the camping season extends from mid-April to late October. Ten state parks remain open for camping the year around: Fort Stevens, Cape Lookout, Beverly Beach, Jessie M. Honeyman Memorial, Bullards Beach, and Harris Beach, all on the Oregon coast; Champoeg, in the Willamette Valley; Valley of the Rogue, in Southern Oregon; Hilgard Junction and Farewell Bend, along I-84 in northeastern Oregon.

Campsites at many state parks are available on a first-come, first-served basis, but 13 of the large, popular parks operate on a reservation system from Memorial Day weekend through Labor Day. Campsite reservation applications should be sent directly to the park concerned. Unreserved sites are available to the traveling public.

For a guide to state parks and information on campsite reservations, fees, and regulations, contact the state tourism office (see page 9) or Oregon State Parks, 525 Trade Street S.E., Salem, OR 97310; telephone (503) 378-6305.

A Campsite Information Center operates from the first Monday in March to Labor Day weekend. Staff members are on duty weekdays from 8 to 4:30 to provide current information on state park campsite availability and other recreation activities. No reservations can be made through the Center, but cancellations are accepted. To make toll-free calls within Oregon, phone 1-800-452-5687; Portland and out-of-state residents should call (503) 238-7488.

Forests & wilderness areas

Oregon's 13 national forests offer almost unlimited chances to enjoy the outdoors. Forest roads wind through the trees to wooded campgrounds, fishing streams, tree-rimmed lakes, lava flows, and other attractions. Trails lead hikers and horseback riders to remote lakes and waterfalls in mountain wilderness areas.

In 1984, new legislation created more than 20 new wilderness preserves in Oregon's national forests and amended the boundaries of many existing areas. Largest of the new preserves are Mount Thielsen Wilderness and Sky Lakes Wilderness in the Cascade mountains, and North Fork John Day Wilderness in Umatilla National Forest.

For general information on recreational opportunities in Oregon's national forests, write to the U.S. Forest Service, P.O. Box 3623, 319 S.W. Pine Street, Portland, OR 97208; telephone (503) 221-2877. Maps of each national forest and many wilderness and recreation areas can be obtained by mail or in person for $1 per map.

Recreational information on BLM lands is available from the Bureau of Land Management, P.O. Box 2965, Portland, OR 97208; telephone (503) 231-6273.

For information on recreational use of state forest lands, write or telephone the Oregon Department of Forestry, 2600 State Street, Salem, OR 97310; telephone (503) 378-2567.

Hiking & cycling along scenic routes

Hikers and cyclists enjoy a feast of scenic routes in all parts of Oregon. A statewide system of hiking, biking, and riding trails is being developed cooperatively by state agencies and citizen groups.

Marked trails wend through state parks and national forests, across other public lands, along rivers and ocean, through the high mountains, and across the desert. Trail guides are available for some routes; check with the appropriate Federal or state agencies for additional information.

Major hiking trails. Most challenging of the lengthy routes is the Pacific Crest National Scenic Trail (see page 82); it winds through high peaks and forests from Canada to the Mexico border. More than 400 miles of the 2,400-mile alpine route traverse Oregon's Cascade Range.

Encircling Mount Hood is the Timberline Trail (see page 87), a 37½-mile path around Oregon's highest peak.

Spectacular coastal panoramas await hikers on the Oregon Coast Trail (see page 45). When completed it will stretch nearly 350 miles from the Columbia River south to the California border.

Two long hiking trails follow sections of the Rogue River as it flows across Oregon's southwestern corner. Northwest of Grants Pass, the 40-mile Rogue River Trail (see page 76) follows the river from Grave Creek Bridge downstream to Illahe through the Federally designated Wild section of the Rogue.

The 69-mile route along the upper Rogue (see page 77) links Lost Creek Reservoir and the Pacific Crest Trail north of Crater Lake National Park.

A 27-mile footpath, beginning east of McKenzie Bridge, follows the upper McKenzie River (see page 89). It traverses part of the Cascade lava beds, skirts a pair of scenic waterfalls and Clear Lake, and ends south of Fish Lake near U.S. Highway 20.

Rugged backpackers gain a special perspective of Hells Canyon on a trail winding high above the river's churning waters (see page 113).

A 150-mile desert hiking route has been mapped across the state's southeastern corner (see page 124). Part of a proposed national desert hiking trail, it cuts north from Denio, Nevada, across Steens Mountain, and down the Blitzen Valley.

Cycling routes. Bikeway development receives strong public support in Oregon, where cyclists enjoy a network of pleasant routes—along Willamette Valley back roads, through state parks, and on long-distance routes. For more on cycling, see page 61.

Fishing & hunting

Trout fishing and seasonal runs of salmon and steelhead attract the most attention, but dedicated anglers can fish at any time of year somewhere in Oregon waters. Coastal harbors offer deep-sea fishing for salmon, and clam, crab, and mussel hunting along the shore.

Anglers, resident and nonresident alike, need to purchase fishing licenses; season, 10-day nonresident, or 1-day licenses are available. Salmon and steelhead anglers need tags for their catch.

Hunters in Oregon try for blacktail deer and Roosevelt elk west of the Cascades, mule deer and Rocky Mountain elk east of the mountains. Other hunters seek upland game birds or migratory waterfowl. Hunting licenses are

Snow-etched Wallowa Mountains loom abruptly above wheat ranch near Joseph in eastern Oregon.

Framed by greenery, Multnomah Falls plummets 620 feet in a pair of lovely waterfalls. Hikers cross footbridge to view lower falls.

Early-rising salmon anglers get first glimpse of sun peeking over coastal mountains at Tillamook Bay.

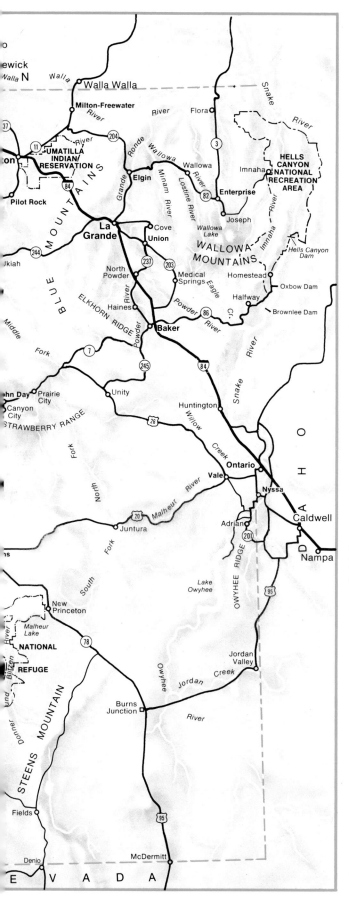

required for nongame as well as game animals and birds. Tags are necessary for big game.

Current information on fishing and game regulations, licenses, and tag fees is available at Oregon sporting goods stores or from the Oregon Department of Fish and Wildlife, 506 S.W. Mill, Portland, OR 97201; telephone (503) 229-5403.

For a free directory of licensed guides operating fishing and hunting trips, river runs, and pack trips, write to Oregon Guides and Packers Association, P.O. Box 3797, Portland, OR 97208; telephone (503) 234-2173.

Boating on Oregon's waterways

If you enjoy life on the water, Oregon offers plenty of lures. You can cruise along the Willamette or Columbia, challenge white-water rivers in a rubber raft or high-sided drift boat, sail or water-ski on broad lakes and reservoirs, or paddle your canoe or kayak down a placid stream or across a wilderness lake.

Portions of nine rivers—the Rogue, Illinois, Sandy, Clackamas, Deschutes, John Day, Minam, Owyhee, and North Fork of the Middle Fork of the Willamette—and Waldo Lake are state-designated scenic waterways.

Small boats can safely navigate many Oregon waterways; river runoff information is available from the River Service of the National Weather Service in Portland, telephone (503) 249-0666.

Commercial operators and Oregon river guides conduct white-water excursions through several challenging river canyons. White-water guides are listed in the Oregon Guides and Packers directory (see above). For information on Rogue River excursions, write to Rogue River Guide Association, P.O. Box 792, Medford, OR 97501. Other operators advertise in outdoor publications.

For information on boating facilities and laws, write to the Oregon State Marine Board, 3000 Market Street N.E., Suite 505, Salem, OR 97310; phone (503) 378-8587. To learn more about recreational facilities on reservoir lakes, contact the U.S. Army Corps of Engineers, Box 2946, Portland, OR 97208; phone (503) 221-6021.

For more information

Travelers will find a network of visitor information centers throughout the state; large blue and white signs direct you to sources of local information. State welcome centers are open April through October at border points on main highways leading into the state—at Portland and south of Ashland on I-5, at Astoria, Seaside, and Brookings on U.S. 101, south of Klamath Falls on U.S. 97, at Umatilla on State 730, and at Ontario on I-84.

For general information on Oregon's attractions and activities, write to the state's Tourism Division, 595 Cottage Street N.E., Salem, OR 97310; or you can phone toll free 1-800-547-7842 (national) or 1-800-233-3306 (inside Oregon) weekdays from 8 to 5.

Along highways I-5, I-84, U.S. 101, and U.S. 97, travelers can stop at unstaffed Travel InfoCenters for information on nearby scenic and recreational attractions and travel-related services. At these gazebos, special telephones enable travelers to make free calls for local reservations, emergency service, or other visitor assistance.

City's dramatic skyline towers above RiverPlace complex and Tom McCall Waterfront Park along the Willamette River south of Hawthorne Bridge. Marina is only public moorage in downtown Portland.

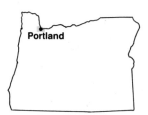

PORTLAND, THE RIVER CITY

Parks and flowers highlight an attractive and busy port

Portland, one of the West's most attractive cities, lies at the confluence of Oregon's two major rivers—the Columbia and the Willamette. Known as the City of Roses, it glows with flowers in spring and summer as rhododendrons, azaleas, and roses burst into bloom. Dozens of parks stud the city with greenery.

The fertile Willamette Valley was the goal of most pioneers who wended their way westward on the Oregon Trail. In the winter of 1844–45, two New England emigrants—A. J. Lovejoy of Boston and Francis Pettygrove of Portland, Maine—laid out a 16-block town site on the west bank of the Willamette and tossed a coin to see which one would name the new town. Pettygrove won. Commerce flourished in the settlement, spurred by the discovery of gold—in California and, later, in Oregon—and the development of steamboat transportation on the rivers.

Today Portland is one of the busiest ports on the West Coast. It is not only the gateway to the vast Columbia River Basin, but also one of the important centers for trade with Pacific Rim nations.

First Impressions

Described by one writer as "the biggest small town in the West," Portland is a medium-size metropolis of about 370,000 people, hub of a metropolitan area of more than 1,325,000 population. Spectacular towers are changing the city's skyline, yet many splendid 19th century structures are being preserved and restored. Portland is a friendly, progressive city, of manageable size.

Dominating the city are its rivers and its greenery.

Visitors find themselves constantly crossing the Willamette on one of the 10 highway bridges that span the busy river. A forested greenbelt of parks covers the city's western hills. Mature trees add a gracious note to downtown parks, and landscaped plazas dot the business district. Greenery and blooming plants also thrive in neighborhood parks and home gardens.

Portland's site at the mouth of the Willamette Valley, sheltered on west and east by the Coast and Cascade mountain ranges, enjoys a mild climate seldom disturbed by extreme temperatures. Though Portland lies at the same latitude as Minneapolis, its climate is warmed by the Japan Current flowing south off the Oregon coast.

Sliced by its river

Though snow-capped Mount Hood is often visible from the city's higher points, Portland is oriented to the Willamette River, a watery life line dividing the city.

The west bank is old Portland, containing the downtown business district, the principal parks, and perhaps a fifth of Portland's residential area. Its hilly terrain offers marvelous views of river and mountains.

Most Portlanders sleep east of the river. Generally the east bank area is level, but it does include a pair of lofty parks (Rocky Butte and Mount Tabor). Here, too, are Portland International Airport, Memorial Coliseum, and several large shopping centers.

City residents enjoy easy access to the Willamette at Tom McCall Waterfront Park downtown and at many other city parks along the river. Commercial developments such as RiverPlace and John's Landing offer additional ways to utilize the riverfront.

Brightened by parks & gardens

Portland is renowned for its parks and greenery; some 160 civic gardens provide welcome open space for city dwellers. Rhododendrons and azaleas brighten parks and home gardens in spring, and extensive rose plantings bloom from late spring to early autumn. Downtown, park blocks and landscaped plazas adorn the business district. Numerous preserves border the Willamette River. In the residential areas, neighborhood parks offer walkways and benches for adults and playgrounds for children.

Along the west-side hills, a chain of parks provides a forested band extending for 9 miles. Much of the land remains undeveloped—a thick virgin forest only a few minutes from the city center. At one end of this vast urban green belt is busy Washington Park, hub of the city's outdoor activities; at the other is untamed Forest Park, laced with hiking trails.

An event-filled summer park program features outdoor plays and concerts, nature studies, sports events, art and craft classes, and special events.

Highways radiate from the city

Major highways skirt Portland's central district and fan out in all directions (see map on page 13). Interstate Highway 5—Oregon's main north-south highway—links the city with the Willamette Valley and southern Oregon. Interstate Highway 84 cuts eastward through the Columbia River Gorge and across northeastern Oregon, paralleling the overland route of the Oregon Trail.

Other highways lead west to the coast, east to Mount Hood and other Cascade peaks, and south to prosperous Willamette Valley towns.

Finding Your Way Around

Portland is divided into five districts, cut by three arteries—the Willamette River, Burnside Street, and N. Williams Avenue (see map insert on page 13).

For suggestions on city sightseeing, scenic drives, tours, and regional attractions, stop at the Visitor Information Center at 26 S.W. Salmon Street, across from Tom McCall Waterfront Park.

If you're exploring the city using public transit, you can travel around by Tri-Met bus or light rail, or by taxi. Sightseeing bus tours include most of Portland's best-known attractions.

Exploring by public transit

Most Portland destinations and nearby suburban communities can be reached by Tri-Met, the region's public transit network. Tri-Met operates more than 70 lines serving Multnomah, Washington, and Clackamas counties, and Vancouver, Washington. The newest addition to Tri-Met service is the Metropolitan Area Express (MAX), a light rail line linking downtown Portland with the town of Gresham 15 miles to the east.

Buses arrive and depart from the handsome downtown Portland Mall on S.W. 5th and 6th avenues. MAX crosses the Portland Mall on S.W. Morrison and Yamhill streets, tying the retail and business core to the historic Old Town/Chinatown districts.

Tri-Met passengers may ride free on buses and MAX within a 340-square-block area called Fareless Square, bounded on the north by N.W. Hoyt Street, on the east by the Willamette River, and on the west and south by Interstate Highway 405. For more information on sightseeing by Tri-Met, see page 17.

Scenic drives offer city view points

From the wooded west-side hills, you can see the city laid out below—the sparkling river and its bridges, downtown skyscrapers, and the residential districts sprawling to the east and south.

Take S.W. Vista Avenue south of Canyon Road (U.S. 26) through the city's older, close-in, elegant residential districts to see gracious houses and well-tended gardens ablaze with flowers. The city's highest point—1,074-foot Council Crest—offers expansive views.

Or drive up Burnside Street into the western hills, through forest rarely found so near the heart of a busy city.

Ask at the Visitor Information Center for a map detailing scenic drives of the city's three districts: west side, east side, and northwest. The sign-marked routes pass most of Portland's main attractions, wind through attractive residential areas, and skirt busy industrial districts.

Local sightseeing tours

Many operators offer local sightseeing tours of Portland and regional attractions, including the Columbia River Gorge, Mount Hood, and the Oregon coast. Gray Line Sightseeing operates scheduled tours daily from May through mid-October, and at other times when demand warrants.

Several tour companies offer sightseeing flights over Mount St. Helens and the Columbia River. You can also join yacht and sternwheeler cruises on the Columbia, winery tours, balloon flights over the Tualatin Valley, and customized tours for small groups. Portland Walking Tours conducts guided walks of downtown Portland and the Old Town district for groups of ten or more.

For information on current tour offerings and operators, inquire at the Visitor Information Center.

Downtown Portland

Like most cities, Portland is constantly changing. In recent years, exciting developments have been taking place downtown and along the waterfront.

Portland's urban renaissance began with the development of Portland Center, the attractive remodeling of Civic Auditorium, and construction of delightful Ira's Fountain. Revitalization of the retail district and comple-

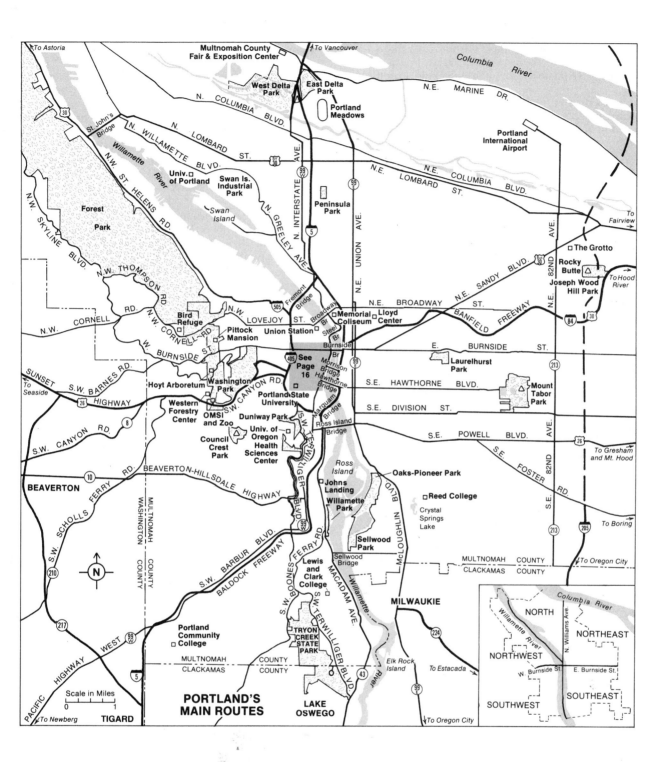

PORTLAND'S MAIN ROUTES

Scale in Miles
0   1

tion of a handsome transit mall followed. Mile-long Tom McCall Waterfront Park (see page 19) opens new opportunities to enjoy the Willamette River as it flows through the heart of the city.

Portland's evolving skyline includes many bold new commercial buildings, yet people have not been forgotten; each tower includes street-level activity space—shops, restaurants, galleries, open plazas—and sculpture and art are integral parts of the design. Many of Portland's fine old historic buildings have been renovated for use as shops and offices. Roam around Portland and take a look at some of these innovations.

Downtown greenery & open space

With excellent foresight, early city fathers set aside complete downtown blocks as landscaped open space. Today these unique park blocks, graced by mature trees, offer greenery in the city's center. Further opening up the downtown area are spacious new plazas, brightened by flower-filled containers, fountains, and bold sculptures.

Business district. In the heart of the city, stately old Elk Fountain separates Lownsdale and Chapman Squares, two downtown blocks donated to the city in 1852; they are bounded by S.W. 3rd and 4th avenues and Salmon and Madison streets. Originally, Lownsdale Square was used exclusively by men and was the debating ground of the city's soap-box orators; Chapman Square was reserved for women and children.

Schrunk Plaza lies directly south, between S.W. Madison and Jefferson streets, facing City Hall and the Federal Office Building.

Pioneer Courthouse Square faces the historic structure across S.W. 6th Avenue between Morrison and Yamhill streets. Dedicated in 1984, it is a popular gathering spot. Office workers lunch on its steps, performers entertain on the plaza below, and strollers scrutinize the inscribed paving bricks underfoot (each bears the name of a contributor who helped to finance the square's construction). Incorporated in the design is the iron gate of the elegant Portland Hotel, which occupied this site for nearly 70 years; tall terra-cotta columns link a row of modern transit shelters.

Another favorite lunchtime gathering spot is O'Bryant Square, a brick plaza bordering S.W. Park Avenue between S.W. Stark and Washington streets. A three-tiered fountain shaped like a rose dominates the square; nearly 250 rose bushes surround it.

Ira's Fountain. Across from the Civic Auditorium at S.W. 3rd Avenue and Clay Street, tumbling waterfalls delight strollers, shoppers, and children. It's a pleasant spot to relax and watch youngsters captivated by the frothy pools and cascades.

Park Blocks. West of the commercial center are the South Park and North Park blocks, also set aside more than a century ago as part of a park belt girdling the city's business district. You'll enjoy a stroll through the South Park Blocks (see page 17), which extend 13 blocks along Park Avenue from S.W. Salmon Street south through the Portland State University campus. Stately elms and maples impart an old-fashioned air to this area.

North Park covers six blocks, bounded by N.W. Glisan and S.W. Ankeny streets.

Landmarks old & new

Traditional old public buildings intermingle with dramatic new towers in Portland's downtown district. You'll discover shopping arcades, restaurants, atriums and roof gardens, art and sculpture displays. First stroll along the brick-patterned Portland Mall, on S.W. 5th and 6th avenues north of Madison; then branch out to other downtown areas.

New on Portland's skyline. A trek to view the city's bold new architecture should begin with the Portland Building at 1120 S.W. 5th Avenue. Designed by Michael Graves, this controversial structure has stirred architectural debate and earned acclaim for its innovative design.

Commanding the entrance is the dynamic hammered copper statue *Portlandia*. Pick up a booklet describing the building at the information desk. Art exhibits are presented in the second-floor gallery.

Diagonally north at 1001 S.W. 5th Avenue is the Orbanco Building; mirrored reflections of nearby buildings shimmer on its walls.

Inside the towering Pacific First Federal Center at 811 S.W. 6th Avenue, you gaze upward through three mezzaninelike floors to a striking skylight. Along the Broadway side, the building is recessed to allow a view north to the 1912 Jackson Tower clock.

An easy landmark to identify at the north end of the commercial district is the U.S. Bancorp Tower at 111 S.W. 5th Avenue, an iridescent pink building of reflective glass and pink polished granite.

North of W. Burnside Street is One Pacific Square, a silvery blue-green glass structure topped by a truncated pyramid; it is the first structure in a major urban renewal project, Five Pacific Square, now underway in Old Town.

Anchoring the south end of the business district is the striking KOIN-TV Center/Fountain Plaza at 222 S.W. Columbia Street, which is reminiscent of Manhattan's tiered skyscrapers of the 1920s.

Commissioned art works embellish the stately Justice Center, which houses the Portland police headquarters, courts, and jail. Visitors enter from S.W. 3rd Avenue, between Main and Madison streets. On the 16th floor, the Portland Police Museum features an old-time precinct station with fascinating police memorabilia.

Diagonally south of the Portland Building is PacWest Center, located at 1211 S.W. 5th Avenue between Madison and Jefferson streets. You'll recognize it by its alternating bold bands of silver aluminum and tinted black glass.

Old favorites. Polished granite columns support the circular portico of Portland's City Hall, a stately, four-story Italian Renaissance structure at 1220 S.W. 5th Avenue between Madison and Jefferson streets. Built in 1895, its distinctive exterior details recall an earlier, more ornate architectural era.

Built between 1909 and 1914, the colonnaded granite Multonomah County Courthouse, on S.W. Salmon Street between 4th and 5th avenues, contains county offices.

Formerly the grande dame of Portland's movie and vaudeville theaters, the old Paramount Theater has been renovated and refurbished to create a performing arts center at S.W. Broadway and Main Street. Now called the Arlene Schnitzer Concert Hall, it is the new home of the Oregon Symphony Orchestra. Next door is the restored Heathman Hotel, listed on the National Register of Historic Places.

Many local and touring musical groups perform in the handsome Civic Auditorium, located at S.W. Clay Street and 3rd Avenue. Wood paneling and Italian marble are used throughout the interior of the auditorium. Modern paintings and sculpture decorate the glass-fronted foyers overlooking Ira's Fountain.

A fine example of carpenter's Gothic architecture, Old Church stands a few blocks west of the business district at S.W. 11th Avenue and Clay Street. Now maintained by a secular society, Portland's oldest existing church (1883) is open to visitors Tuesday through Saturday

Children rush from Tri-Met bus at Washington Park stop near rose gardens. In addition to flowers, city's popular park includes Japanese garden, Oregon's Museum of Science and Industry, the World Forestry Center, and excellent zoo.

Light rail service, known familiarly as MAX (for Metropolitan Area Express), links downtown Portland's transit mall with suburban Gresham 15 miles to southeast.

On sunny days people congregate at multilevel Burnside Bridge pier to fish, watch river traffic, eat lunch, or just work on their tans.

from 11 to 3. Free organ concerts are performed Wednesdays at noon on the old organ that was brought around Cape Horn.

Other downtown landmarks. Also worth a special look is Willamette Center, 121 S.W. Salmon, a streamlined, three-block complex near the river between S.W. Taylor and Main streets. Sky bridges and escalators link different sections, which include a large theater and a carousel.

An urban renewal project of the 1960s, Portland Center is a handsome 54-block area south of Market Street, bounded by S.W. Front and 4th avenues and extending south to Interstate Highway 405. Apartment towers overlooking the river are linked to office buildings and shopping arcades by pedestrian malls. Seek out small Pettygrove Park, a delight of grassy mounds and tree-lined paths, and Lovejoy Fountain, where cascading waters create a refreshing retreat.

Sometimes called the "Ivory Tower," the streamlined white First Interstate Tower at 1300 S.W. 5th Avenue was the first building to raise Portland's skyline to new heights.

To learn the current weather forecast, look to the beacon atop the Standard Plaza Building at 1100 S.W. 6th Avenue. A white light signals colder temperatures expected; red, warmer; green, less than 5 degrees change; blinking beacon, precipitation; steady beacon, no precipitation.

Shoppers enjoy a visit to the Galleria at 921 S.W. Morrison, where a turn-of-the-century department store has been imaginatively remodeled into a delightful indoor marketplace. Galleries lined with shops, restaurants, and offices face an airy, skylighted atrium.

Morgan's Alley is a charming little shopping arcade at 515 S.W. Broadway (between Washington and Alder streets). Restaurants and shops open onto the cobblestone gallery—especially pleasant to visit on a rainy day.

At the Yamhill Marketplace, colorful open-air produce and food stalls along S.W. 2nd Avenue recall the farmers' market that once occupied this site. Shops and numerous short-order ethnic eateries wrap around the building's large skylit court at S.W. 2nd Avenue and Yamhill Street. Ride the glass-walled elevator to the rooftop observatory, where plaques identify nearby landmarks. Produce market hours are 8 to 6 daily; most other shops are open from 10 to 6.

Old Town makes a comeback

In the 19th century, the downtown waterfront was Portland's commercial center, and the area displayed its finest architecture. But as the river city grew, its business center shifted and classic buildings deteriorated.

In recent decades, however, Portland rediscovered its architectural treasures. Two downtown historic districts have been designated: the Skidmore–Old Town area at the western end of the Burnside Bridge, and the smaller Yamhill district a few blocks south. Entrepreneurs have renovated and refurbished many of the fine old buildings, cleaning weathered bricks and facades and polishing the cast-iron embellishments. Lively specialty shops, restaurants, galleries, and professional offices now mingle with long-established businesses.

Explore the market. On weekends from April through Christmas, you can combine a look at historic architecture with a visit to Old Town's lively outdoor market. Nearly 300 local craftspeople and vendors set up stalls at the west end of Burnside Bridge; street musicians and entertainers add to the fun. Shops overflow to the nearby New Market Village and adjacent plaza and the Skidmore Fountain Building. The original Saturday Market has expanded to Sundays, too; market hours are 10 to 5 Saturdays, 11 to 4:30 Sundays.

Theme museums. To learn about Portland's architectural history and restorations, stop at the Oregon Historic League, 26 N.W. 2nd Avenue. Hours are Tuesday through Friday from 10 to 3, Saturday from 10 to 4, and Sunday from noon to 4.

Ships and maritime history are the focus of the Oregon Maritime Center and Museum at 111 S.W. Front Street; it's open Friday and Saturday from 11 to 4, Sunday from noon to 5.

Also in the historic district is the fascinating American Advertising Museum at 9 N.W. 2nd Avenue. Open Wednesday through Friday from 11 to 5 and Saturday and Sunday from noon to 4, it chronicles the advertising industry's development since the late 1600s in print, radio, and television.

A stroll through the district. You'll discover Portland's fine old buildings for yourself on a walk through the Skidmore–Old Town Historic District. Many facades are constructed with handsome arches or columns. Cast-iron embellishments add lavish decoration—replicas of noble faces, festoons of greenery, and garlands of fruit and flowers.

Skidmore Fountain, at S.W. Ankeny Street and 1st Avenue, is a sentimental link with Portland's gaslight era; its plaza was a favorite meeting place in turn-of-the-

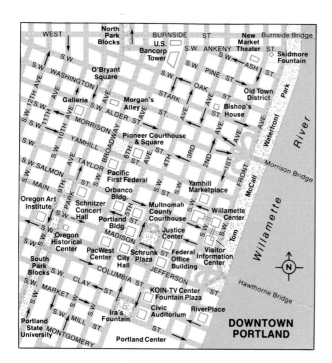

century Portland. The Skidmore Fountain Building, built in 1891, has been converted into a marketplace.

The elegant facade of the New Market Theater on S.W. 2nd Avenue at Ankeny Street, dating from 1872, now sets the stage for the New Market Village cluster of shops.

One of the first buildings to be restored was the handsome Bishop's House, built in 1879 at 219 S.W. Stark Street. Other restored buildings of special interest include the Glisan Building at 112 S.W. 2nd Avenue near Ash Street, built in 1889; and the Failing Building, 235 S.W. 1st Avenue at Oak Street, which has rich paint colors highlighting its simple cast-iron designs.

North of Burnside Street, take a look at these buildings:

The Blagen Block, 34 N.W. 1st Avenue at Couch Street, is a fine restoration of a large 1888 commercial building. Nearby at 53 N.W. 1st Avenue the 1877 Norton House was once a thriving waterfront hotel. Erickson's Saloon, at N.W. 3rd Avenue and Couch Street, claims the world's longest bar—684 feet long. The Italianate style of the Merchants Hotel, 200 N.W. Davis Street, dates from the 1880s.

Union Station on N.W. 6th Avenue is a rambling, red brick building topped by a handsome tile-roofed clock tower. The station welcomed its first passenger trains in the 1890s; now Amtrak trains stop here daily.

Along the South Park greenbelt

Museums featuring art and Oregon history face the South Park Blocks at S.W. Jefferson. Walk south along S.W. Park Avenue for a look at Portland State University.

Oregon Art Institute. Housed in a classically simple red brick building, the Institute offers a vigorous program. The complex, located at 1219 S.W. Park Avenue, is open Tuesday through Thursday from 11 to 7, Friday from 11 to 9:30, and Saturday and Sunday from noon to 5.

The Portland Art Museum is noted especially for its permanent collections of Asian art, contemporary American and European prints, and Northwest Coast Indian art. Works by several sculptors are displayed in an outdoor court on the north side of the museum.

Temporary exhibitions change every 4 to 6 weeks. Oregon artists are presented in one-person and group shows, and their works are featured in the rental-sales gallery. Art books, prints, and museum reproductions can be purchased in the museum shop.

The Oregon Art Institute also includes the Northwest Film & Video Center, which circulates film programs and offers classes on the technical and creative aspects of film making; and the Pacific Northwest College of Art, which provides classes and professional training in the visual arts.

Oregon Historical Center. If you'd like to learn more about the colorful history of Oregon and the Pacific Northwest, stop in for a look at the exhibits here. The headquarters of the Oregon Historical Society is open Monday through Saturday from 10 to 4:45 (closed major holidays).

The museum offers permanent exhibitions on early Northwest exploration, Oregon Indians, and the pio-

TRAVELING BY TRI-MET BUS & RAIL

For visitor or resident, the buses and trains of Tri-Met (Tri-County Metropolitan Transportation District of Oregon) offer an easy and pleasant way to get around Portland and to visit city and suburban destinations.

More than a decade ago, the city revamped its central business district, constructed an innovative transit mall, established a free riding zone, and developed bus and rail service covering the three-county (Multnomah, Clackamas, and Washington) Portland metropolitan area and Vancouver, Washington.

The rail service itself, dubbed MAX (the Metropolitan Area Express), has become a popular tourist attraction. The 15-mile line connects downtown Portland and the southeast suburb of Gresham.

The heart of the transit service is the downtown Portland Mall along 11 blocks of S.W. 5th and 6th avenues between S.W. Madison and W. Burnside streets. Designed for people and buses to share, the $16-million mall has wide brick walkways landscaped with trees, flower-filled containers, benches, fountains, and sculpture. Covered passenger kiosks offer protection from the weather and provide extensive information on trip planning and transit service.

You can ride without charge if you board and disembark within a 340-square-block downtown area called Fareless Square. The area is bounded by Interstate 405 on the south and west, N.W. Hoyt on the north, and the Willamette River on the east. Elsewhere, fares vary according to the distance traveled. Outside of Fareless Square, riders pay as they enter a bus. MAX riders purchase tickets from automatic ticket machines located on MAX platforms. Bus and MAX service operates from 5 A.M. to 1 A.M.

Trip planning assistance is available at the Tri-Met Customer Assistance Office at #1 Pioneer Courthouse Square. (701 S.W. 6th Avenue) on weekdays from 9 to 5. You can purchase Tri-Met's *Transportation Guide & Map* here; it shows all Tri-Met bus and MAX routes on a color map and contains all schedules. Printed timetables are also available here and at more than 200 other public places.

Riders will also find information on Tri-Met service in the Yellow Pages of local telephone directories; Call-A-Bus route and schedule information is available 24 hours a day.

Captain Hook, Peter Pan, and children wave to the crowd from their floral float during annual Rose Festival in June.

Blaze of color greets springtime visitors to the American Rhododendron Society test gardens in Crystal Springs Lake Park. Blossoms are at their peak in April and May.

Tugboats nudge ocean freighter toward pier at busy Port of Portland. Located downstream from Fremont Bridge, port handles specialized cargoes and operates ship repair facilities. Free tours are conducted on Saturdays in summer.

neers of the Oregon Trail. An original 1845 covered wagon is displayed along with pioneer artifacts, and a collection of miniature historic vehicles offers a delightful record of early land transportation. Changing exhibitions focus on different aspects of the Northwest's history and contemporary development.

The Society publishes many popular and scholarly books on regional history, architecture, biography, and other subjects. Posters, maps, and books published by the Society can be purchased in the building's bookstore.

Scholars and other visitors make extensive use of the vast regional research library collection, which includes thousands of books, maps, historical manuscripts, more than 2 million photographs, and millions of feet of historic film.

Portland State University.   Walk south along the green South Park promenade to the peaceful downtown campus of Portland State University, a young and vigorous college with an enrollment exceeding 15,000. The campus extends from S.W. Market Street south to Jackson.

Ancient elms shade the broad lawns where students relax. Chess and checker players compete across tile-topped game tables, and on sunny days entertainers often stage noontime performances.

Rediscovering the Willamette

For decades Portlanders caught only glimpses of their river. Buildings, docks, and warehouses cut the Willamette off from public view and access.

The city's vitality is particularly evident along the riverfront, where ambitious projects are now underway.

Stroll beside the river

One of the exciting new developments in downtown Portland is Tom McCall Waterfront Park, a narrow riverfront esplanade stretching 22 blocks along the Willamette's west bank from the Steel Bridge south to S.W. Columbia Street. Named in honor of a former governor, the park provides residents and visitors plenty of opportunities to enjoy the Willamette as it flows through the center of Portland.

Trees and lawns planted between S.W. Front Avenue and the river set off city traffic, and a landscaped waterfront promenade invites strollers. It's a great spot for people watching; you may see joggers, roller skaters, artists, or entertainers. Anglers cast for trout, salmon, and steelhead from fishing platforms along the shore. Riverfront hotels, shops, restaurants, and a marina invite you to stop.

Each spring U.S. and Canadian naval ships tie up along the seawall during the Rose Festival, and the park is the site of Portland's lively 62 KGW Neighborfair in July, a summer maritime festival, an August food-tasting bazaar, the September Autumnfest, and other events.

Across the river, the East Bank Esplanade extends between the Steel and Hawthorne bridges, a distance of about 1½ miles. Separating the river and I-5, this landscaped park strip offers a spectacular but noisy place to walk, fish, cycle, or just sit admiring the city skyline or watching river traffic. To reach the promenade, walk up the ramp that begins near S.E. Belmont and Water streets at the east end of the Morrison Bridge.

Walk across a bridge

In Portland you can expect to cross the Willamette again and again. Ten traffic bridges span the river, linking the city's west-side business districts with east-side commercial and residential areas (see map, page 13). Built and rebuilt over the past century, Portland's bridges vary considerably in style and character.

Walkways on the downtown bridges (on all except the Marquam and Fremont freeway spans) give pedestrians a splendid view of the river and its traffic. Best bets for walkers are the Morrison and Burnside bridges; each has a wide walkway and is accessible from the central part of Tom McCall Waterfront Park. Walkways are narrow on the Hawthorne, Steel, and Broadway bridges.

Each of the walkable bridges can open to allow lofty ships to pass; the river is deep enough to handle all but the largest ocean-going vessels. Tugboats push loaded barges, maneuver freighters, or tow log rafts along the busy waterway. Pleasure craft of all types and sizes share the river with the larger ships. Drawbridges open on signal from approaching traffic on the Willamette.

The Steel and Hawthorne bridges are vertical-lift spans; a wide section in the middle of each lifts up, by a system of cables and counterweights, on a pair of steel towers. The Broadway, Burnside, and Morrison bridges are all double-leaf bascule bridges. Their center spans split in the middle and each half can be drawn up to nearly vertical.

A look at Portland's busy port

Downstream from Fremont Bridge is the Port of Portland, which transforms Portland from a medium-size inland city into an international port.

The Port of Portland operates five marine terminals that handle general and bulk cargoes in a variety of specialized shipping methods—including containerization, roll-on roll-off traffic, and river and ocean barging. Other specialized cargoes handled here include imported automobiles, logs, and bulk grain and ore shipments.

The Port of Portland contains much more than ocean shipping docks. It also operates five industrial parks, a ship repair yard (housing the largest floating drydock on the West Coast), a dredge, Portland International Airport, and three smaller airports.

From June through September, free guided bus tours of the Port are conducted each Saturday. To reserve a seat, contact the Port's Community Relations Office, phone (503) 231-5000, ext. 268; or write to P.O. Box 3529, Portland, OR 97208. The 3-hour port tour includes a walk through Portland International Airport, and a view of cargo handling, grain elevators, automobile unloading docks, and the ship repair yard.

To see river traffic from a different perspective, consider one of the scheduled cruises by yacht or stern-wheeler that operates out of Portland. Check with the Visitor Information Center, 26 S.W. Salmon Street, for information on current trips.

RiverPlace & Johns Landing

Two mixed-use developments along the Willamette's western bank—RiverPlace and Johns Landing—offer a look at ways in which recreational use of the riverfront can be combined with commercial and residential aspects.

RiverPlace. This inviting complex south of the Hawthorne Bridge has a 200-slip marina, the only public moorage in downtown Portland. Boat rentals and lessons in sailing and rowing are available here.

Downtown joggers trot along the esplanade. Tree-shaded benches invite strollers to stop to relax. Commercial diversions include a new hotel, several restaurants and cafés, and a small collection of retail shops.

Johns Landing. One of the early projects in Portland's riverfront revival, the 70-acre Johns Landing was designed as a self-contained riverfront village. Stretching for nearly a mile along the waterfront southwest of the Ross Island Bridge, between S.W. Flower and Carolina streets, it restored one of the city's oldest industrial areas to active use.

Remodeling transformed a former furniture factory at 5331 S.W. Macadam Avenue into the Water Tower, a nostalgic marketplace of about 50 specialty shops and restaurants and a floor of offices. Its namesake water tower still looms above the building, retaining the sturdy, rambling charm of the old factory. Shops are open weekdays from 10 to 9, Saturday from 10 to 6, and Sunday from noon to 5.

Parks along the Willamette

As the Willamette River has been revitalized, Portlanders have gained new enjoyment from recreation on and along the water. You'll find picnic areas, boat ramps, a garden of rare plants, an amusement park, and view points for watching the ever-changing parade of river traffic.

Just offshore from the city of Milwaukie, Elk Rock Island is a 16-acre wooded park in the middle of the Willamette River. The Portland-owned island is accessible by boat and—in summer—by wading from Milwaukie. You can watch boaters and water-skiers or follow winding footpaths amid the island park's rare plants and trees.

The Oaks Amusement Park opened in 1905 to coincide with the Lewis and Clark Exposition, and it has provided fun for several generations of Portland families. Located on the east bank of the Willamette just north of Sellwood Bridge, the private park has an old-fashioned charm. Families enjoy its rides and midway attractions, large roller-skating rink, and shaded picnic areas overlooking the river.

Sellwood Riverfront Park, located on the east bank just north of Sellwood Bridge, has benches overlooking the river and an excellent view of the downtown skyline. The park has a small wildlife habitat pond, a large lawn area, and—in summer—a sandy beach.

On the west bank of the river north of Sellwood Bridge, Willamette Park offers a public boat ramp and a fine spot to picnic and watch boats.

Located beneath the northeast end of St. Johns Bridge, Cathedral Park derives its name from the tall pointed arches supporting the bridge. The park has a grand view of river traffic, a boat ramp, fishing dock, bike and foot paths, picnic tables, and a rose garden.

Kelley Point Park lies at Portland's northwestern tip, where the Willamette joins the Columbia. From I-5, take the N. Marine Drive exit (near the Multnomah County Fair and Exposition Center) and drive west about a mile. Picnickers can spread their lunches in a grassy meadow or cook on barbecue grills; beach fires are also permitted. You can watch river boats from the shore.

The Western Hills

The forested hills west of the Willamette contain some of Portland's most inviting residential districts and an outstanding collection of city parks. Here you can hike through wilderness, enjoy flower gardens, study Northwest native trees and shrubs, tour an elegant mansion, visit an excellent science museum, stroll through a wildlife sanctuary, and drive through forest corridors.

Activities abound in Washington Park

One of Portland's oldest and best-loved parks, Washington Park offers varied diversions for all ages. Summer evening outdoor concerts are a Portland tradition. Tennis players enjoy night-lighted courts. Forests and broad grassy lawns give way to two outstanding gardens in the park's northeast corner.

In the southern part of the park are the popular Oregon Museum of Science and Industry (OMSI), the Western Forestry Center, an energy-efficient model house, and the Washington Park Zoo.

International Rose Test Gardens. Most outstanding of the city's rose gardens, this 4½-acre site is a Northwest showplace during the June Rose Festival; roses continue to bloom until early fall. More than 4,000 rose bushes—including some 400 varieties—are planted on a terraced slope overlooking the city. New varieties are tested in the middle terrace area.

On summer weekends you often see a wedding party clustered in a secluded part of the garden. The view of the city from the Queen's Walk, at the end of the garden, is considered the best in Portland.

Japanese Garden. A roofed gate beckons you into a quiet oriental world of weeping willows, stone lanterns, and gently falling water, all captured in five classic gardens. Developed entirely from private donations, the garden meanders over 5½ acres of woodland, opening onto views of the Portland skyline. Cherry trees blossom in April. The garden is open year round, but closed on major winter holidays. For information on hours and fees, phone (503) 223-1321.

Oregon Museum of Science and Industry. Science is fun for both children and adults at this fascinating museum, a unique local institution whose influence extends far beyond Portland. Popularly called OMSI, it is located north of U.S. 26 at 4015 S.W. Canyon Road. The museum is open daily from 9 A.M. to 5 P.M., with extended hours on weekends and in summer.

Visitors often participate in the engrossing science exhibits, which include electricity demonstrations, planetarium shows, and a transparent woman dramatizing parts of the human body. You can tour the aerospace hall; command the pilot wheel of a ship's bridge; study Oregon fossils; see how the heart works from a walk-in model; and learn about modern agriculture from an indoor greenhouse, an operating beehive, and a chick incubator.

OMSI exists solely on donations—of money, time, materials, and services—and wide popular support. School and family programs offer science enrichment classes, summer camps, field trips, and opportunities for laboratory research. OMSI's science shop has field guides, science equipment, and kits for young researchers.

World Forestry Center.   Across from OMSI, three majestic wooden buildings offer intriguing exhibits on forestry, production techniques, and the many uses of wood. Located at 4033 S.W. Canyon Road, the center is open daily from 10 A.M. to 5 P.M.

In the main exhibit hall, two floors of displays—dioramas, motion pictures, and automated exhibits—illustrate the forest's life cycles and multiple uses, the forestry industry's harvesting and manufacturing operations, and the wide array of products derived from wood. The center's best-known attraction is a 70-foot "talking tree," which illustrates how trees feed and grow. The "Forests of the World" presentation discusses the six types of forests found throughout the world. In the Exhibit Hall, the Jesup Wood Collection assembles examples from the 505 trees native to North America.

Special monthly events and shows, classes, lectures, and other educational activities take place in the annex buildings.

Tera I.   Across the street from the World Forestry Center, an experimental energy-efficient house and laboratory illustrate the home of the future. Operated by Pacific Power and Light, the exhibit shows how solar collectors work, which appliances best conserve energy, and how nature can help heat and cool a house. Tera I is open 12:30 to 4:30 weekdays and noon to 5:30 weekends.

Washington Park Zoo.   One of the oldest zoos in the country (since 1887), the Washington Park Zoo covers a 61-acre site at 4001 S.W. Canyon Road, just north of U.S. 26. The zoo opens daily at 9:30 A.M.; closing hours vary by season. For information on fees, schedules, and special events, phone (503) 226-1561.

The zoo is best known for its successful Asian elephant breeding program; more than 20 babies have been born here since 1962, so there is a good possibility you'll see a little one scurrying around with the herd. A museum showcases elephants in history and focuses on the zoo's famous herd.

Main exhibits show animals in their native environments. A colony of Humboldt penguins from Peru inhabit a penguinarium with surf, cliffs, and rocky shores. Grizzly bears, wolves, and other Alaskan natives prowl the Alaska Tundra Exhibit. A trail through woods and past a waterfall leads to the Cascades Exhibit, where you'll see beavers, otters, trout, and other wildlife amid plants native to the Pacific Northwest. A tunnel leads you into the dark, arctic winter, where you'll see large polar bears swimming in deep pools beneath the polar ice.

Children can mingle with small animals in the children's zoo and see baby animals in the nursery.

Miniature trains of the Washington Park and Zoo Railway take zoo visitors on a winding 4-mile route through the park's woodlands, stopping near the International Rose Test Gardens and Japanese Garden. Ask for a stop-over pass if you want to visit the gardens. Weather permitting, the trains operate daily from spring through fall, weekends only in winter.

A walk through Hoyt Arboretum

If gardening is your pleasure, don't miss outstanding Hoyt Arboretum. Native Northwest trees, shrubs, ferns, and wildflowers have been collected in a hilly woodland adjacent to Washington Park.

Eight miles of cool, shady trails weave through the trees; identification markers enhance the enjoyment of the casual visitor as well as the botanist. More than 400 tree species from around the world are planted here.

S.W. Fairview Boulevard divides Hoyt Arboretum into two sections: conifers are planted west of the road, deciduous trees to the east. Self-guided nature trails begin near the administration building; pick up a trail guide before you depart. Guided tours of the arboretum begin at 2 P.M. on weekends from April through October. Picnic tables and a shelter with a fireplace are located across from the administration building.

The splendid Pittock Mansion

In a parklike setting high in the city's western hills, a 22-room mansion built in French Renaissance style reflects the elegant standards of early 20th century craftsmanship. Built between 1909 and 1914 at 3229 N.W. Pittock Drive, the dwelling was once the private estate of Portland newspaper tycoon Henry Pittock.

Graceful terraces and stone balustrades distinguish the mansion's exterior. Dominating the interior is a magnificent central staircase finished with a polished hardwood handrail and bronze supports. Ornamental plaster work, marble and hardwood floors, and hand-carved mantelpieces complement the mansion's elegant furnishings and art objects. The building has a central vacuum cleaning system, an elevator to all floors, and room-to-room telephones.

A modest fee is charged to tour the house, but Pittock Acres Park grounds are open without charge; they offer a sweeping view over the city and Willamette River to the Cascades. Hours vary by season; phone (503) 248-4469 for information.

To get to the Pittock mansion, go west on Burnside; a mile beyond N.W. 23rd Avenue, turn right on N.W. Barnes Road; then make another right turn on N.W. Irving Avenue and follow signs into the park.

A bird refuge & wildlife exhibits

Bird watchers enjoy a visit to Pittock Bird Sanctuary at 5151 N.W. Cornell Road. More than 1½ miles of trails wind through the grounds, which are kept in their natural state. You'll probably see small mammals as well.

Inside the visitor center (open daily from 9 to 5) you can study natural history exhibits ranging from butterfly collections to paintings of western birds.

Forest Park, a city wilderness

A vast city wilderness offers hikers and equestrians more than 30 miles of trails just a few minutes northwest of downtown Portland. The 5,000-acre park follows the shoulder of the Tualatin Mountains for some 6½ miles. Trails link Forest Park with other parks in the western hills. A trail map is available from Portland's Parks and Recreation department, 1120 S.W. 5th Avenue, Room 503; call (503) 796-5193 for information.

Wildwood Trail, designated a National Recreation Trail, winds 14 miles through the natural forest corridor of the western hills. Beginning near the Western Forestry Center in Washington Park, it heads north through park woodlands to end near N.W. Springville Road. Hikers occasionally see deer in the woods; seasonal wildflowers and autumn foliage accent luxuriant greenery.

When road and fire conditions permit, motorists can drive through the park along Leif Erikson Drive, a primitive, graded dirt-and-gravel road. Allow at least an hour to drive the 11-mile route, which begins near N.W. Thurman Street. Turnouts allow you to picnic or enjoy views.

Other west-side parks

Among several dozen parks in the western hills, here are a few of special interest:

Wooded Macleay Park, located between Pittock Acres and Forest Park, is a good choice for picnicking and hiking. Turnouts along N.W. Cornell Road, which traverses the park, provide access to hiking trails.

Since Council Crest Park, atop a hill in the southwest district, is the highest point in the city, it offers fine views in all directions.

If you're a lilac fancier, plan a May visit to Duniway Park, located at S.W. 6th Avenue and S.W. Sheridan Street just south of I-405. If you're a jogger, go there any time to run on the park's quarter-mile track.

Terwilliger Boulevard Park is a forest corridor following the mountain ridge between I-405 and State Highway 10. Joggers exercise at trailside fitness stations, and motorists gaze over the city panorama from turnouts along the east side of the boulevard. Cyclists enjoy the Terwilliger Bike Trail, an 8-mile scenic route linking the downtown area and Lake Oswego. It follows a wooded ridge with skyline views, passes through dense forest in Tryon Creek State Park, and ends near Lake Oswego.

Tryon Creek State Park is Oregon's first metropolitan state park, a 600-acre wilderness preserve bordering a lushly wooden canyon between Portland and Lake Oswego. Accessible only by trail, the park is a haven for urban hikers, cyclists, and horseback riders; each group has its own paths. A trail guide is available at the nature cen-

ter, open daily from 8 to 5 at 11321 S.W. Terwilliger Boulevard. When you're there, view exhibits on park plant and animal life—a naturalist is on duty Wednesday through Sunday. For information on guided walks, lectures, slide shows, and other events, phone (503) 636-4550.

East-side Destinations

In contrast to the forested hills west of the Willamette, Portland's east side stretches across a flat valley toward the Cascades. Dozens of neighborhood parks pepper the residential area.

Modern Portland International Airport is located along the south shore of the Columbia River in northeast Portland; more than 300 flights arrive and depart daily. Marine Drive parallels the Columbia shore; during sailing season, yachts maneuver in the mile-wide river.

Busy Lloyd Center

One of the Northwest's first shopping complexes, Lloyd Center is a sizable retail center east of the Willamette River.

More than 100 specialty shops and several department stores open onto landscaped pedestrian malls. Changing exhibits highlight arts and crafts, flower displays, or youth activities. At the covered, open-air ice-skating rink you can watch students practice or take to the ice yourself. Restaurants, banks, and professional offices round out Lloyd Center's facilities.

Mount Tabor, an extinct volcano

A favorite for family picnics, this large park in southeast Portland has its own extinct volcano; the north end of the crater is used in summer as an outdoor amphitheater. Geologists say the volcanic activity occurred about 10 million years ago.

The road circling Mount Tabor's grassy summit affords sweeping views of the distant downtown area, the rivers, and the lower Willamette Valley with Mount Hood looming on the eastern skyline.

Urban wilderness in Laurelhurst Park

Cyclists, joggers, and strollers enjoy Laurelhurst Park as a bit of lush urban wilderness. Located one block south of E. Burnside Street on S.E. 39th Avenue, the park abounds with trees, flowers, and trails. Art shows are held in a natural theater, and you can feed the ducks that inhabit a small lake in the park.

An outdoor cathedral

The tranquility of an outdoor cathedral impresses those who visit the Grotto, located at N.E. 85th Avenue and Sandy Boulevard. An elevator transports visitors to the upper level; this 64-acre woodland contains flower-lined trails and a panoramic view of the Columbia River. Grounds are open from 8 A.M. until dusk.

Lush vineyards sweep over crest of hill in Tualatin Valley, only minutes west of Portland. Wine tasting is a popular weekend activity; most wineries are small and welcome visitors.

Eager fishers wade into Sandy River, long-handled dip nets in hand, to scoop up silvery smelt during early spring run. Lewis and Clark State Park, near river's mouth, is a favorite destination for Portlanders.

Mass is held daily in the chapel, and on Sundays from May to September in the outdoor Grotto; call (503) 254-7371 for information about and times of services.

Exploring the neighborhoods

Perhaps the best way to get acquainted with an area is by walking. Here are three distinctive neighborhoods on Portland's east side that offer intriguing discoveries:

Sellwood's Antique Row. About 35 antique stores and specialty shops draw browsers to Portland's old Sellwood district, along a 12-block area of S.E. 13th Avenue southeast of Sellwood Park. Many of the shops are housed in old gingerbread-decorated buildings. Browsers discover vintage treasures, including classic American furniture, jewelry, lamps, glassware, rare books, and Old West memorabilia. Most shops are open Wednesday through Saturday from 11 to 5, Sunday and Tuesday by chance.

S.E. Hawthorne's eateries. Another district that is being revived, S.E. Hawthorne Boulevard has varied architecture and an interesting array of shops; its trademark, however, is its eateries. Bakeries, delis, and other food shops and restaurants offer edible temptations that may be hard to resist. Interesting shops are scattered along S.E. Hawthorne between S.E. 12th and 55th avenues; you'll find an excellent concentration between S.E. 32nd and 39th avenues.

Ladd's Addition. With its unusual hub-and-spoke street pattern, its wide-ranging mix of architecture, and its many parks and broad, elm-lined streets, this local historic conservation district is one of Portland's most distinctive neighborhoods.

It was designed in 1891 by William S. Ladd, who promoted it as a "residential community for cultured people." It still looks remarkably old-fashioned—you'll see few driveways, and iron rings for tethering horses still decorate curbs.

S.E. Ladd Avenue, the main street, cuts diagonally through the area from S.E. Hawthorne Boulevard and 12th Avenue to S.E. Division Street and 20th Avenue. The center of the neighborhood is Ladd Circle, a small rhododendron-filled park; the district also has four small rose gardens.

Rhododendrons & roses

Gardeners and other flower lovers will enjoy spectacular seasonal displays at a couple of Portland parks.

More than 2,500 rhododendrons are planted in the Portland test gardens of the American Rhododendron Society in Crystal Springs Lake Park. Located near S.E. 28th Avenue and Woodstock Boulevard southwest of Reed College, the gardens cover a wooded island in the lake as well as part of the mainland park. A footbridge links the areas, and pathways wind through the gardens. Blossoms are at their peak in April and May, when annual shows attract large crowds.

Roses abound in Peninsula Park, a short detour east of I-5 in north Portland. More than 700 varieties of roses—more than 10,000 bushes—bloom in the Sunken Rose Garden from late May into autumn. A Victorian bandstand presides over the city's largest rose garden, located in the southern part of the park near the corner of N. Ainsworth Street and N. Albina Avenue.

Picnic at Blue Lake Park

Families and groups enjoy this popular Multnomah County park, located 15 miles east of Portland off I-84 near Fairview. The park's 900 picnic sites get heavy use, as does the lake, where visitors swim, fish, and go boating. The children's play area features imaginative playground equipment.

Activities & Events

Metropolitan Portland has activities of all types going on year round—operas and symphony performances, dramatic and musical plays, art shows and craft exhibits, professional and amateur sports events, tours of local industries, and many seasonal festivities.

For information on events, check with the Visitor Information Center of the Greater Portland Convention and Visitors Association, 26 S.W. Salmon Street, phone (503) 222-2223.

Opera, symphony & theater

Portland's major peforming arts events take place in Arlene Schnitzer Concert Hall, S.W. Broadway and Main Street, and the Civic Auditorium, 222 S.W. Clay Street.

The Oregon Symphony Orchestra presents a full season of classical and pops concerts from September through June in Arlene Schnitzer Concert Hall. Productions of the Portland Opera are presented in the Civic Auditorium. Other local and touring groups present classical, rock, jazz, country, and folk concerts, as well as ballets, Broadway musicals, travel films, and children's programs.

Chamber Music Northwest, Portland's summer chamber music festival, draws musicians from all over the nation for a 5-week concert season in June and July, presented at Reed College and the Catlin Gabel School.

The Portland Civic Theatre presents a year-round schedule of Broadway musical shows, dramas, mystery, and comedy in Portland's oldest and largest live theater at 1530 S.W. Yamhill Street. Portland's only professional Equity theater, the Willamette Repertory Theater, presents its productions at 25 S.W. Salmon Street.

Sports, shows & expositions

Portland takes an active role in professional sports, with league entries in basketball, ice hockey, and baseball. The city also hosts many other events.

Memorial Coliseum, 1401 N. Wheeler Avenue is the site for indoor athletic events, conventions, ice shows, major animal shows, rock band concerts, circuses, and fairs; it is located on the northeast side of the Willamette between the Broadway and Steel bridges.

Large shows and expositions take place in the Multnomah Exposition Center, a sizable area at 2060 N. Marine Drive, on the Columbia's south bank. Among the major shows are the spring Home & Garden Show, the Multnomah County Fair, and the annual Pacific International Livestock Exposition.

Soccer, football, and baseball games are played in Portland Civic Stadium at S.W. 18th Avenue and Morrison Street. In season, you'll find horse racing at Portland Meadows, greyhound racing at the Multnomah Kennel Club in Fairview Park, and motocross and sports car races at the Portland International Raceway near West Delta Park.

A half-dozen public golf courses are located within the city, and many others are only a short drive beyond. In the city parks you'll find tennis courts, swimming pools, and children's playgrounds.

Check Portland newspapers for current information on sailboat racing, ice-skating competitions, hiking trips, bicycle excursions, and other sports activities.

Crafts & carousels

Among other activities, you might explore Portland's busy arts and crafts scene or seek out one of the city's many carousels.

Galleries specialize in regional arts and crafts, original photography, Indian and western art, sculpture, and works in wood, fiber, glass, and metal. The Oregon Art Institute sponsors many events (see page 17). The Oregon School of Arts and Crafts offers day and evening classes at its campus at 8245 S.W. Barnes Road; visitors can watch resident artists and students at work; phone (503) 297-5544 for information.

You'll find vintage carousels at the World Forestry Center, Jantzen Beach Center, Willamette Center, Oaks Park, and at 7601 S.W. Barbur Boulevard. The Portland Carousel Museum adjacent to the Willamette Center Carousel is open daily from 11 to 4. For more information, check with the Visitor Information Office.

Rose Festival heads events

In early June, Portland honors the rose in a 2-week civic celebration climaxed by a tremendous floral parade. Events include a queen coronation, sports competitions, and a rose show. Naval ships hold open house along the Willamette seawall in downtown Portland, and Indians from many western tribes gather in East Delta Park for an Indian Pow Wow and Pageant.

Major summer celebrations include the 62 KGW Neighborfair, a cultural celebration with ethnic foods, crafts, music, and dancing at Tom McCall Waterfront Park; and the Multnomah County Fair at the Exposition Center. The Washington Park Summer Moonlight Festival features outdoor concerts and performances in the Rose Garden Amphitheater.

September highlights are the Artquake, with literary, visual, and performing arts in the South Park Blocks; and the Autumnfest, a festive gathering in Tom McCall Waterfront Park and the Old Town district. In October, the Pacific International Livestock Exposition is held at Multnomah Exposition Center.

HISTORIC SAUVIE ISLAND, A RURAL RETREAT

Just 20 minutes northwest of downtown Portland lies Sauvie Island, an unspoiled wedge of greenery at the confluence of the Columbia and Willamette rivers. Separated from the city's busy industrial fringe, the island is a pastoral retreat.

You can watch ocean-going freighters sail along the Columbia, hike the island's beaches, canoe its waterways, cycle along level roads, picnic in sunny meadows, shop for farm-grown produce, and visit a historic territorial homestead. Often anglers simply set up a chair on the sandy beach, throw a line in the river, and relax. Island lakes and marshes teem with birds and other wildlife.

Long before white settlers arrived, Indian tribes from the Columbia and Willamette valleys gathered here. Lewis and Clark landed on Sauvie Island in 1805; later, the island was the site of a Hudson's Bay Company fur trading post (Fort William) and a pioneer dairy.

Early settlers lived an isolated, self-contained life. Near the south end of the island is the Bybee-Howell house, a territorial homestead built here in 1846; it is open daily in summer.

Pre-Civil War furnishings reflect life in the Oregon country on the eve of statehood. Fruit trees found in early Oregon orchards are planted behind the house, and native plants have been collected in the pioneer garden. Equipment and tools used on 19th century farms are displayed in an agricultural museum.

On the last Saturday of September, a "wintering-in" festival at the Bybee-Howell house re-creates traditional pioneer harvest events, including pressing cider from apples grown in the homestead's orchard.

Half of the island is fertile farmland. Farmers' "you-pick" signs line the roads all summer, and produce stands offer island-grown produce from June through October. On autumn weekends, hayrides are available, and families come here to choose the perfect Halloween pumpkin.

The lake-dotted north half of the island is a state wildlife area, a good place to watch migrating and resident birds. In season, sandhill cranes, Canada geese, and bald eagles can be seen; inquire at the refuge headquarters to locate the best vantage points.

Columbia Gorge vista near Hood River unfolds for travelers on Interstate Highway 84 as the road skims alongside river. Scenic Highway (page 31) winds along cliff high above water.

ALONG THE COLUMBIA RIVER

Follow the Pacific Northwest's historic water highway

No single physical feature has influenced the development of the Pacific Northwest more than the Columbia River and its tributaries. Rising in the Canadian Rockies, the river meanders through British Columbia and eastern Washington. It then veers westward, carving an awesome channel through the Cascade Mountains on its 1,243-mile journey to the sea.

Long before the first white men sailed up the Columbia, prehistoric tribes recorded their own presence by carving petroglyphs on the cliffs above the river. Indian tribes settled near the Columbia, fishing for salmon, trapping animals, and trading among themselves.

The entrance to the great river of the West was not discovered until 1792, when a Yankee sea captain and trader, Robert Gray of Boston, sailed several miles upstream on his ship *Columbia*. Five months later Lieutenant William Broughton, an English naval officer serving under Captain George Vancouver, explored the river nearly 100 miles inland.

Early exploration and settlement of the Oregon Territory depended in large part on the Columbia—the only water-level route from the country's interior to the sea. Explorers and fur trappers paddled their canoes along the river highway. Tired pioneers completed their grueling overland journey by rafting their wagons and livestock through the Columbia's hazardous gorge.

Beginning in the 1850s, steamboats transported passengers and freight along the Columbia and other rivers, linking the scattered settlements, farming areas, and mining districts.

As you drive along Oregon's great river, you'll see a cross section of the state's geography—sandy beaches, quiet farm lands, industrial ports, forested mountains, sparkling waterfalls, valleys of fruit orchards, vast wheat fields, livestock ranges, and arid plateau.

Visible, too, is the hand of man shaping the river to his needs. Commercial ships and pleasure craft can navigate 464 miles inland to Lewiston, Idaho, on the Snake River. Huge freighters load lumber and wheat for foreign ports, and tugboats maneuver barges and log rafts along the waterway. Massive dams barricade the river for power and irrigation. Numerous roadside parks invite you to enjoy the river's many moods.

The Lower Columbia

In the years following Lewis and Clark's epic overland journey, fur traders arrived. Members of John Jacob Astor's Pacific Fur Company sailed up the Columbia in 1811 and established a fur trading post—Fort Astoria—on the south shore.

Astoria became the first permanent settlement and trading center in the Oregon country. Its major growth and the settlement of other lower Columbia river towns occurred in the 1840s and '50s as overland immigrants arrived and ships entered the harbor in growing numbers. By its 100th birthday, Astoria was the second largest city in Oregon.

From Astoria, U.S. Highway 30 follows the twisting river upstream to Portland. You follow the route of the Lewis and Clark Trail. Small towns are scattered along the route, but it's a quiet drive through wooded countryside and farm lands until you're near Portland.

Astoria has a maritime flavor

At the turn of the century, Astoria rivaled San Francisco in size and splendor, and a hint of those glory days remains. Wealthy merchants and sea captains built elegant wooden frame houses on the hills overlooking the river. Though much of the old town was destroyed by fire in 1922, more than a dozen handsome old Victorian houses remain along Exchange, Franklin, and Grand streets. For a map showing historic buildings, stop at the Chamber of Commerce office at Marine Drive and Hume Street.

A large commercial fishing fleet anchors in the shadow of the massive 4-mile-long toll bridge linking Oregon and Washington. On weekends, small vessels ply the channel or head westward toward the rougher waters near the Columbia Bar. Each August, sport fishers compete for the biggest catch during the Astoria Regatta, a week-long civic party that includes water sports events, street dances, fireworks, a salmon barbecue, and a twilight boat parade.

Warrenton, a thriving community west of Astoria, is the charter-boat center for salmon fishing. From June to September, ocean trawlers take people out for the day to fish for Chinook or silver salmon. Private boats can be launched in Astoria, Hammond, and Warrenton.

Many Astoria residents are of Scandinavian ancestry. Annually in mid-June the city hosts a Scandinavian Midsummer Festival featuring music and folk dancing, arts and crafts demonstrations, booths displaying Scandinavian articles, a pancake breakfast, and a Scandinavian dinner.

Astoria Column.   Orienting yourself in Astoria is best done from the vantage point of Astoria Column, crowning 635-foot Coxcomb Hill. A pictorial frieze spirals around the outside of the 125-foot column depicting major events in Astoria's history—the discovery of the Columbia, the arrival of the Lewis and Clark expedition, the founding of Astoria, and the settlement of the territory.

If you're willing to climb the enclosed spiral staircase —166 steps—to the top of the monument, your reward will be a magnificent panorama. You can see the city en-circled on south and east by wooded hills, the Columbia River with its docks and wharves, the great span of the interstate bridge, the Pacific Ocean, and Young's Bay.

Marine exhibits.   The history of the Columbia River and its ports dominates the Columbia River Maritime Museum, now housed at 1792 Marine Drive on the Astoria waterfront. The museum is open daily from 9:30 to 5; it is closed Mondays from October to April.

Exhibits in seven galleries focus on different features of the entire Columbia River system; restored craft and other items are displayed in the museum's great hall. You'll see sailing ship models, early sea charts, whaling and fishing equipment, and figureheads and hardware salvaged from historic vessels and ships wrecked at the mouth of the Columbia.

A prominent feature of the maritime museum is an actual seagoing vessel, the lightship *Columbia*, moored at the foot of 17th Street in Astoria Maritime Park next to the museum site. The ship marked the mouth of the Columbia River for more than 30 years before being retired in 1979. The Coast Guard ship *Resolute* is moored alongside.

Historical treasures.   The Clatsop County Historical Society has developed the former home of Captain George Flavel as a Victorian museum, filled with elaborate furnishings reflecting the life of a wealthy family of the 1880s. Located at 441 8th Street between Duane and Exchange streets, the house is a two-and-a-half story frame building constructed in Queen Anne style and set amid spacious landscaped grounds. A three-story tower rises at one corner, and a frosting of wood filigree trims the building. The mansion's six elaborate fireplaces, all different, were built of imported rare-wood panels shipped around Cape Horn. Fireplace tiles came from various European and Asian countries.

Admission also includes entrance to the Heritage Center and Historical Museum at 16th and Exchange streets, which houses exhibits of the Clatsop County Historical Society.

Both buildings are open daily from 10 to 5 from May to September; the rest of the year visitors are welcome daily from 11 to 4.

Fort Astoria.   At 15th and Exchange streets, a historical marker and a partially reconstructed fort indicate the site of the first permanent American outpost west of the Mississippi River. During certain periods, there's a "living history" presentation here, with a man dressed as a French fur trader describing the founding of Astoria. Check at the Chamber of Commerce office for information.

Side trips from Astoria

Astoria's prime location offers a choice of excursions— roaming nearby beaches, traveling inland to wooded hills, or tracing the footsteps of Lewis and Clark.

Hardy souls willing to gamble on the weather find the Clatsop Spit beaches near the mouth of the Columbia a quiet world of sand dunes and beach grass. Only the clang of ocean buoys and the trill of meadowlarks break the silence. The oceanside road leads to a lookout with an elevated viewing platform. From here you watch waves

ASTORIA SIDE TRIPS

Scale in Miles
0 2 4

crashing against the enormous South Jetty boulders and see freighters moving cautiously past the treacherous sandbars that have claimed many vessels at the mouth of the Columbia. Clatsop Spit is a good place to catch Dungeness crabs, and clam diggers harvest razor clams south of the jetty when there's a minus tide.

A fine picnic spot near Astoria is Young's River Falls County Park, located about 15 miles south of the Young's River Loop Road. You drive through rich green dairy country along the river; daisies and buttercups dot lush pastures in spring. From the parking area, a path descends to the base of the falls. You can hike, swim, and fish in the park.

From Astoria, State Highway 202 follows the North Fork of the Klaskanine River southeast, climbing through coastal rain forests of spruce and hemlock, to reach Fishhawk Falls County Park. On the eastern slope of the Coast Range, you enter the pastoral Nehalem Valley at Jewell.

Fort Clatsop National Memorial

Six miles southwest of Astoria, on the western bank of the Lewis and Clark River, you can visit the site of Fort Clatsop, headquarters of the Lewis and Clark expedition during the winter of 1805–06.

A full-scale replica of the original fort has been constructed, based on the floor plan and dimensions drawn by Captain Clark. It is open daily from 8 A.M. to 5 P.M. in winter, to 6 P.M. from mid-June through Labor Day. Admission is free. Picnic tables are located on the grounds. For information, phone (503) 861-2471.

The explorations of Meriwether Lewis and William Clark provided the first detailed knowledge of the Northwest, awakening an interest that lured trappers and settlers into the region and helped make Oregon an American—rather than a British—territory.

Lewis and Clark's journals provide a valuable record, vividly chronicling not only their explorations and struggle for survival but also their detailed study of the surroundings. They observed and carefully described the trees, birds, animals, and fish they found, often accompanying their writings with drawings. Members of the local Clatsop, Chinook, and Tillamook tribes were frequent visitors to the fort, and the journals record their dress, appearance, customs, and way of life. The expedition's maps were the first accurate records of the topography of the regions through which the group journeyed.

In the Visitor Center you will see equipment used by the expedition, maps tracing its route, and audio-visual programs on the Lewis and Clark journals and the expedition's stay at Fort Clatsop. Books and pamphlets about the expedition, frontier exploration, and natural history can be purchased here.

A replica of the original fort, built of the "streightest and most butifullest logs," was constructed on the site to mark the expedition's 150th anniversary. In its sheltered clearing, the reconstructed fort appears surprisingly small. Only 50 feet square, it housed 33 people through the winter. A 15-star flag flies atop the flagpole. In summer, costumed rangers describe the life of expedition members and demonstrate frontier skills and tasks.

Short trails, corresponding to those used by members of the expedition, lead to the camp's fresh-water spring and the canoe landing. A 32-foot dugout canoe, similar to those used for river travel, can be seen near the river below the fort.

Up the Columbia

Driving up the Columbia from Astoria, you catch occasional glimpses of the water. From Clatsop Crest, savor a final view before U.S. 30 winds up into the forested hills of the Coast Range. Picnickers enjoy the woodsy setting of Bradley State Wayside. At Westport, a toll ferry transports Washington-bound cars across the Columbia.

Clatskanie. Trees shield river views as you follow the Oregon shore east through dairy and farm lands toward Clatskanie. Located in a wooded valley on the Clatskanie River, the town was named for a small tribe of Indians that once lived nearby. Boating and fishing are popular on both the Columbia and Clatskanie.

High on a hill above Clatskanie is a castlelike structure, built about 1900 by Thomas Flippen, an early logger and sawmill owner. Now a National Historic Site, it has been restored and furnished, and is open for tours daily except Monday from 11 to 5.

State Highway 47 goes south from Clatskanie to the Nehalem Valley, meeting State 202 at Mist. Hub of this scenic recreation area is Vernonia, nestled in the hills of the Coast Range. Visitors can learn about the early days in a historical museum, picnic or swim along the Nehalem River and its tributaries, or seek agates along Clear Creek and Rock Creek.

Rainier. Another fine old dwelling with a new lease on life is the 1888 House, once the home of George Moeck, a German merchant who supplied Columbia river boats. The restored Moeck house, located on U.S. 30 in Rainier, contains two restaurants and a half-dozen specialty shops.

Lewis and Clark Bridge—the only bridge between Astoria and Portland—spans the Columbia at Rainier, providing access to Longview's mills and other industries on the Washington shore. From the hill west of Rainier, you have a fine view of the river, the cities several hundred feet below, and Mount St. Helens to the north.

Learn about nuclear power

The curved cooling tower of the Trojan nuclear power plant has become a landmark along the lower Columbia. Located 42 miles northwest of Portland between Rainier and Goble, the uranium-fueled plant is a major source of electrical energy for the region.

Visitors learn about energy sources during a stop at the Visitor Information Center, just off U.S. 30 near the plant entrance; it is open Wednesday through Sunday from 9:30 to 5. Fascinating exhibits, models, and film presentations explain various energy alternatives, including solar, wind, and nuclear power.

Public tours of the Trojan plant are conducted for visitors, within security regulations; for information and tour reservations, telephone (503) 226-8510.

An adjacent 75-acre recreation area, open from 10 to 8 in summer, offers picnic facilities, play equipment, a sports field, and a wildlife-viewing shelter. A large natural lake, wintering ground of migratory whistling swans and other birds, has been kept in its natural state.

Old river settlements

Pioneer loggers from New England first settled in Columbia City and St. Helens in the 1840s. As the towns grew, businesses clustered along the waterfront. From U.S. 30, side streets lead several blocks east to the river, where the towns' older sections retain the informal charm of a slower-paced era.

Columbia City. One of the most attractive 19th century houses along the river is the Caples House, situated at First and I streets to overlook a scenic stretch of the Columbia. Built in 1870, the house (originally the home of a pioneer doctor) and several outbuildings have been restored and furnished as a museum. From February through November, the buildings are open afternoons daily except Monday.

St. Helens. Named for the volcanic peak in Washington often visible to the northeast, St. Helens is not only a river port and market center but also the county seat. The downtown riverfront area is a designated historic district. The Columbia County Courthouse, built in 1906 of locally quarried stone, has been a lower Columbia landmark for decades. A historical museum on the upper floor is open Friday and Sunday afternoons. The courtroom resembles a setting from a western movie.

The town's oldest structure is the Knighton House. built by the town's founder in 1847. Spared in the 1904 fire that burned many of the town's wooden buildings, the house has been moved from its original site near the courthouse to 155 S. 4th Street.

Pastoral retreat. Historic Sauvie Island (see page 25) lies just northeast of U.S. 30 on the western outskirts of Portland where the Willamette River enters the Columbia.

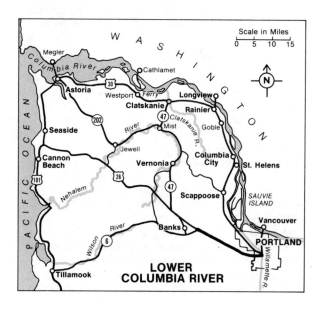

The Columbia River Gorge

The most spectacular stretch of the Columbia River Highway lies upriver from Portland. East of Troutdale, the river slashes through the Cascade Range. Clear streams tumble down the wooded hillsides, plunging over the steep basaltic cliffs in jubilant waterfalls. Columbia River Gorge National Scenic Area was created in 1986.

Two highways follow the river route—Interstate Highway 84, the water-level freeway, and the Columbia River Scenic Highway, a pleasant detour that traces a section of the original Columbia River Highway, winding across forested slopes high above the river.

Several state parks in the gorge offer picnicking and rest areas; campsites are available in Ainsworth State Park. Roadside stops along the scenic route have trails to waterfalls and view points. Near the riverside freeway, Rooster Rock and Benson parks feature water sports.

The scenic Sandy River

A favorite destination for family outings, the Sandy River flows from Mount Hood's glaciers through foothills east of Portland to join the Columbia near Troutdale. In 1805, Lewis and Clark named it the Quicksand River.

Riverside parks. Those scouts' explorations are commemorated in Lewis and Clark State Park, 16 miles east of Portland near the mouth of the Sandy River. During the spring smelt run, anglers scoop up the small silvery fish in long-handled dip nets. Shad fishing is good here in late May and June; in autumn anglers cast for steelhead. A nature trail features plants discovered and noted by Lewis and Clark. Broughton Bluff, a target of rock climbers, towers several hundred feet above the river.

A few miles upstream is Dabney State Park, 19 miles east of Portland. Farther south, Oxbow County Park offers campsites and hiking and bridle trails. Dodge Park, a day-use park north of Sandy, has picnic tables, fishing access, and a playground.

Pristine gorge. If you want to really see the river, venture a do-it-yourself float trip. A 6½-mile stretch of the river, from Dodge Park downstream to Oxbow County Park, is wild and isolated, accessible only by boat. For information on raft and canoe rentals, contact River Trails, 336 E. Columbia, Troutdale, OR 97060, phone (503) 667-1964. Fees include all equipment and shuttle service.

Steep 400-foot cliffs protect this wilderness corridor where deer and elk browse and water birds dive for fish along the rocky shore. Quiet pools alternate with whitewater rapids. Federal and state agencies and the Nature Conservancy, a private organization, have joined forces to preserve the gorge as a semiwilderness recreation area.

In spring and early summer, this part of the river runs high and fast with plenty of challenging rapids. Expert river runners use kayaks and enclosed canoes, but less experienced river runners are safest in a raft. Downstream from Oxbow to Dabney (5 river miles) or Lewis and Clark (9 miles), the going is easy with only minor riffles, ideal for canoeing.

Lone hiker pauses on footbridge across Multnomah Falls, Oregon's highest waterfall. Winter snow outlines green canyon walls around lower falls.

Brilliant autumn foliage gilds wooded slopes along Columbia River Scenic Highway. Narrow route links waterfall vistas and shady picnic areas. Moss-covered masonry of local basalt blends with region's topography.

Columbia River Scenic Highway

The old Columbia River Highway is an engineering classic—the first paved road across Oregon's Cascades and one of the most ambitious and scenic roads ever built in the Pacific Northwest. Opened in 1916, it remained until 1950 the only route along the steep Oregon cliffs of the Columbia Gorge. Now called the Scenic Highway, it is still one of the Northwest's loveliest drives. Cyclists also have discovered its charms.

You can poke along at a leisurely rate—enjoying river views from high overlooks, catching the spray of wispy waterfalls, and exploring some of the inviting forest trails. Moss-covered sections of the highway's original walls and railings add a charming note.

Two sections of the old road remain. The 22-mile western segment departs from I-84 at Troutdale, 16 miles west of Portland. It winds through rural country, then climbs to the Crown Point view point more than 700 feet above the river. Vista House, a Gorge landmark, is on the National Register of Historic Places; it was erected as a memorial to early explorers and the Oregon pioneers. A 9-mile eastern segment of the old route lies between Mosier and The Dalles (see page 34).

Larch Mountain. A favorite destination of Portland residents is Larch Mountain, approximately 38 miles east of the city. The Larch Mountain Road branches off the Scenic Highway east of Corbett, passing through hilly farm land and tree-lined corridors on its way to the summit. Pickers gather huckleberries here in late summer.

A short, steep trail leads from the picnic area to Sherrard Point, where a vast panorama encompasses five major Cascade peaks, the Columbia River, and Portland. A 7-mile trail descends along Multnomah Creek to the Scenic Highway.

Waterfalls in abundance. The 24-mile scenic route is enjoyable in itself, but the best rewards are found at the stops. Waterfalls, formed by tributary streams, cascade over the cliffs toward the river. Short trails lead to the falls and view points; walks of just a few hundred feet take you into the forest.

One of the finest falls, Latourell, drops straight and narrow into a shadowy pool. The names of Bridal Veil Falls, Mist Falls, Wahkeena (Indian for "most beautiful") Falls, and Horsetail Falls offer hints of their appearances. One of the best, Oneonta Falls, cannot be seen from the road; the 800-foot route to the falls lies up the stream bed, between canyon walls green with moss and ferns.

Best known of the waterfalls are the two drops of Multnomah Creek; at 620 feet, Multnomah Falls is the highest in Oregon. Near the base of the falls is a display with multilingual commentary. A trail curves up and across the often-photographed footbridge spanning the chasm; it continues to the top of the cliff, where a side trail leads to a viewing platform at the top of the falls.

Inside the Nature Center near the base of the falls, you learn about the geology, history, and Indian legends of the Columbia Gorge; hours are 1 to 5 Tuesday through Friday, 10 to 6 Saturday and Sunday.

Meals are available in the recently renovated Multnomah Falls Lodge, a traditional stopping point since 1925.

A hiker's paradise

For the hiker, the forest trails of the Columbia Gorge offer a virtual feast of choices—you can walk a few hundred feet to a waterfall view point, tuck a picnic in your knapsack and head up a creek trail on a day hike, or strike off on a weekend backpacking trip. The Oregon portion of the Pacific Crest Trail begins west of Cascade Locks.

In 1984, 39,000 acres of rugged forested slopes above the river were set aside as the Columbia Wilderness. The area contains about 200 miles of trails, including the Eagle Creek Trail and a segment of the Pacific Crest National Scenic Trail; key access points are from I-84 and Wahtum Lake. For information on trails and recreation facilities, contact Mount Hood National Forest offices at Troutdale, Gresham, or other locations. You can obtain information sheets on favorite trails and special area maps such as "Forest Trails of the Columbia Gorge."

Horses are allowed on some trails, but many routes are reserved exclusively for hikers. Large sign-maps at trailheads indicate the routes, and trails are well marked.

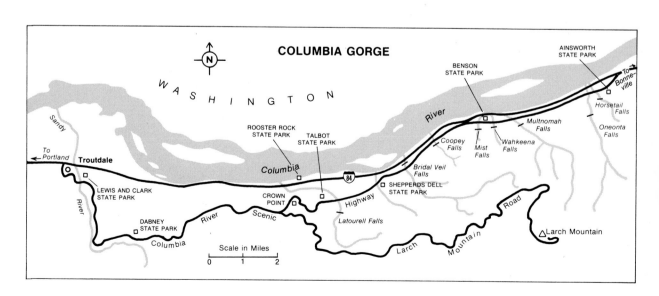

Among several short family excursions are the trails up Wahkeena, Multnomah, and Horsetail creeks. On the delightful route through Oneonta Gorge, you make your way from rock to rock through the narrow canyon; water is shallow in late summer, so a misstep isn't serious.

Longer trails follow the rim of the gorge or descend from Larch Mountain. Backpackers enjoy beautiful Eagle Creek Trail with its numerous waterfalls, Herman Creek, or other trails connecting with mountain lakes on the eastern ridges of the Cascades.

Bonneville Dam

First of the massive Federal dams to harness the power of the mighty Columbia was Bonneville, built about 40 miles east of Portland in the late 1930s. It was named for Captain Benjamin L.E. Bonneville, who explored the Northwest a century earlier. A 96-acre historic site here is listed on the National Register of Historic Places.

Originally constructed in two sections, Bonneville barricades separate river channels on either side of Bradford Island, an ancient Indian burial ground. The original powerhouse lies between the Oregon shore and the island; the spillway dam stretches from Bradford Island north of Cascades Island. A second powerhouse and adjoining visitor center connect Cascades Island to the Washington shore.

On the Oregon side of the river, picnic sites overlook the Columbia. Inside the visitor center on Bradford Island, exhibits explain the area's history, the operation of the dam, and fish migration. Guided tours are conducted in summer. You can watch the fish through underwater viewing windows or walk alongside the fish ladders.

From a canalside walkway, visitors can watch boats and barges pass through the 500-foot-long navigation lock along the Oregon shore. Preliminary work has begun on a larger navigation lock.

Immediately downstream, a state hatchery raises millions of young salmon for release. A self-guided tour shows you how the hatchery works, and teaches you about fish found in the Columbia.

The upper gorge

Angling for salmon and steelhead is popular just below the dam and on Lake Bonneville. Waterside parks provide boat launching ramps and facilities for camping, picnicking, fishing, and water sports.

Indian legends tell of an ancient natural bridge that once arched across the Columbia near Cascade Locks. Today the manmade Bridge of the Gods spans the river.

Cascade Locks. Numerous rapids or cascades blocking the gorge of the Columbia proved a serious hazard to pioneer wagon trains and river traffic. Until navigation locks were completed in 1896, travelers were forced to portage around this hazardous area. In late summer, the community celebrates Portage Days with an Indian-style salmon bake, arts and crafts booths, and a flea market.

Cascade Locks Marine Park, a National Historic Site, borders the site of the old Government Locks. The former canal lock is popular with anglers; Indians still fish here with long-handled dip nets as their ancestors did. In the lock tender's residence, built in 1905, a museum contains mementoes of local Indians and early settlers, the old portage road, and 19th century steamboats and railroads. Outside you'll see the diminutive Pony Engine, the Northwest's first steam locomotive.

For more than 70 years, colorful paddle-propelled steamboats plied the Columbia and other Oregon rivers. Learn more about this legendary era at the Sternwheeler Museum, located in the Cascade Locks visitor center at the east end of Marine Park. Eyewitness accounts of steamboat races and other events amplify displays of early photos and navigation equipment.

From mid-June through September, you can take a 2-hour cruise on the sternwheeler *Columbia Gorge*, a replica of the steamers that once plied Northwest rivers. The boat departs on three scheduled trips daily from a dock near the visitor center. From October to mid-June, the boat is moored in Portland. For cruise information, contact the *Columbia Gorge*, P.O. Box 307, Cascade Locks, OR 97014, phone (503) 374-8427 or (503) 223-3928.

Historic hotel. West of Hood River, the restored Columbia Gorge Hotel was built in 1921 by Simon Benson, a timber tycoon and tourism promoter, to serve travelers journeying along the recently completed Columbia Gorge Scenic Highway. Once again serving motorists, the elegant clifftop villa features individually decorated rooms, bountiful meals, parklike grounds, and its own 207-foot waterfall plunging toward the river.

The fertile Hood River Valley

The town of Hood River lies at the foot of an extremely scenic and fertile valley. South of town, the snowy cone of Mount Hood rises dramatically. Thick forests and dozens of sparkling streams descend its flanks. Vast fruit orchards spread across the valley floor.

The 20-mile-long Hood River Valley is Oregon's largest apple-growing region; additional thousands of acres are planted in pear and cherry trees. Hood River celebrates a Blossom Festival on the last weekend in April and a Harvest Festival in October, both good times for touring the orchard country. From August to December you can watch local fruit being processed for canning and packing.

Table wines and fruit wines are produced by several local wineries. For information on tours and tasting, contact the Oregon Winegrowers Association (see page 77) or the Hood River County Chamber of Commerce.

The Columbia Gorge becomes a virtual wind tunnel in summer, when windsurfers come by the hundreds from around the world to take advantage of steady winds and opposing river currents. Some international competitions take place here. Big race weekends offer quite a show as brilliantly colored sails skim across the river at speeds as high as 35 mph. Races and festivals are held here on weekends from mid-March through mid-August.

Hood River also hosts an old-fashioned Fourth of July celebration, the Hood River County Fair in late July, and the Columbia River Cross Channel Swim on Labor Day.

Port Marina Park. Tourist information is available in the visitor center in Port Marina Park. The Hood River

County Museum here focuses on the settlement of the Hood River Valley and its development as a famous fruit center; the museum is open from Blossom Day through October from 10 to 4 (closed Monday and Tuesday).

If you want to give windsurfing a try, equipment rentals and lessons are available. The park has a small marina, a swimming beach, and a picnic area.

Touring the fruit country. A 35-mile scenic tour guides visitors through the best of the valley. From Panorama Point you'll enjoy a sweeping vista of apple and pear orchards stretching toward the base of Mount Hood. The route leads through farm lands and orchards, and past appealing picnic sites beside the Hood River. In autumn some farms have roadside stands offering cider and freshly picked fruit to passers-by. Southwest of Parkdale, unimproved roads lead to lava beds along the northeastern slope of Mount Hood. The route returns through Parkdale and Dee to Hood River.

Lost Lake. Another fine drive leads to Lost Lake, about 28 miles southwest of Hood River in Mount Hood National Forest. Mount Hood rises in glacial majesty behind the lake. In summer the woods are full of pink rhododendrons; huckleberries ripen in autumn. The road to the lake is closed by snow in winter.

A Forest Service campground is located on the lake shore. In summer, groceries and fishing supplies are available at a small store, where boats and canoes can be rented in season. No motorboats are permitted on the lake. Fishing is good in nearby streams, and hikers enjoy views of Mount Hood on the trail encircling the lake.

East of the Cascades

Beyond Hood River the forest thins, and you become increasingly aware of a change in climate and topography. As you enter the semiarid plateau region east of the Cascades, the great banded cliffs stand out more sharply above the river, and the hills take on the warm yellows and delicate greens of wheat and grass.

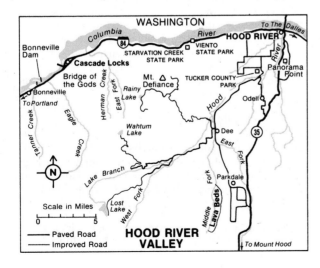

On its winding journey through the desert areas of eastern Oregon and Washington, the Columbia follows the rugged channel that it has cut during many centuries.

East of Hood River at Mosier, signs lead motorists off I-84 onto the Rowena Loops, a 9-mile scenic route encompassing part of the old Columbia River Scenic Highway. It climbs through ponderosa pine, scrub oak, and groomed orchards to Rowena Crest, a bluff nearly 750 feet above the river. The view point is part of Mayer State Park, which also offers picnic tables down by the river and facilities for swimming, boat launching, and fishing.

In April and May visitors enjoy a spectacular wildflower display in Tom McCall Preserve, about 100 feet north of the Rowena Crest parking lot. Footpaths weave through the terraced fields and past ponds to a river overlook.

Memaloose State Park, 11 miles west of The Dalles along I-84, has camping and picnic sites. It overlooks Memaloose Island, once an important Indian burial ground but now almost submerged by the reservoir.

The Dalles, end of the Oregon Trail

Bordering a great crescent bend of the Columbia, The Dalles lies approximately 189 miles from the river's mouth and 82 miles east of Portland. The historic town is the trading hub of north-central Oregon's thriving agricultural economy. Vast fruit orchards (primarily sweet cherries) begin at the city's outskirt; in late April, The Dalles celebrates a Northwest Cherry Festival featuring blossom tours, a parade, and a street fair.

The Dalles gained its main fame as the town at the end of the Oregon Trail. Yet thousands of years before the trappers and emigrant wagon trains arrived, primitive groups migrated down from the Bering Straits and scratched strange picture writings on the rocks overlooking the Columbia. Later, generations of Indian tribes gathered near Celilo Falls to trade and fish for salmon. In 1805 Lewis and Clark camped here overnight after taking their large canoes through the frightening rapids.

Two missions had been established by the time the first pioneer wagon train arrived in 1843—the vanguard of a vast overland migration that streamed across the plains for several decades. Most of the emigrants trudged on toward the rich lands of the Willamette Valley.

Gold was discovered in Idaho and eastern Oregon in the early 1860s. Miners surged into The Dalles, and the town boomed as an outfitting center. Wagons piled high with freight lumbered through on their way to the mines and livestock ranges. Steamboat service on the Columbia increased. Stages rumbled in from Canyon City, Umatilla, and other interior settlements.

During the third week in July, the town recalls that bygone era with Fort Dalles Days, a city-wide festival featuring fiddlers' contests, street dances, cowboy breakfasts, a chili cookoff, a rodeo, and a huge Western parade.

Explore The Dalles

The Dalles today combines its pioneer heritage with the demands of a modern agricultural center. Barges loaded with wheat and other cargo maneuver along the river.

Passengers get a different perspective of the river as sternwheeler *Columbia Gorge* churns under Bridge of the Gods. Summer cruises depart from Cascade Locks; nearby Sternwheeler Museum exhibits mementoes of steamboat era.

Salmon and steelhead leap up fish ladders at Bonneville Dam during annual spawning migration up the Columbia. Exhibits inside Visitor Center explain fish life cycle and dam operation.

Leaflets available at the Visitor Information Center, 404 West 2nd Street, outline a walking tour of the central district and suggested driving tours of the region.

Old courthouse. Built in 1858, the original Wasco County Courthouse is now located adjacent to the Visitor Center on West 2nd Street. It housed a sheriff's office and three jail cells on the first floor and a courtroom upstairs. In the early years, the building also served as a public meeting place and church; later it was used as the town's City Hall. Visitors are welcome daily from 10 to 5 in June, July, and August, and from 11 to 5 Tuesday through Friday the rest of the year. History exhibits, slide shows, and lectures take place here.

Historic churches. Two 19th century churches have been preserved. St. Paul's Church, built in 1875 at 5th and Union, now houses Episcopal church offices. Services are still held in the chapel each Wednesday noon.

St. Peter's Landmark, at Lincoln and West 3rd, is a red brick Gothic church built in 1897. Gargoyles glare from downspouts on the steeple, and a bronze rooster weather vane tops the spire. The church is open for tours Tuesday through Saturday from 11 to 3. It contains six rose windows and 34 vertical stained-glass windows, most of them given in memory of pioneer families. The pipe organ is constructed of rare tigerwood, the railing and altars of Italian marble, and the ceilings of stamped aluminum.

Art Center. Art exhibits and classes are held in the former Carnegie Library, 220 E. 4th Street. Open Tuesday through Saturday from 10 to 4, it also features a sales gallery containing work by local artists.

Riverfront Park. Sheltered by offshore islands, this park offers access to a fine area for beginning windsurfers; board rentals and lessons are available from shops in town. The nearby Boat Basin has boat rentals as well as launching and moorage facilities. Guided fishing trips are available here, or you can fish from shore.

Fort Dalles Museum. The old post surgeon's quarters, built in 1856 during the Yakima Indian wars, houses a museum of pioneer memorabilia. Located south of the business district at 15th and Garrison streets, it is the last remaining building of Fort Dalles. From May through September, the museum is open from 10:30 to 5 daily except Monday; the rest of the year, hours are noon to 4 Wednesday through Friday, 10 to 4 Saturday and Sunday.

Distinguishing the two-story board-and-batten structure are pointed shingles lapped in a design, a gabled room extending over an entry porch, and square-topped windows of leaded glass hooded with decorative cornices. Inside, handsome manteled fireplaces and period furniture decorate the rooms. Historic photos and possessions of pioneer settlers illustrate the settlement's early days. Outside, sheds house a variety of horse-drawn wagons, stagecoaches, and other early vehicles.

Scenic drive. A road loops high above town to a view point, where you can gaze upriver to The Dalles Dam. Sorosis Park is an oasis under the pines containing picnic tables, a children's play area, horseshoe pits, tennis courts, a jogging trail, and a rose garden.

The Dalles Dam— an old fishing site

Three miles east of The Dalles stands a link in the Columbia's chain of multipurpose dams. Completed in 1960, The Dalles Dam is primarily a hydroelectric project, yet its contributions to river transportation are more interesting.

Until recent decades, the turbulent waters—climaxing in the rocky gash of Celilo Falls—formed a major obstacle to river traffic on the Columbia. Passengers and cargo had to bypass the falls—first along Indian trails, then on a portage wagon road, and after 1863 by a 13-mile rail trip from The Dalles to Celilo. Finally in 1915 an 8½-mile canal replaced the railroad. In 1958 Celilo Falls and the old canal were submerged by water backed up behind The Dalles Dam; now, a navigation lock aids river traffic around the dam.

From June through Labor Day, guided tours to The Dalles Dam depart daily from 10 to 4:30 from a visitor center in Seufert Park, east of U.S. Highway 197 just south of The Dalles Bridge. A brightly painted engine and passenger car transport visitors to the dam. On this train tour, you visit the powerhouse, and you see scale models explaining how the dam works, exhibits on the Lewis and Clark Expedition and local history, and fish migrating up the fish ladders.

Many recreational opportunities are available along Lake Celilo, a 24-mile-long reservoir above the dam. You can picnic, fish, swim, water-ski, or windsurf. Celilo Park marks the site of old Indian fishing grounds, where generations of tribal fishermen speared or netted salmon from the river while perched precariously over the frenzied white water. Indians still fish in the traditional way on platforms behind the Portage Inn.

At Deschutes State Park, near the mouth of the river, the Oregon Trail Exhibit Shelter shows pioneers bringing their wagons across the river at this same spot.

At Biggs another bridge crosses the Columbia to Maryhill on the Washington shore. Maryhill Museum of Fine Arts displays one of the most diversified art collections in the Pacific Northwest.

Harnessing water power at John Day Dam

Upon its completion in 1968, the John Day Dam marked the final step in harnessing the waters of the lower Columbia. It crosses the river near Rufus, about 25 miles upstream from The Dalles, just below the mouth of the John Day River.

The dam has an awesome power-generating capacity—one of the largest of any single hydroelectric dam in the world; at peak production, it produces 59 million kilowatt hours daily.

Interstate 84 skirts the dam and the south shore of Lake Umatilla. Visitors can take a self-guided tour through the powerhouse and into the underwater fish-viewing room where displays identify fish species.

The navigation lock (near the Washington shore) can lift ships 105 feet in about 15 minutes. Towboats deftly nudge the unwieldy barges into the lock, through which more than 3.5 million tons of commercial cargo pass each year.

Numerous recreation areas dot the shores of Lake Umatilla, stretching some 76 miles upriver. Part of the reservoir is managed as a wildlife refuge, where migratory waterfowl stop on their flight along the Pacific Flyway. Philippi Park, on the John Day River, is a camping and picnicking area accessible only by boat.

During building of the dam, several towns had to be relocated. The entire town of Boardman was moved, as well as the business districts of Arlington and Umatilla. Highways and railroads were rerouted and buildings were transferred from the area now under water.

Up the lonely river

In the vast wheat lands and livestock ranges of eastern Oregon, settlements are smaller and farther apart. State rest areas are located along I-84 near Boardman.

For years Boardman was a sleepy settlement known as a highway gas stop in the midst of sagebrush and tumbleweeds. Relocated during the building of John Day Dam, Boardman today teems with agribusiness development—large-scale farming and cattle ranching, potato processing plants, and a modern industrial park. Construction of a $520 million coal-powered generating plant has stimulated additional growth. A large riverside park offers camping and picnicking facilities, a swimming area, boat ramp, and protected small craft harbor.

Beyond Boardman, U.S. Highway 730 forks northeast toward Umatilla and Washington's tri-cities area. Irrigon Park offers picnic sites, boat ramps, an enclosed swimming area, and an imaginative children's playground.

Umatilla, named for a local Indian tribe, is a busy water sports center. Umatilla Park and Marina is one of the most modern moorages on the Columbia; the complete marina includes overnight camping facilities and trailer hookups, boat ramps and docks, a picnic area, and a gravel swimming beach. A wildlife park near the interstate bridge provides good bird watching.

McNary Dam & Lake Wallula

Easternmost of the four dams along Oregon's northern border is McNary Dam, built in the 1950s just east of Umatilla and 292 miles upstream from the mouth of the Columbia. Access to the dam is from U.S. Highway 730.

Picnic sites, boat ramps, and swimming areas are available near the dam along the Oregon shore. At stopping points along a self-guided tour, recorded messages explain the dam's features. You can watch the fish through viewing windows in the fish ladders on both sides of the dam. From a gallery in the powerhouse you see the dam's 14 generator units.

To reach the navigation lock, you must cross the Umatilla Bridge to the Washington side of the river and take a side road from State Highway 14.

Hat Rock State Park, bordering the shore of Lake Wallula 9 miles east of Umatilla, is reached by a spur road off U.S. 730. The large monolith was a landmark often mentioned in the diaries of explorers and early-day travelers. Water sports enthusiasts enjoy the reservoir's numerous picnic sites, sheltered swimming beach, and boat ramps. Lawns and trees add refreshing greenery.

THINGS TO SEE AT COLUMBIA DAMS

The four dams along Oregon's Columbia River—Bonneville, The Dalles, John Day, and McNary—are part of the vast Columbia Basin Project harnessing the river and its far-flung tributaries for electric power, river navigation, irrigation, flood control, and recreation. Dams are operated by the U.S. Army Corps of Engineers. Each dam has special attractions, but all share common features.

Public areas are open daily during daylight hours. When you arrive, inquire at the visitor center about tours, recreation facilities, and special activities. Displays and brochures provide information about the dam, the river and its fish, recreation, and nearby attractions.

From March to November you can watch salmon, steelhead, and shad as they migrate from the ocean up the Columbia, heading for upstream spawning grounds. The major salmon migration occurs in autumn. Walkways extend along the outdoor fish ladders, and underwater viewing windows allow a close look at the fish.

To reach reservoir waters above the dam, the fish ascend fish ladders—a stairlike series of pools with submerged openings—that allow the fish to swim from one pool to the next until they reach the top of the dam. Fish counting stations identify each fish and record its passage.

At each dam you can watch river traffic pass through a navigation lock, going upriver or downstream around the dam. Changing the water level in the lock will lift or lower the boats and barges. The navigation lock at John Day Dam, with a maximum lift of 113 feet, is the highest single-lift lock on the Columbia. Lock passage is free to all vessels.

Loaded barges transport petroleum products and agricultural chemicals inland and move grain downstream for shipping to world markets. Tugboats push the barges and log rafts through the locks, and small pleasure boats cruise from one reservoir to another.

Each reservoir has riverside parks along both the Oregon and Washington shores. You can picnic or camp beside the river, launch boats, and enjoy water sports. Anglers pull in salmon (primarily Chinook and coho), steelhead, rainbow trout, American shad, walleye catfish, and bass. In spring and autumn, migratory waterfowl pause along the shores of Lake Umatilla.

Heceta Head Lighthouse, one of nine remaining lighthouses along Oregon's coast, flashes warnings from a rocky headland jutting far into surf. Its powerful beacon can be seen by ships as far as 21 miles out at sea.

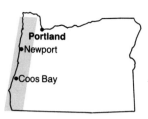

DOWN THE OREGON COAST

Explore or just relax along this inviting and varied shore

Oregon's ever-changing shoreline is rich in contrasts—broad, sandy beaches and rugged promontories, dense forests and rolling dunes, sheltered coves and grassy headlands, towering mountains and hidden lakes. U.S. Highway 101 closely parallels the 400-mile shoreline.

In the bracing sea air, vacationing families spend long days roaming quiet beaches, clambering over rocky promontories, beachcombing for driftwood and agates, and gazing into hidden tidepools. They frolic in the surf, build sand castles, fly kites, hike coastal trails, dig for clams, picnic in sheltered parks, or cast fishing lines in the nearest surf or stream. For a change of pace, they visit art galleries and cheese factories, drive or bicycle inland roads, ride horseback, play a round of golf, or take a boat trip. Winter brings the thrill of storm watching from coastal view points, and whale watching from excursion boats or headlands as gray whales migrate between the arctic waters of the Bering Sea and the lagoons of Baja California.

Coastal communities bustle with visitors from mid-June through Labor Day, but generally the best coastal weather comes in autumn, after the crowds depart. In summer, winds can be chilly on even the sunniest days, and low-hanging fog often blankets the coastal belt in mornings and evenings. Winter storms lure hardy beachcombers and storm watchers.

Accommodations range from elegant resorts and modern motels to housekeeping cabins. The northern half of the coast has been more extensively developed, but travelers find ample lodging along the entire shore.

State parks are normally open for day-use activities throughout the year, but some campgrounds are closed from November to mid-April. Nine coastal state parks remain open for year-round camping—Fort Stevens, Nehalem Bay, Cape Lookout, Beverly Beach, Washburne, Jessie M. Honeyman, Bullards Beach, Harris Beach, and Loeb. In summer, nine of the larger coastal park campgrounds operate on a reservation basis (see page 6). Primitive camp-sites for hikers and bikers are located in about 20 coastal state parks. Most private camping parks along the coast are open year round.

Travel packs containing brochures on attractions and events along the entire coast are available for $2 (for postage and handling) from the Oregon Coast Association, P.O. Box 670, Newport, OR 97365.

The Historic North Coast

Less than 2 hours from Portland, the northern Oregon coast attracts numerous vacationing families with its forested headlands, long sandy beaches, and varied activities. Coastal sites recall the historic Lewis and Clark Expedition, Indian legends, and tales of marine adventure.

Migrating salmon attract anglers to north coast streams from late spring into autumn. Good steelhead rivers include the Nehalem, Trask, Necanicum, Kilchis, and Nestucca. In many coastal ports, charter boats and guides are available for fishing on the rivers or sea.

Art galleries have sprung up in many coastal towns, especially around Cannon Beach and Lincoln City, and a number of crafts people make their headquarters along the coast. Local visitor information centers can direct you to galleries displaying the work of Oregon artists.

Numerous routes link Portland and the Willamette Valley towns with the main coastal centers. Roads pass through rolling farmland and cut through Coast Range forests; some follow meandering rivers to the sea.

Fort Stevens State Park

Nine miles west of Astoria, Fort Stevens State Park stretches 4 miles along the shore south of the Columbia (see map, page 28). Beachcombing, clam digging and surf casting engage beach visitors; at low tide, the battered hulk of the *Peter Iredale*, a British schooner that ran aground in 1906, beckons explorers.

Inland, several long, shallow lakes attract swimmers, boaters, and fresh-water anglers. A 2½-mile trail follows the wooded shore of Coffenbury Lake. Eight miles of paved bicycle trails wind through the park.

The park includes most of the old Fort Stevens Military Reservation that guarded the mouth of the Columbia from the Civil War until 1947. Battery Russell was fired on by a Japanese submarine in 1942—the only recorded attack on a mainland U.S. fortification since the War of 1812. Replicas of the original guns recreate the appearance of World War II emplacements. In the Visitor Center, a movie, displays, and historic photographs recount the fort's history. Ask for a map outlining a self-guided tour.

South of Fort Stevens, you can walk in solitude for miles along the wide, windswept beach. Wherever the surf beats in unhampered, razor clams are abundant. Or you can look for crabs cut off from the sea by the ebbing tide, or try surf fishing.

Stroll along Seaside's mall

If you haven't visited Seaside lately, you'll find the town has been revitalized with an attractive new mall along Broadway, its main street. A convention center as well as a favorite family resort, Seaside offers lively entertainment and a broad, sandy beach. You can stroll along the beachfront promenade—locally called the Prom—for nearly 2 miles, past impressive, large family beach houses.

A turnaround at the ocean end of Broadway marks the end of the Lewis and Clark Trail. Nearby, an aquarium exhibits marine life. Near the south end of the promenade, on Lewis and Clark Way, a reconstructed salt cairn marks the site where members of the famed expedition boiled sea water to provide salt for the group's return trip.

The Necanicum River flows through the center of town; it's a good stream for sea-run cutthroat, salmon, and steelhead. If you'd like to go riding along the beach, you can arrange for saddle horses in Seaside.

Activity-minded Seaside schedules events the year round—including a marathon and 8-km run in February, the Miss Oregon Pageant in July, a beach volleyball tournament and an arts and crafts show in August, and a month-long "Yuletide at Seaside" celebration.

Alpine blooms atop Saddle Mountain

Four miles south of Seaside, U.S. 26 sweeps inland along the Necanicum River through the thickly forested Coast Range toward Portland. Off U.S. 26 just east of Necanicum junction, a paved road climbs about 8 miles north to Saddle Mountain State Park.

You have two good reasons to hike the 3-mile trail to the top of 3,283-foot Saddle Mountain—an outstanding view and rare alpine wildflowers in spring. Only the final ½ mile is steep. Wear hiking boots if you have them, carry water, and bring a jacket; no water is available on the trail, and it's likely to be cold and windy on the summit.

If you have a wildflower identification book, bring it along. Botanists consider Saddle Mountain's peak an island of rare alpine flora isolated by Ice Age glaciers. Look for unusual blooms tucked amid the high rocks and crags.

Build sand castles at Cannon Beach

Named for a cannon washed ashore in 1846, the community of Cannon Beach extends along a scenic 7-mile strand between Tillamook Head and Arch Cape. Surf fishers, swimmers, clammers, and kite flyers enjoy the long, curving beach. Offshore stands Haystack Rock, a massive monolith rising 235 feet above the sea. Gulls and other sea birds nest in its crevices, and starfish and sea anemones hide in tidepools around its base.

In recent years, this attractive beach community has become a coastal art center. In summer Portland State University sponsors the popular Haystack program for adults—a selection of 1- and 2-week workshops and seminars in music, writing, and visual arts. A separate young people's program emphasizes art and outdoor activities. For more information, write to Haystack, Box 1491, Portland, OR 97207, phone (503) 229-4812.

Plays are performed in the town's Coaster Theater. Highlighting the events calendar are a spring Sand Castle Contest, where competitors create fanciful architectural masterpieces and sculptured figures from wet sand, and a December Dickens Festival and Christmas play.

North of Cannon Beach, a narrow paved road climbs west from U.S. 101 up the southern bluff of Tillamook

NORTH COAST

Head to Ecola State Park, perched above the sea. Extending along the coast for more than 6 miles, Ecola has two sandy beaches along its southern edge. Rock fishing is excellent in a sheer-walled cove on the north side of Ecola Point, the main picnic area. Farther north you'll find interesting tidepools along Indian Beach and Indian Point; often you'll see surfers at Indian Beach. From the picnic area, look out to the old Tillamook Lighthouse, clinging to a wave-swept rock a mile offshore.

Neahkahnie's legendary treasure

Arch Cape marks the beginning of rugged coastal scenery. U.S. 101 tunnels through the massive rock, then climbs high above the sea as it curves around Neahkahnie Mountain. Local legends hint of Spanish treasure buried on the mountain by the crew of a mystery ship.

Ten miles south of Cannon Beach, Oswald West State Park memorializes the foresighted governor who in 1912 preserved the coastal beaches for the people of Oregon. Campers can load their gear on park-supplied wheelbarrows for the short trek through lush coastal rain forest to the walk-in campground.

Fishing, crabbing, clamming, and driftwood hunting are outdoor pursuits at Nehalem Bay. Indoors, visitors stroll through art galleries and taste Oregon wines. More than 100 artists display their work at the Nehalem Arts Festival in July. Access to Nehalem Bay State Park on the spit is from the village of Manzanita.

Plan a coastal picnic

Inviting parks and roadside seafood stands often tempt travelers to picnic along the coast, but nowhere is it easier than in northern Tillamook County. Enjoy wine tasting and cheese sampling as you shop for your banquet; more than a half-dozen local food producers and suppliers encourage visits.

Southbound travelers begin their wine and food tour at the Nehalem Bay Winery, housed in a converted cheese factory a mile east of U.S. 101 on State Highway 53 at Mohler (open daily from 10 to 5). Pick up fresh seafood —crab, shrimp, or oysters—and freshly baked bread and pastries in Garibaldi, and stop for locally made sausages and smoked meats in Bay City.

Oregon's best-known Cheddar cheese materializes before you at the Tillamook County Creamery, 2 miles north of Tillamook on U.S. 101 (open daily 8 to 6). A mile farther south, Brie cheese is produced at the Blue Heron Cheese Factory, housed in a handsomely renovated barn (open daily 9 to 6). Both have delicatessens where you can supplement your picnic supplies.

Along the shore of Tillamook Bay

Rockaway Beach, largest of several towns between Nehalem Bay and Tillamook Bay, hosts a Kite Festival each spring. You can enter the competition or watch the proceedings from a wayside park along U.S. 101.

Barview Jetty County Park offers good rock fishing and skin diving from the jetty and surf fishing from the shore; camping and picnicking facilities are available.

Commercial and pleasure fishing boats sail from Garibaldi's harbor. You can launch, rent, or charter boats here or remain ashore to inspect the catch as it's processed.

Back road explorers will enjoy a 14-mile drive inland, up the quiet wooded valleys of the Miami River and Foley Creek. Another scenic byway is the Kilchis River Road; anglers come here for trout and steelhead.

Reclaiming the Tillamook Burn

In the summer of 1933, a vast forest fire, whipped by vicious winds, turned the wooded hills of Tillamook County into a roaring inferno. In 1939 and 1945 other fires broke out in the same area. More than 500 square miles— 13½ million board feet—of Oregon's finest timber was destroyed, some of it more than 400 years old.

Today the young trees of Tillamook State Forest are gradually covering the burned hills.

You can camp or picnic in a number of forest parks along State 6, and trails wind through the young Douglas firs. At Gales Creek Park, 4 miles west of Glenwood Junction, a 2-mile hiking trail winds north along Gales Creek. For information, contact the Oregon State Forestry Department office at 801 Gales Creek Road, Forest Grove.

The Tillamook Valley

Large barns, grazing cows, and lush pastures identify the Tillamook Valley as dairy country. Serene and relatively uncrowded, southern Tillamook County offers a magnificent coastline, pastoral river valleys, and wooded mountains. Five rivers flow into Tillamook Bay.

One of the most popular stops on the coast is the Tillamook County Creamery, which some 700,000 people visit each year to watch cheese being made, tour a museum, and taste the famous cheese.

The fascinating Tillamook County Pioneer Museum is housed in the 1905 county courthouse at 2106 Second Street. Three floors of exhibits provide intimate glimpses of Tillamook County life and history. Exhibits include a replica of a pioneer dwelling, Indian artifacts, photographs of settlers and early logging operations, and an outstanding natural history display. Many of the 500 specimens of animals and birds are displayed in habitat settings. From May through September the museum is open Monday through Saturday from 8:30 to 5, Sunday from noon to 5; the rest of the year, it is closed on Monday.

Craft demonstrations are featured at Tillamook's Arts and Crafts Fair in early July. A notable attraction at the Tillamook County Fair in August is the unique Pig 'N' Ford Races; drivers race around a dusty track in stripped-down Model T Fords while clutching squealing pigs.

Three Capes Loop

Travelers speeding along U.S. 101 have little hint of the magnificent 35-mile coastal drive west of Tillamook. The Three Capes Loop connects a trio of rugged promontories—Cape Meares, Cape Lookout, and Cape Kiwanda—where tall forests meet the sea, waves thunder against basalt headlands, and secluded beaches await the beachcomber. The loop rejoins U.S. 101 south of Tillamook.

Cape Meares. Head west from Tillamook along the south shore of Tillamook Bay. Bayocean Peninsula attracts clammers and crabbers. You can also fish, hunt for agates, or search for driftwood and glass fishing floats.

In Cape Meares State Park, trails lead through the rain forest to the Octopus Tree (a venerable multitrunked Sitka spruce) and to the historic lighthouse at the tip of the headland. In summer, the lighthouse is open to visitors (see page 53). The headland is a good site for whale watching in winter and early spring.

South of the cape, beachcombers explore tidepools and surf-carved caves and search for driftwood and agates. Offshore, sea lions frolic in the waves and sea birds soar and swoop near Three Arch Rocks.

Oceanside and Netarts are quiet seaside towns. On fair-weather weekends, hang-gliders float over the rocks and beaches near Oceanside. In March, residents host a Beachcombers' Fair. Anglers often hook flounder, perch, and sea trout in Netarts Bay; you can also go clamming and crabbing here.

Cape Lookout. One of the most prominent headlands on the coast, Cape Lookout juts almost 2 miles into the sea like a rugged basalt finger. A popular year-round campground, Cape Lookout State Park offers access to a broad sandy beach, many trails, clamming, and surf fishing. You can picnic overlooking the beach or back beneath gnarled, moss-draped trees.

From the summit of the ridge, a 2½-mile trail winds through a dense coastal rain forest, past a monument commemorating the 1943 crash of a World War II patrol plane, toward the tip of the cape. Since heavy rains make trails difficult to travel, hiking boots are a wise idea. Many kinds of birds nest on the rugged walls of the headland.

Sand Lake. Dune buggies, four-wheel-drives, and motorcycles take to the dunes near Sand Lake—roaring, spinning, leaping, and sliding over the sand. Regulations for off-road vehicles are posted, and visitor use permits are required in advance for summer holiday weekends (available from the Siuslaw National Forest office in Hebo).

A natural channel breaches a low coastal berm, letting the ocean flow inland to create the small lake. Coastal plants flourish along its shore, and migrating ducks and geese winter here. Try crabbing or flounder fishing from the bridge or channel bank.

Cape Kiwanda. Southernmost of the three headlands, Cape Kiwanda shelters the beach at Pacific City. Hang-glider enthusiasts often work off the high dunes just behind the cape. One of the finest marine gardens on the coast lies just south of Cape Kiwanda.

Pacific City. With no protected harbor or boat basin, local fishermen launch their flat-bottomed dories through the surf directly from the beach, then head for offshore fishing grounds. Charter trips can be arranged. Prime quarry is the salmon, caught from June through September; bottom fishing for cod and halibut is good around Haystack Rock and off the nearby reef.

The Nestucca River area offers not only deep-sea fishing but excellent surf and river fishing for salmon, trout, and steelhead. Try your luck clamming or crabbing near the river mouth or search for driftwood along the spit curving south of Pacific City.

Along U.S. 101 to Cascade Head

Pastoral valleys and wooded mountains present restful vistas in southern Tillamook County. County parks and forest campgrounds dot the coastal river valleys; for a recreation map, stop at the Tillamook County Chamber of Commerce office, 2105 First Street, Tillamook.

You catch glimpses of the ocean again near the family resort of Neskowin, one of the oldest beach towns. Adults can enjoy a round of golf at either of two public courses; children wade in the sun-warmed creek, frolic on the beach, and ride horseback on sandy trails. Surf fishing often yields good catches of sea perch, trout, and flounder.

Just south of town, the 10-mile Neskowin Scenic Drive veers inland from U.S. 101, following a section of the old coast road along Neskowin Creek. It cuts a narrow corridor through the lush greenery of Cascade Head Experimental Forest; informational signs indicate points of interest. The route meets U.S. 101 north of Otis Junction.

Hills, forest, and ocean meet on the wild mountainous Cascade Head ridge. Though much of the rugged headland is now protected as a scenic research area, hikers can sample it on several trails. Near the summit, Forest Road 1861 leads west to the start of the Nature Conservancy North Trail and the Harts Cove Trail. Just north of the Salmon River, Three Rocks Road leads west from U.S. 101 to the beginning of the Nature Conservancy South Trail. Off Three Rocks Road is the Sitka Center for Art and Ecology on Cascade Head Ranch.

The Scenic Central Coast

South of Lincoln City, U.S. 101 skims the ocean shore. State parks and scenic waysides come one after another. You have your pick of wide, sandy beaches—favorite destinations of agate hunters and driftwood collectors. From December through May, migrating gray whales appear off the coast, drawing visitors to rocky headlands.

Many of the coastal towns cluster near the mouths of rivers—the Yaquina, Alsea, Yachats, Siuslaw, and Umpqua—and streams where anglers cast for sea-run cutthroat trout or steelhead. A half-dozen golf courses dot this section of the coast.

Lincoln City is the center of a busy oceanside strip of resorts, motels, galleries, craft and gift shops, and tourist-oriented attractions.

Sizable commercial fishing fleets moor in harbors at Depoe Bay and Newport. Here, too, are sport-fishing boats that depart in search of salmon in summer and carry whale-watching groups in winter.

Florence is the northern gateway to the Oregon dunes, a scenic recreation area marked by miles of windswept sand dunes.

Resort and condominium complexes overlook the sea. Many motels and cottages are also available; some offer kitchens, fireplaces, and decks with ocean views.

Hang gliders catch the wind, soaring aloft from high sand dunes
behind Cape Kiwanda. Destinations are landing spots
on beach beside surf far below.

Tug glides beneath bridge
spanning the Columbia River
between historic seaport of Astoria
and the state of Washington.

Groping for gapers is fun for the whole family.
Springtime low tides lure throngs of clam diggers
to the broad, sandy beach at Seaside.

Oregon Coast   **43**

Lincoln City—five towns in one

A consolidation of five small coastal towns, the tourist center of Lincoln City stretches 7½ miles along U.S. 101 between forested mountains and the sea.

North of town you can visit Lacey's Doll and Antique Museum (open May through September), located near the junction of U.S. 101 and State Highway 18. Art galleries and gift shops cater to visitors.

Center of boating, water-skiing, and windsurfing activities is Devils Lake; sheltered picnic areas and campsites dot its tree-lined shore. You'll see rowboats, sailboats, and canoes on the lake, along with faster models. On windy days from spring through fall, kite flyers put on a daily show at D River Wayside Park.

Residents fish during their lunch hour at Devils Lake or along the D River, the lake's ¼-mile-long outlet to the sea (and reputedly the world's shortest river). You can rent a boat and tackle at the lake.

Anglers of all ages have a grand time fishing off the Taft public dock at the narrow mouth of Siletz Bay. Salmon and smaller fish—perch, flounder, greenlings—are hauled in here. If you heave a crab ring over the side while you fish, you might catch the fixings for a hearty seafood stew.

Along the winding Siletz

Homeland of the Siletz Indians and once the scene of a booming logging and sawmill industry, the Siletz River is best known today as steelhead country. Fish begin moving upriver in May.

State Highway 229 parallels the Siletz upriver from U.S. 101—first through a pastoral valley and then along a narrow river canyon where forests are thick with ferns and moss-draped trees. The meandering river imposes its relaxed atmosphere on the valley. Anglers can launch or rent boats at several moorages. Small riverside parks are located along the route.

Salishan and salmon vie for attention

Queen of the coastal resorts is luxurious Salishan Lodge, situated on a promontory overlooking Siletz Bay and the sea. Renowned throughout the Northwest for its resort and conference facilities, Salishan also offers an 18-hole golf course and indoor and outdoor tennis courts. West of U.S. 101, a new shopping mall—called The Marketplace at Salishan—offers a variety of shops and services.

Fogarty Creek State Park includes one of the state's most accessible ocean beaches. From wind-protected picnic sites east of U.S. 101, a path beneath the highway provides easy access to the beach. Each September several thousand visitors gather for an Indian-style salmon bake here; fish are split and fastened onto a framework of green branches, then propped near open fires to bake.

Rockfishing is popular at Boiler Bay Wayside. A ship's boiler that washed ashore here in 1910 can still be seen at low tide. Marine gardens are also uncovered when the tide is out.

Depoe Bay's fame rests chiefly on its small, rock-bound harbor and its colorful fleet. Commercial boats unload their catch on the south side of the harbor, while sightseeing and deep-sea fishing trips depart in summer from the north wharf. Salmon fishing is good from May through mid-October; tuna fishing is best from mid-June through September. Whale-watching boat trips depart in winter. Each Memorial Day, the Fleet of Flowers ceremony honors men who have lost their lives at sea.

Stroll along Depoe Bay's promenade (look for spouting water west of the sea wall) or watch boats negotiate the narrow, rock-lined channel beneath the bridge. A salt-water aquarium exhibits sea animals and fish.

South of Depoe Bay, Whale Cove attracts surfers, skin divers, and rock hunters. Rumrunners landed cargoes of illicit whisky here during Prohibition.

Cape Foulweather's splendid vistas

The highway reaches a height more than 450 feet above the sea as it climbs Cape Foulweather, a headland named by Captain James Cook in 1778. Take the Otter Crest Loop—part of the old highway curving west of U.S. 101 around the tip of the headland—for spectacular panoramas. You can picnic above the churning waves at Devils Punchbowl State Park; a trail leads down to the beach.

During the spring and autumn gray whale migrations, whale watchers scan the sea from atop Foulweather and other high coastal peaks and headlands in search of spouting white puffs of vapor.

You can watch surf fishers at Rocky Creek, camp at Beverly Beach State Park, hunt for agates and driftwood near the mouths of rivers and creeks, and peer into tidepools and caves north of Otter Rock and below the Yaquina Head lighthouse. The community of Agate Beach attracts rockhounds, surfers, and golfers.

CENTRAL COAST

Scale in Miles
0 5 10

—— Paved Road
—— Unpaved Road

The rural Yaquina Valley

Pleasant U.S. 20 winds through the Coast Range between Corvallis and Newport, paralleling the Marys River on the eastern slope and the Yaquina on the western.

At Chitwood the highway passes a restored covered bridge, still in daily service, then continues west to the hillside mill town of Toledo and on to Yaquina Bay. There's another old covered bridge south of U.S. 20 at historic Elk City.

Newport's lively waterfront

Busy capital of Lincoln County, Newport stretches along a bluff on the north shore of Yaquina Bay. A revitalized bayfront and a large commercial fishing fleet contribute both to Newport's color and to its prosperity.

To get acquainted with Newport, take the town's scenic drive, which includes Yaquina Bay State Park at the north end of the bridge, as well as the lively bayfront. Here, commercial canneries mingle with waterfront restaurants, art galleries, specialty shows, and other attractions. In the Nye Beach area, Newport's oldest quarter, works by local artists are displayed at the Arts Center facing the ocean.

Two buildings of the Lincoln County Historical Museum, at 545 and 579 S.W. 9th Street, feature intriguing exhibits on pioneer life and the logging industry, nautical memorabilia, Siletz and other Northwest Indian cultures, and other topics. In summer the museum is open daily from 10 to 5; winter hours are 11 to 4 (closed Mondays). Ask for a free county historical map.

In late February, Newport's Seafood and Wine Festival showcases Northwest specialties. Fishing boats are colorfully decorated for the Blessing of the Fleet ceremony in early March. During the annual Loyalty Days and Seafair Festival in early May, visitors can board naval ships.

Along the bayfront. Overlooking the estuary from the wooded bluff is the Yaquina Bay Lighthouse, built in 1871 but used only 3 years. Its light tower and lightkeeper's living quarters are combined in the same structure. Restored and refurnished with items typical of the 1870s, the lighthouse is open in summer (see page 53). Picnickers find sheltered tables near the parking area. A trail leads down to the beach and north jetty.

The bayfront road winds past the Coast Guard station and under the bridge. Salt-water aromas and a forest of masts guide you to the busy, mile-long waterfront.

You can buy crabs out of a steaming pot or enjoy seafood specialties at several dockside restaurants. Deep-sea trollers make regular sightseeing and fishing trips in search of salmon, bottom fish, tuna, and crabs. Fish processing plants handle the catch.

A look beneath the sea at Undersea Gardens, 267 S.W. Bay Boulevard, reveals marine animals, fish, and plants in a natural habitat.

Bring your imagination to Mariner Square on the bayfront. Ripley's Believe It or Not! features a world where truth is stranger than fiction. Next door, the Wax Works creates scenes from history and fantasy. Both attractions are open daily from 9 to 8 in summer, 10 to 5 in winter.

HIKING THE OREGON COAST

Hikers are getting a spectacular coastal trail that, when completed, will stretch nearly 350 miles from the Columbia River south to the California border. It provides a marvelous opportunity for intimate glimpses of this varied coast.

The northernmost portion of the Oregon Coast Trail—from the Columbia River's South Jetty 62 miles south to Barview County Park at Tillamook Bay—was dedicated in 1975. Tall cedar signposts have been placed along the route, and a map brochure is available. Detailed trail information is available in *A Hiker's Guide to the Oregon Coast*, available for $2 from the State Parks and Recreation Division in Salem (address on page 6).

Many parts of the trail are not new. Before the Coast Highway (U.S. 101) was completed in the 1930s, travelers made their way along the packed sand beaches on foot and by car, ferrying across estuaries and heading inland only when stopped by rocky headlands. Early-day hikers and pack animals followed Indian trails across coastal capes.

Today's hiking trail follows many of these traditional paths; it ascends Tillamook Head following the route taken by members of the Lewis and Clark Expedition, and it climbs the slope of 1,700-foot Neahkanie Mountain along an old Indian route. New sections of trail are under construction to link existing segments.

The trail can be enjoyed on a day trip or on longer outings. Autumn offers the best hiking weather—the sun is warm, the north wind dies away, and mornings and evenings are clear. Experienced hikers prefer to walk with the prevailing winds—from north to south in summer, the reverse in winter. Trails may be slippery in wet weather.

Hikers are cautioned to carry a canteen of water (especially on long beach stretches), to be prepared for wind and rain, and *never* to turn their backs on the ocean. ("Sneaker" waves or "high rollers" sweep several people out to sea every year.) Binoculars, a map, tide table, and extra socks and shoes may add to your enjoyment.

Primitive campsites for hikers and cyclists have been set aside in 20 coastal state parks. Most state campgrounds are open mid-April through October; nine (see page 39) operate the year around.

Sea lions bask on offshore rocks north of Florence. Visitors view these year-round residents more closely inside nearby Sea Lion Caves.

Anglers count the catch when boat docks in Depoe Bay's small harbor. Vessels exit to sea through narrow entry below highway bridge.

Wild rhododendrons and beach grass provide colorful counterpoint to golden sand. Oregon dunes stretch more than 40 miles along coastline between Florence and Coos Bay.

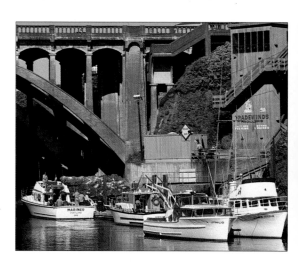

If you follow the north shore of Yaquina Bay inland toward Toledo, you soon leave the tourist waterfront behind to pass the commercial fishing fleet, private cruisers, ocean freighters loading lumber, commercial oyster farms, and tidal flats where clammers dig at low tide. Frequently you'll see yachts gliding across windy Yaquina Bay.

South Beach. Cross the Yaquina Bay Bridge and another treat awaits—the outstanding Mark O. Hatfield Marine Science Center, operated by Oregon State University.

Most visitors find this a fascinating stop. In the public area, marine fish and invertebrates are displayed in tanks designed to show the creatures' natural habitat. Displays explain various marine subjects—coastal geology, tides, and estuary life are highlights. In the handling pool, visitors touch and examine an octopus, anemones, starfish, and other intertidal animals. Brochures and inexpensive field guides are available in the bookshop. The Center is open daily from 10 to 4, in summer from 10 to 6. The summer Seatauqua program offers public workshops, field trips, films, and talks on the marine environment.

Ten miles south of Newport at Seal Rock, humorous "chainsaw sculpture" is displayed at Sea Gulch.

South to Waldport and Yachats

On the route south to Alsea Bay, state parks and waysides offer an ample number of picnic sites and beach accesses for coastal travelers. If you'd like to meet some of the local artists and crafts people, stop at the Seal Rock Art Co-op (open Wednesday through Sunday from 11 to 5).

Waldport, a friendly little town on the south shore of a broad estuary, is a popular fishing, crabbing, and clamming center. Inland along State Highway 34, riverfront parks and marinas bordering the Alsea River draw trout, salmon, and steelhead fishermen. Waldport celebrates Beachcombers' Days in mid-June with 3 days of festivities. A salmon derby is held on the Alsea River in early October.

Farther south, rugged rocks jut into the crashing surf at Yachats (YAH-hots); often you'll see fishers here, bracing themselves as they cast lines into the incoming tide. Site of a summer smelt run, Yachats organizes a Silver Smelt Fry in July. The town also hosts an arts and crafts fair in mid-March. South of the Yachats River, a broad sandy beach invites a brisk walk or run; a kite-flying contest is held here in October. The town also promotes a Christmas in Yachats celebration.

Pause awhile at Cape Perpetua

This magnificent headland—created by several ancient lava flows and also named by Captain James Cook during his historic 1778 voyage—is part of Siuslaw National Forest and the hub of the Cape Perpetua (Per-PET-u-ah) Scenic Area.

First stop for most travelers is the Forest Service visitor center south of the cape, just off U.S. 101. From late May to mid-September it is open daily from 9 to 6; off-season hours are 10 to 4 Friday through Sunday. A 15-minute movie and diorama introduce visitors to the natural forces at work on the coastal environment and the area's plant and animal life.

Hiking trails branch out from the visitor center to driftwood-strewn beaches, lush rain forest, shell mounds, and tidepools (all marine life is protected in the area). Don't miss the spectacular view from atop Cape Perpetua, accessible by car and trail; whales, seals, sea lions, and porpoises are sometimes visible from the headland.

A self-guided 22-mile auto tour begins just north of the visitor center and winds through wooded hills and coastal valleys, returning to U.S. 101 at Yachats. Ask for a descriptive brochure at the visitor center.

Two small wilderness preserves are located between Cape Perpetua and Heceta Head: Cummins Creek Wilderness and, a short distance south, Rock Creek Wilderness. A third protected area, Drift Creek Wilderness, is located northeast of Waldport. All three preserves are steep and heavily forested with Sitka spruce, western hemlock, and other coastal vegetation. Streams support chinook and coho salmon and steelhead trout. For information on the areas, contact the Waldport district office of Siuslaw National Forest.

Sea lions and a landmark lighthouse

Ten miles south another splendid headland thrusts far into the restless surf. Marked by its often-photographed lighthouse, Heceta (Huh-SEE-ta) Head was named for Spanish sea captain Bruno Heceta, who sailed along the coast in 1775.

The lighthouse is not open to the public. Heceta House has been acquired by the Forest Service and is being restored. You can picnic, hike, or fish in Devils Elbow State Park just south of Heceta Head Lighthouse. The best views are from headlands to the south.

Campers head for Washburne Memorial State Park just north of the headland; the park has a good swimming beach, surf fishing, and gravelly patches where beachcombers often find agates.

About 12 miles north of Florence, sea lions cluster around Sea Lion Caves where they live the year around, mating and rearing their pups. In spring, bull sea lions select—and sometimes battle for—their harems of 10 to 20 cows. Pups are usually born in June. The barking of the sea lions resounds in the large marine cave at the base of the cliff. Visitors can descend into the cavern by elevator to a viewing area daily from 9 A.M. to dusk. In stormy weather most of the animals stay inside the cave, but when the sun comes out, they bask on a long rocky ledge outside or frolic in the waves. Many shore birds nest on the cliffs or inside the cave.

One of the coast's more unusual attractions is Darlingtonia Botanical Wayside, an 18-acre state preserve 5 miles north of Florence. It has been set aside exclusively for the protection and observation of the native *Darlingtonia californica* (also known as the cobra lily or pitcher plant). You can see hundreds of the cobralike plants from a wooden walkway built above the marshy area.

At Indian Forest, 4 miles north of Florence on U.S. 101, a footpath leads through coastal pines to full-size replicas of Indian tribal dwellings. Buffalo roam inside a corral, and handmade Indian arts and crafts are sold in the trading post. The attraction is open from May through mid-October; hours are 10 to 4 in spring and autumn, 8 to dusk in summer.

Florence, rhododendron capital

Pink blooms of the coast rhododendron brighten the roads around Florence each spring, providing the theme for a community-wide Rhododendron Festival on the third weekend in May. This friendly port town at the mouth of the Siuslaw River offers a stimulating diversity of outdoor recreation possibilities.

Shopkeepers and crafts people have rejuvenated Florence's Old Town area, a three-block strip of Bay Street east of U.S. 101 along the Siuslaw riverfront. Bypassed by the coast highway, the area languished for years, but the refurbished buildings and interesting shops now make this a pleasant place to browse. A small commercial fishing fleet is moored upriver, and you'll often see lumber being loaded in port.

Rhododendron Drive heads west from Florence along the river to Harbor Vista County Park, overlooking the Siuslaw bar, then loops north to Heceta Beach. Tiny huckleberries ripen along coastal roads in late summer.

Sea-run cutthroat return to tidewater in July and August, salmon and steelhead migrate up the Siuslaw in autumn to spawn, and clams and crabs populate the bay.

One mile south of Florence on U.S. 101, the Siuslaw Pioneer Museum and the Gallery of Local Arts occupy a former church. Museum exhibits focus on the town's settlers, coastal Indians, the early logging industry, and natural history. From mid-May through September, the museum is open from 1 to 5 daily except Monday; off-season hours are 1 to 5 Tuesday, Saturday, and Sunday; in January through March, from 1 to 5 Tuesday only.

On the building's lower level, the Siuslaw Gallery of Local Arts exhibits and sells the work of 20 area artists and crafts people. The gallery is open daily except Tuesday—from 10 to 5 from mid-May through October, noon to 4 the rest of the year.

Dunes Country

Vast shifting mountains of sand, smoothed or wave-rippled by coastal winds, rim the coast for more than 40 miles between Florence and Coos Bay. Relentlessly, the wind-blown sand moves slowly eastward, creating islands of pine forest and blocking the flow of fresh-water streams to make a chain of coastal lakes.

A 41-mile stretch of this unusual region has been designated the Oregon Dunes National Recreation Area, a 32,000-acre preserve administered by Siuslaw National Forest officials. Between the Siuslaw River and Coos Bay, the dunes extend inland from 1 to 3 miles and rise to heights of 300 feet. Roads and trails branch west into the dunes area from U.S. 101. Twelve miles north of Reedsport, the Oregon Dunes Overlook offers informational signs, trails, and spacious views over the dunes and coastal forest to the ocean. Many state park and Forest Service campgrounds dot the area.

Stop at the headquarters office in Reedsport, just south of the Umpqua River bridge, for a map of the area and information on campgrounds, beach access, hiking and nature trails, off-road vehicle (ORV) driving tips and regulations, and special activities.

Exploring the Oregon Dunes

You can enjoy the dunes area in a number of ways—sliding down hills of sand or riding dune buggies over the sandy slopes; fishing in fresh-water lakes, from jetties or piers, or casting into the surf; boating and canoeing on the lakes; hiking trails near the ocean or beachcombing for driftwood. Dune buggy trips depart south of Jessie M. Honeyman Memorial State Park.

In the north dunes, the best area for backcountry activity lies between the Siltcoos and Umpqua rivers; since most of this area is closed to ORV cross-country travel, vegetation is diverse. In the southern part of the dunes, the tallest and widest dunes are found from the Umpqua Lighthouse south to Tenmile Creek.

Look for deer and raccoon tracks near wooded areas in early morning; beavers inhabit the lake areas. You'll see gulls and other shore birds on the beaches, blue herons around wooded lakes and ponds, and migratory waterfowl in the marshy areas.

A chain of coastal lakes

Just behind the dunes, a chain of about 2 dozen coastal lakes offers a pleasant change of pace. Some are small, choked with lily pads and hidden from the highway. Larger lakes—such as Woahink, Siltcoos, Tahkenitch, and Tenmile—have long fingers penetrating far into the canyons, Most of the lakes are stocked with fish. Several larger lakes have marinas with boat rentals.

Sheltered from the ocean winds, lake waters are warm enough for pleasant midsummer swimming. Bathhouses are located at Cleawox and Woahink lakes (both bordering Honeyman State Park) and at Eel Lake (William M. Tugman State Park); you can swim in other lakes as well. Sailboats, rafts, canoes, and rowboats dot the lakes on pleasant days.

Along the lower Umpqua River

Logging and forest products provide the livelihood for many residents in western Douglas County; paper and plywood mills are located in Reedsport and Gardiner.

The region's big annual celebration is the Ocean Festival, held on the last weekend of July. Events include a parade, outdoor arts and crafts display, 5 km and 10 km runs, and tours of Umpqua Lighthouse (usually closed to visitors).

Winchester Bay's prosperity is linked to its small boat marina—Salmon Harbor—liveliest in summer as Chinooks and silvers show up outside the bar and start to move upriver. Charter trips can be arranged.

The Umpqua has a well-deserved reputation as one of the state's best fishing streams. In tidewater areas of the Umpqua and Smith rivers, anglers pull in striped bass, Chinook salmon, and shad. Smelt migrate upriver in February. Clammers dig in the Umpqua tidelands and along coastal beaches north of the river. Crabbing is also good near the river mouth.

Upstream, riverside turnout areas along State Highway 38 invite travelers to picnic or saunter along the bank. Anglers fish in the riffles.

Sleepy Scottsburg provides few clues to its lively past. In the early 1850s, it was a rip-roaring boom town, largest in southern Oregon and principal outfitting point for the Siskiyou gold mining camps. Tall-masted schooners from San Francisco transported miners and supplies up the Umpqua to Scottsburg.

Exploring the Coos Bay Area

U.S. 101 zips quickly through the towns of North Bend and Coos Bay, but the best attractions of this lively region lie off the highway—west to a trio of splendid parks, and inland through placid river valleys.

Coos Bay separates two entirely different types of coastal terrain: shifting sand dunes rim the coast north of the bay, whereas rugged cliffs and rocky coves line the shore south to Cape Arago. The best natural deep-water harbor between Puget Sound and San Francisco, Coos Bay is a busy commercial waterway as well as a recreational delight. Small boats cruise its protected waters, and clammers and crabbers scour their favorite grounds.

Forest products dominate the region's economy, and timber is shipped from the port of Coos Bay to worldwide markets. Southwestern Oregon is also myrtlewood country; you can watch this distinctive hardwood being shaped into decorative items at several south coast factory-shops.

Regional events include the North Bend Jubilee and North Bend Airshow in June; the Oregon Coast Music Festival in July; Coos Bay's Blackberry Arts Festival and the Coos County Fair in Myrtle Point in August, and the Bay Area Fun Festival in September.

A stop in North Bend

North Bend's Simpson Park occupies the northern end of a wooded peninsula that extends into the bay. Picnic tables and a visitor information center are located here. Another attraction is the Coos Historical Museum, which contains exhibits of Indian and pioneer mementos. The museum is open daily except Monday; hours are 10 to 4 from Tuesday through Saturday, noon to 4 Sunday. A steam-powered logging locomotive and donkey engine are displayed outside.

North Bend's Pony Village Shopping Center is the largest covered shopping mall on the Oregon coast.

Coos Bay attractions

Coos Bay's showplace is the Coos Bay Mall, a 4-block section of Central Avenue in the heart of the business district. Bordered with trees and flower beds, the covered pedestrian mall is a pleasant place to stroll and shop. At one end is the elegant old City Hall, built in 1923 and modernized with covered front walkways and a fountain; the building now houses shops and restaurants. You can see other restored buildings on a city walking tour.

Regional art is featured at the Coos Art Museum, 235 West Anderson, open 11 to 5 Tuesday through Friday, noon to 4 Saturday and Sunday. Art classes and shows by emerging and established Northwest artists are held here.

In mid-July, Coos Bay's 9-day Oregon Coast Music Festival draws music lovers to the south coast. Programs range from chamber and symphonic to folk, jazz, concert band, and dance music. Related events sponsored by other groups include art exhibits, seminars, nature programs, and a music camp for young people. For information, write to the Music Enrichment Association, P.O. Box 663, Coos Bay, OR 97420.

Along the coast to Cape Arago

Superb state parks and other coastal attractions lure travelers west of U.S. 101 along the Coos estuary. Clammers find good digging in vast tide flats between Empire and South Slough. From Coos Head to Cape Arago the coastline is a succession of eroding sandstone headlands, offshore reefs, and driftwood-strewn beaches. During winter storms, huge waves crash against the bluffs, sending great bursts of spray high into the air.

Campgrounds are located west of Charleston at Sunset Bay State Park and at Bastendorff Beach County Park.

Charleston. Commercial and charter fishing boats operate out of the busy Charleston Boat Basin. Peak season is mid-July through September, when deep-sea anglers troll offshore for silver and Chinook salmon. You can have your catch smoked or canned near the docks. Rental boats and crab rings are available. Visitors are welcome daily from noon to 4 at the nearby Coast Guard Station.

Visitors are welcome daily from noon to 4 at the nearby Coast Guard Station.

South Slough. Fresh water from coastal streams meets and mingles with salt water of the ocean in South Slough, site of the nation's first estuarine sanctuary. Though pri-

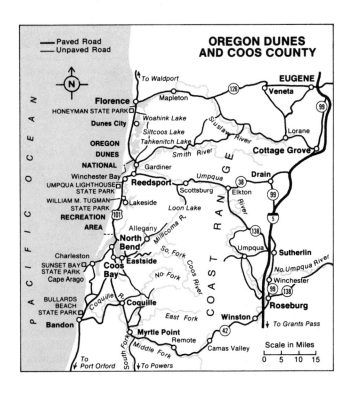

marily a reserve for research and education, the area has trails, a canoe launch area, and an interpretive center with ecological displays. Located 5 miles south of Charleston, the center is open from 8:30 to 4:30 daily from June through August, weekdays only the rest of the year.

Sunset Bay State Park. Precipitous sandstone cliffs curve protectively around this miniature bay, sheltering it from ocean winds. Small children frolic safely in gentle water near shore while their parents enjoy the broad sandy beach for sunning or sunset watching. At low tide, look at the eroded troughs in the wave-cut bench rock and at sea life in acres of tidepools. A 3-mile hiking trail leads from the campground through the grounds of Shore Acres to Cape Arago State Park.

Shore Acres State Park. Unique in Oregon's state park system, Shore Acres encompasses the former estate of a 19th century timber and shipping tycoon. His sailing ships brought hundreds of exotic plants from distant lands to be planted in the estate's formal English garden, now fully restored, and in other display areas.

An interpretive center contains exhibits and historic photos. Visitors can picnic or walk along the sculptured sandstone bluff, fish from the rocks, or watch wave action from a glassed-in viewing area.

Cape Arago State Park. Southernmost of the three parks, Cape Arago offers a commanding view of the coast and of ships entering and leaving the Coos Bay harbor. Barking sea lions loll on wave-washed Simpson Reef, a tilted sandstone shelf just north of the cape. Trails lead down the bluff to rock-fishing areas, tidepools, and sheltered coves. Migrating whales can be seen offshore in spring.

Seven Devils coast. West of the Charleston bridge, the Seven Devils Road provides access to a trio of remote, rock-strewn beaches between Coos Bay and Bandon. Side roads lead to Agate Beach, Merchant's Beach, and Whiskey Run Beach, site of an 1853 gold rush. Headlands separate the beaches. At low tide, beachcombers can walk for 6 miles along the shore, looking for agates, jasper, and petrified wood among the rocks.

Inland river valleys

Country roads fan inland, through dairy land marked by spacious old barns and along the banks of placid coastal rivers. Anglers troll the tidewaters of the Millicoma and Coos rivers for shad and striped bass.

To drive up the Millicoma Valley, turn east from U.S. 101 in south Coos Bay and follow Coos River Highway signs through Eastside. Beyond Allegany the paved road ends, and the gravel route narrows and worsens as you begin to climb. You can picnic in a grove of myrtle trees 4 miles northeast of Allegany at Nesika County Park. Six miles beyond, a pair of 200-foot-high waterfalls make Golden and Silver Falls State Park a scenic delight. You can hike and picnic here (no drinking water).

South of Coos Bay, State Highway 42 forks southeast through more farming and dairy country to Coquille, hub of southern Oregon's myrtlewood area. The highway follows the river upstream for more than 30 miles. Myrtle

trees decorate the coastal foothills, and you can picnic in a riverside myrtle grove at Hoffman Memorial Wayside, 3 miles south of Myrtle Point.

The Coquille Valley Art Center is open from 1 to 4 Wednesday through Sunday. The Coos County Logging Musuem is located in Myrtle Point.

Along the South Coast

U.S. 101 touches the coast again at Bandon. Oregon's superb southern shore has fewer access highways, and fewer visitors, but it offers some of the coast's most spectacular scenery. Side roads branch east from the highway up tranquil river valleys. Wildflowers brighten the coastal hills and spur roads from March to August, but they're at peak bloom in May and June.

Accommodations cluster around the larger towns— Bandon, Port Orford, Gold Beach, and Brookings—that have become vacation and sport-fishing centers.

Bandon, Oregon's cranberry capital

Bandon, located at the mouth of the Coquille River, has an active art colony and several excellent galleries. Its restored Old Town invites strolling. In September, Bandon hosts a Cranberry Festival with a full weekend of activities including a cranberry food fair.

Just north of town, Bullards Beach State Park is a year-round campground bordering the river and ocean. Beyond the picnic area, a road leads to the restored lighthouse on the spit overlooking the river's treacherous bar. The historic lighthouse, built in 1896, is open to visitors in summer (see page 53).

Departing from Bandon's Boat Basin daily at 12:30 and 3 P.M., the sternwheeler *Bold Duck* makes 2-hour boat trips up the Coquille River. Weekend dinner cruises are also scheduled. For information, call the ticket office at (503) 347-3942 between 11 and 3.

The Beach Loop Road winds along the bluff southwest of town; offshore seastacks of somber black rock mark the seascape. You'll find wind-sheltered picnic tables and beach access at Bandon State Park.

Farther south, U.S. 101 passes several myrtlewood factory-shops where travelers can watch wooden articles being made. Children can feed tame deer and small animals in natural surroundings at the West Coast Game Park Safari about 7½ miles south of Bandon.

Picnic near a century-old lighthouse

Occupying Oregon's windy westernmost tip is the Cape Blanco Lighthouse, reached by a 6-mile access road from U.S. 101 from a point north of Port Orford. In continuous operation since 1870, the brick lighthouse has walls 6 feet thick at the base. Now automated, the light is closed to the public.

The cape has interesting rock outcroppings offshore. Wind-protected camping and picnic facilities are available

Sunset softly colors beach and coastal rocks south of Cape Sebastian. U.S. Highway 101 hugs the coast along this rugged and wild section, providing magnificent ocean views.

With balletlike movements, lumberman corrals logs, directing them toward mill at Coos Bay to be trimmed and shaved into mountains of chips.

With a splash of spray, jet boat heads up forest-bordered Rogue River. White water trips penetrate 52 miles upstream from Gold Beach. Passengers pause for hearty lunch at riverside lodge.

Oregon Coast **51**

at the state park here, and a trail leads down to the drift-wood-littered beach. After winter storms, beachcombers search amid the driftwood for glass fishing floats. Low tide reveals tidepools near the base of the cape.

South of the Sixes River, forest roads lead inland to Grassy Knob Wilderness. For information, contact Siski-you National Forest officials in Powers or Grants Pass.

Port Orford's historic Battle Rock

Port Orford is a sports center, busiest in the autumn when migrating salmon and steelhead attract anglers to the Sixes and Elk rivers. In spawning season, you can watch salmon lunge up the fish ladders at the state fish hatchery.

Garrison Lake attracts both coast birds and trout an-glers. You can reach the coastal dunes from the state way-side. At low tide, there's good hunting for blue agates and glass floats.

Buffington Memorial Park, west of U.S. 101 in Port Orford, has a picnic area, playground, jogging trail, and horse arena.

Be sure to visit the local harbor, a natural deep water port. Boats have no bar to cross to get to the open sea. Most commercial and sport boats are launched by a con-verted log-loading boom; a paved ramp is also available. In season, you can purchase fresh Dungeness crab, shrimp, bottom fish, and salmon.

Southwest of town, Port Orford Heads State Wayside offers sweeping coastal views from Cape Blanco south to Humbug Mountain. Migrating whales pass offshore, and

you'll often see fishing boats trolling for salmon or check-ing crab pots.

Battle Rock rises above Port Orford's sandy beach like a giant mossy-backed serpent. It was the site of an 1851 conflict when a party of hostile Indians besieged white settlers who took refuge on the rock. The battle is reenacted annually during the city's Fourth of July cele-bration. At low tide, hikers can walk out to the rock and follow a winding trail to its tree-covered crest or explore a tunnel. At high tide, waves surge around Battle Rock, turning it into an island.

Surfers head for beaches south of town at Battle Rock Wayside and Hubbard Creek Bridge.

About 13 miles south of Port Orford, life-size replicas of dinosaurs and other extinct animals lurk in a fern-filled forest setting at Prehistoric Gardens.

South to the Rogue River

From Bandon south to the California border, no paved roads link the coast with interior towns. Most of Humbug Mountain State Park lies on the sheltered inland side of the mountain, but on the north slope, trails lead down to a sandy beach cut by a pleasant creek.

Fishing draws visitors the year around to the twin towns of Gold Beach and Wedderburn, which flank the mouth of the Rogue. Depending on the season, fishers cast for Chinook, silvers, or steelhead from bank, boat, or ocean. In Gold Beach you can rent tackle and boats and arrange for fishing guides. Good clamming areas lie along Bailey Beach and Myers Creek. Agate hunters and beach-combers prowl the long beach below town. Horseback riders can rent saddle horses for trail rides in the Wedder-burn hills.

Jet boat trips. One of the best side trips on the coast is the jet-boat trip up the lower Rogue River. Operators transport passengers and mail upriver in open boats pow-ered by hydro-jets. Travelers have a choice of excursions: a 32-mile trip upstream to Agness or a 52-mile ride up to Paradise Lodge in the "wild river" section of the canyon.

Excursions depart about 8:30 A.M. daily from May through October, pausing for a hearty, family-style lunch at one of the Rogue's riverside lodges before returning to Gold Beach in the afternoon. In winter the mail boat trav-els upriver three times a week. For current information on fares and schedules, contact the Gold Beach-Wedderburn Chamber of Commerce in Gold Beach.

Forested slopes border the rocky canyon. Passengers often see blacktail deer and other wild animals; birds swoop overhead; and clumps of wildflowers add bright touches. Often the boat's pilot will point out geological features or recount tales of river life.

Above Agness the canyon narrows and deepens. Whitewater rapids come one after the other. You might see hikers on the Rogue River hiking trail (see page 76), which parallels this roadless section.

Riverside trails. A forest road, now paved, follows the Rogue's south bank upstream to meet the Powers-Agness road. Hikers can branch off on trails along the Rogue or Illinois rivers in Siskiyou National Forest. Illahe marks the west end of the 40-mile Rogue River trail.

SOUTHWESTERN COAST

Scale in Miles
0   5   10   15

Paved Road
Unpaved Road

A primitive road branches south from the Rogue River road along the Illinois River, known for its clear water, rugged canyon, and excellent steelhead fishing (autumn through spring). The hiking trail begins above Lawson Creek.

Rugged coastal panoramas

Some of Oregon's most wild and rugged coastal scenery is concentrated along U.S. 101 between Cape Sebastian and Brookings. For a nostalgic scenic detour, drive the stretch of the twisting old coast highway that climbs to Carpenterville, the side road southeast of Pistol River.

Samuel H. Boardman State Park, named for the father of Oregon's outstanding state park system, offers splendid seascapes and three picnic areas. The first is on U.S. 101 near 245-foot-high Thomas Creek Bridge. You can look for driftwood near the Whale's Head picnic area or try surf casting or clamming at Lone Ranch picnic area. Short access roads lead to spectacular view points at House Rock and Cape Ferrelo. Hiking trails descend to Natural Bridges Cove and to Indian Sands, where the rust-crusted sculptured dunes extend to the edge of the bluff.

Southernmost of Oregon's state campgrounds, Harris Beach State Park combines sandy beach and rocky shore. Located 2 miles north of Brookings, it attracts surf fishers, hardy swimmers (on incoming tides), and beachcombers. Offshore rocks add drama to ocean views; numerous sea birds dwell on Goat Island. South of the parking lot, a trail rambles over the headland to a tiny cove that becomes one enormous tidepool at low tide.

Azaleas and lilies at Brookings

Just north of the California border, Brookings marks the mouth of the Chetco River. Timber, commercial fishing, and flower bulb farming dominate the economy.

Blooming wild azaleas attract visitors for the Azalea Festival on Memorial Day weekend; the best display is in Azalea State Park, a 26-acre natural park east of U.S. 101. Acres of snowy lilies bloom in July, scenting the air with delicate fragrance, and fields of golden daffodils blossom in February and March.

The productive waters of the Chetco River offer trout in spring, steelhead and salmon in autumn. Licensed guides are available for either stream or ocean fishing, and charter boats depart from Brookings during salmon season. Other anglers enjoy rock fishing, surf casting, or fishing off the jetty at the river mouth. The Brookings-Harbor Chamber of Commerce can direct visitors to good crabbing and clamming areas.

The Chetco River Road leads inland from the coast. Rhododendrons, azaleas, and wild lilacs grow profusely. Amid the heavy stands of Douglas fir in Siskiyou National Forest are scattered some unusual trees and plants, including the rare Port Orford cedar, the Brewer's weeping spruce, myrtle trees, and some of Oregon's few groves of coast redwoods (*Sequoia sempervirens*). Rarest of all is the kalmiopsis, a small rhododendronlike plant protected in the Kalmiopsis Wilderness (see page 73). For information on campsites, picnic areas, and points of interest, inquire at the Chetco Ranger Station in Brookings.

SENTINELS LIGHT THE WAY FOR SHIPS

A century ago their blinking lights pierced the darkness, guiding mariners along the treacherous coast. Today five lighthouses—Yaquina Head, Heceta Head, Umpqua River, Cape Arago, and Cape Blanco—still signal ships far out at sea. Automation has eliminated the lightkeeper's job, but the mystique of the 19th century lighthouse remains.

A walk around one of these timeless sentinels will take you back to days when shipping was a dangerous adventure. From outside the lighthouse, look up at its many-sided lens. As the lens turns, it focuses light from a constantly burning bulb into a bright beam. Each lighthouse has a unique light pattern—such as one flash every 20 seconds or a red and white pattern—that identifies the light to passing ships. The Coast Guard maintains these navigational aids.

Three inactive lighthouses—Cape Meares near Tillamook, Yaquina Bay near Newport, and Coquille River near Bandon—have been restored by the State Parks and Recreation Division and are open to visitors. Each contains exhibits of historic interest.

Cape Meares Lighthouse, 10 miles west of Tillamook in Cape Meares State Park, was built in 1890. A photo mural display is featured in the restored structure. Visitor hours are 11 to 6 daily in summer, by appointment only for groups the rest of the year.

Yaquina Bay Lighthouse was constructed in 1871 to mark the harbor entrance to Yaquina Bay. It was replaced 3 years later by the Yaquina Head Lighthouse 4 miles north; the tower overlooking the bay entrance was never reactivated. It is the only surviving structure in Oregon combining a light tower and keeper's dwelling in the same structure. The lighthouse is open from noon to 5 daily from Memorial Day through September; the rest of the year, it is open on weekends from noon to 4.

Coquille River Lighthouse, constructed in 1896, is at the south end of Bullards Beach State Park, 1 mile north of Bandon. It contains photo and informational displays on the Coquille River and area shipwrecks. The lighthouse is open from June through September from 8 to 6, in winter by appointment through the park office.

Shimanek Bridge near Scio in Linn County carries rural traffic. Unusual because of its color, this covered bridge is one of about 50 still dotting Oregon country roads.

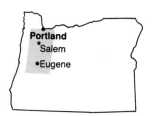

THE WILLAMETTE VALLEY

Historic communities dot Oregon's fertile heartland

The broad and bountiful Willamette Valley extends some 125 miles south of Portland, cradled between the fir-clad slopes of the Coast Range on the west and the Cascade Mountains on the east. Still essentially rural, it contains the state's large cities and major industries and (including Portland) roughly two-thirds of the population. Rolling hills and buttes accent the flat lowlands, which are cut by numerous tributary streams meandering down from the hills to join the main Willamette River.

Interstate Highway 5 bisects the valley, by-passing the cities. Older north-south routes are State Highways 99W and 99E, which link valley towns west and east of the river.

To see the best of the Willamette Valley, you must leave the highways and explore rural routes that wind through small towns and farm lands, up tributary creeks, and into foothills above the valley. Country roads play hide-and-seek with streams, cross covered bridges, and pass 19th century churches and spacious old barns.

Oregon's Heartland

The Willamette Valley was the wellspring of civilization in the Pacific Northwest. In terms of influencing history, the Willamette was to its valley what the Mississippi and Ohio rivers were to mid-America. The history of the Willamette Valley is really the history of Oregon, for the rich valley was the destination of fur trappers and homesteaders from the earliest days.

From the arrival of the trappers and traders until railroads were completed in the 1870s, the Willamette River was the primary carrier of commerce. Towns grew up around its ferry landings, shipping points, and mill sites. Steamboats traveled up the river as far as Springfield— and on tributaries such as the Yamhill and Tualatin— transporting passengers and cargo between riverside settlements.

In the early days, the Willamette Valley was Oregon's center of agriculture, commerce, culture, and social activity. It still is.

Some outsiders mispronounce the name of the valley and river. As one exasperated old-timer told a visitor, "It's will-LAM-it, dammit!"

The pioneers' promised land

The journey west was a long and difficult one. Some early travelers sailed around Cape Horn, but most made the tiring journey by wagon train along the Oregon Trail.

Settlement in the Willamette Valley meant isolation, hardship mixed with pleasure, and occasionally even prosperity; but life was generally uneventful. Most of the settlers were Americans. In the early years, Oregon had little of the cosmopolitan influence that peppered the development of other western states.

The discovery of gold in California in 1848 turned the majority of overland migrants southward, away from the Oregon Trail that had previously led most pioneers to the Willamette Valley. Many Oregon men traveled south to the diggings; some returned with gold, and more than a few valley stores, farms, and businesses were financed by gold removed from the ground in California. Farmers who stayed behind made big money supplying the California merchants who provisioned the miners.

Rich farm land edged by forests

The fertile lands of the Willamette Valley attracted settlers in the 1840s, and this rich farm land still yields an impressive array of crops. As you travel rural roads you can discover fields of strawberries, caneberries, blueberries, hops, peppermint, wheat, flax, beans, corn, bulbs, holly, and nut and other fruit crops (hazelnuts, walnuts, peaches, prunes, and cherries). Most of the nation's northern-climate lawn grass seed is grown here.

Logs are cut on the surrounding hills and mountains, but most of the processing takes place in the valley. The Eugene-Springfield area, at the south end of the valley, is recognized as the lumber capital of Oregon—and as one veteran lumberman put it, "You might as well call it the lumber capital of the world." Sawmills, plywood plants, and paper factories have been joined by a host of allied industries that process bark and wood chips into many useful products.

A river parkway

The Willamette winds through Oregon's most populous region, yet in many stretches it retains a sense of the untouched wild. Most people get only glimpses of this splendid waterway. Many roads and highways cross or touch the river, but no scenic roads parallel its shore for extended distances because early road builders avoided the Willamette's muddy lowlands.

Since 1967 the Willamette has been the focus of an innovative river parkway plan—known as the Willamette River Greenway—that has improved the river's ecosystem and enhanced its recreational uses. Reservoirs near the river's headwaters have tamed the Willamette's rampaging floods, and conservation programs have done much to clean up the river. Fish are thriving again in the Willamette.

Waterside parks dot both banks of the Willamette for some 200 miles, from Cottage Grove Reservoir and Dexter Dam to the Columbia River northwest of Portland; a few are accessible only by boat. To learn about access points, obtain a copy of the Willamette River Recreation Guide from the state's tourism office (address on page 9).

Increasing use of the river and lands bordering the water has brought some problems, for public and private land is not always clearly marked. Inquire locally regarding public access roads, park areas, and boat landings to avoid trespassing on private roads and property.

River recreation. The most enjoyable way to explore the Willamette is by boat. Though essentially a meandering river, it offers canoeists and kayakers the excitement of fast chutes and white water in its upper reaches.

Below Corvallis the river widens, gathering tributaries and dignity as it flows northward. Water activity increases as urban boaters and water-skiers enjoy the river. Most parks bordering the Willamette provide boat ramps, and several marinas operate along urban stretches of the lower river. Canoes and small craft can be rented in some of the larger towns.

As they migrate upstream, salmon and steelhead attract great crowds of anglers. Trout, bass, and other freshwater fish also await the lure.

River ferries. Motorists cross the lower Willamette on three free county-operated ferries. Each accommodates four to six cars—and an occasional cyclist or two—per trip, making continuous crossings during daylight hours. Electrically powered cables operate the ferries.

From Canby on State 99E, take North Holly Street about 3 miles north to the Canby Ferry landing. On the north bank, a county park offers picnic tables and a boat launching ramp.

The Wheatland Ferry crosses the Willamette 12 miles north of Salem. In river boat days, vast amounts of grain were shipped from a settlement here.

Midway between Albany and Salem, the Buena Vista river crossing has had ferry service since 1851. From I-5, drive about 4 miles west from the Talbot turnoff. A county park is located on the west bank.

Birthplace of Oregon

The lower Willamette Valley was the birthplace of American government in the Oregon country. It was here that pioneers settled to farm the rich lands and, in a historic vote at Champoeg, that a majority of settlers voted to cast their lot with the United States.

Oregon City, which grew along the Willamette River at the site of an impressive waterfall, became the center of government west of the Rockies. Settlements grew up along the territorial roads; many of these towns are now linked by State 99W and 99E west and east of the river.

Tualatin Valley byways

Once alive with beaver and a favorite hunting ground of Hudson's Bay Company fur trappers, the fertile Tualatin (too-WALL-a-tin) Valley is now one of the state's fastest-developing areas. The name of the meandering river comes from the Indian word twality, meaning lazy river. Despite its rapid growth, the valley still contains prime agricultural land. Several wineries welcome visitors.

West of Portland, the broad, busy Tualatin Valley Highway (State 8) is Washington County's "main street," linking the towns of Beaverton, Hillsboro, Forest Grove, and smaller communities. A number of research and electronics industries have settled here.

Off State Highway 217, enclosed Washington Square shopping center houses more than 130 retail stores and specialty shops (including six major department stores). Skylights, vaulted ceilings, and landscaped garden courts accent the climate-controlled mall.

Forest Grove is the site of one of the oldest colleges in the West, Pacific University, founded in 1849 as Tualatin Academy. On the campus you can visit the Old College Hall; built in 1850, it was the first frame building on the Tualatin Plains. Constructed of hand-hewn timbers and topped with a graceful bell tower, the building housed classes until 1948, when it was converted into a museum.

Valley byways reveal small communities where 19th century churches come as a pleasant surprise. Several of these churches are located north of U.S. 26 near the West Union Road. About 4 miles north of Hillsboro you'll find the small, white Tualatin Plains Church (locally called the Old Scotch Church), which was built about 1878; almost surrounded by trees, it stands amid gravestones of pioneer settlers. Sequoia trees grouped around Verboort's Catholic Church are the legacy of an unsuccessful gold seeker named John Porter, who returned home from California carrying a sack of cones gathered from the giant redwoods; other redwood trees flank the Washington County Courthouse in Hillsboro and are scattered about Forest Grove and the nearby countryside.

Festive celebrations. Forest Grove turns into a tintype of the 1890s each spring during the town's annual Barbershop Ballad Contest and Gay '90s Festival. Many townspeople dress in period costumes, and surreys and horseless carriages reappear. Barbershop quartet competitions attract groups from all over the Northwest. The town also hosts a Concours d'Elegance in July. During the town's August Corn Roast, visitors enjoy hayrides, watch square dancers perform, and eat corn roasted over open fires.

Hillsboro hosts a Happy Days Celebration in July and the Washington County Fair and Rodeo in August. Sherwood has a Robin Hood Festival in July, and Tualatin sponsors an August Crawfish Festival. On the first Saturday in November, thousands of persons congregate in Verboort (2½ miles northeast of Forest Grove) for the community's Sausage and Kraut Dinner and bazaar.

Trolley Park. From May through October, old-time trolley cars roll again at Trolley Park, an unusual museum tucked away in the forest 38 miles west of Portland, near Glenwood. The park is open daily from 11 A.M. to 6 P.M. Operated by the Oregon Electric Railway Historical Society, it offers trolley rides, an exhibit on American trolley cars, and tours of a car barn. A 26-acre park offers picnic tables, campsites, and swimming and fishing in Gales Creek; for group reservations, phone (503) 642-5097.

Clackamas roads offer discoveries

Southeast of Portland, country back roads follow the Sandy and Clackamas rivers. Many rural delights await the traveler—lily fields coloring the landscape near Sandy in summer, produce stands offering fresh-from-the-farm vegetables, simple roadside signs advertising home businesses or pets for sale. The region's largest shopping mall is the Clackamas Town Center, located off I-205 at Sunnyside Road.

Waterside recreation at Lake Oswego. Lakeside living keynotes the town of Lake Oswego, built around the shores of the 3½-mile-long private lake. Boaters and waterskiers skim through lake waters, and apartment dwellers lean over their balcony railings to feed the ducks. A pleasant town for strolling, Lake Oswego has an interesting selection of shops and restaurants. Each June the town hosts a Festival of the Arts, featuring exhibitions, an arts and crafts bazaar, and performing arts.

At the mouth of Oswego Creek, George Rogers City Park offers a tree-shaded picnic area, a small beach, and a public boat landing on the Willamette River. Cyclists enjoy several bike trails near town. Mary S. Young State Park lies along State 43 about 3 miles south; you can picnic, fish, or hike here.

Learn about local history. In several towns, museums offer insights into the region's lively history. Nineteenth century churches are scattered through the countryside; inquire at Clackamas County chambers of commerce for a historical map indicating points of interest.

Fruit trees that pioneer homesteaders brought across the plains in 1847 prosper near Milwaukie, located on the Willamette's east shore about 6 miles upriver from Portland; in the 1860s, the Bing cherry was developed here. On Saturdays and Sundays from 11 to 3 visitors learn about local history at the Milwaukie Museum, housed in a relocated and restored 1865 farmhouse at 3737 S.E. Adams; an antique streetcar stands nearby. If you like, relax or picnic in peaceful North Clackamas Park.

Gresham's historical museum, housed in the Art Mall building on the campus of Mount Hood Community College, is open to the public on weekdays.

Troutdale also has a historical museum located in a city park on the Sandy River. Old equipment and tools used by pioneer farmers and carpenters can be seen Wednesdays from 1 to 3 or by appointment.

Barlow Road markers. Sandy, located on U.S. Highway 26, marks a waypoint on the historic Barlow Road; beginning in 1846, Sam Barlow's toll road looped south from the Oregon Trail around the flank of Mount Hood, offering emigrants an alternate route to the dangerous river journey down the Columbia. A plaque at Sandy's City Hall and several markers along U.S. 26 commemorate the route.

Southeast of Sandy on State Highway 211 at Eagle Creek is the restored farm house of Philip Foster. Since weary emigrants traveling the Barlow Road were welcomed and resupplied here, Foster's pasture became a famous camping ground.

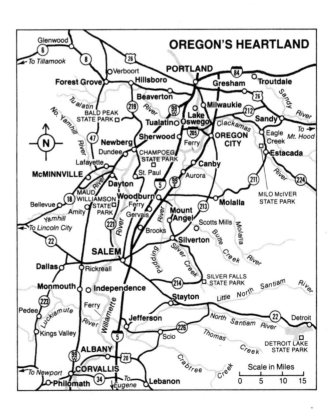

Clackamas River Road. Estacada, at the junction of State Highways 224 and 211, is the gateway to the Clackamas River recreation area. State 224 and forest roads penetrate deeply into Mount Hood National Forest. For information on forest recreation, campgrounds, and hiking trails, contact Forest Service officials in Estacada.

Hiking and equestrian trails, boating, and river fishing attract campers and picnickers to Milo McIver State Park, 5 miles west of Estacada off State 211.

Professional and amateur loggers compete in feats of strength and skill at the Estacada Timber Festival in July.

Oregon City, territorial capital

In 1828 Dr. John McLoughlin, factor (chief agent) and superintendent of Hudson's Bay Company at Fort Vancouver, and British Governor Simpson chose the falls of the Willamette River as the site for a sawmill to process timber for Pacific markets. By the 1840s, Oregon City was the Northwest's major city and capital of the vast Oregon Territory. A transportation industry developed to portage cargo and passengers around the 41-foot falls to upstream settlements. At 5th and Washington streets, the "End of the Oregon Trail" interpretive center is open Wednesday through Saturday from 10 to 4, Sunday from noon to 4.

Oregon City lies 12 miles south of Portland near the confluence of the Clackamas and Willamette rivers. The town's business district borders the river on the east bank; its residential area lies atop a high bluff. Pedestrians are conveyed between the two levels by a free public elevator at 7th Street and Railroad Avenue.

Historic houses. Atop the bluff at 713 Center Street, the former dwelling of Dr. John McLoughlin is open to visitors as a monument to the man who has been called "the father of Oregon." He encouraged American emigrants to settle in the fertile Willamette Valley and supplied many of their needs. The elegant, two-story, white clapboard house has been restored and refurnished with late 18th and early 19th century pieces originally brought around Cape Horn from England, including many of Dr. McLoughlin's personal articles. The house is open daily except Monday from 10 to 4, to 4:30 in summer. The graves of Dr. McLoughlin and his wife are located just north of the house.

Next door is another historic house, the former residence of Dr. Forbes Barclay, a civic leader from 1850 to 1872.

The 1907 Mertie Stevens residence at 603 6th Street is furnished in period style and includes exhibits of the Clackamas County Historical Society. It is open Thursday and Sunday from 1 to 5 P.M.

Riverside parks. Good sites for river recreation are Clackamette Park, at the confluence of the Clackamas and Willamette rivers, and Willamette Park, on the west bank at the mouth of the Tualatin River. You can picnic, swim, launch a boat, fish from shore or craft, or water-ski at both parks. Willamette Park also has a playground.

Willamette Falls & its locks

When salmon migrate upriver in spring, fishermen in boats congregate in foaming water near the base of the horseshoe-shaped Willamette Falls.

Boats bypass the 41-foot falls by means of a series of four locks along the river's west bank, behind the paper mill. Operated by the U.S. Army Corps of Engineers, the locks are open 7 days a week from 8 A.M. to midnight. Once a boat enters, it takes about 45 minutes to pass through the locks.

More than a million tons of river traffic pass through the locks each year. Rafted logs, paper, and paper products make up most of the commercial traffic. Pleasure boats and other small craft also pass through the locks. Passage is free to all craft.

To see the locks in operation, cross the bridge from Oregon City to West Linn and turn left. A walkway down to the river leads to the lockmaster's office and several good view points.

Rare plants at West Linn

An island of rare plants occupies a 22½-acre site atop West Linn's high basalt bluff. The Camassia Natural Area lies immediately east of West Linn High School.

Isolated by the glacial Missoula Flood at the end of the Ice Age approximately 15,000 years ago, the small natural area contains more than 300 species of plants rare to this part of the Northwest. Early bloomers such as trillium begin flowering in late March, but the main show comes in late April and early May. The flood also deposited several erratic boulders and gouged ponds in the meadows.

Lively events attract visitors

From Oregon City, State Highway 213 arcs south through pastoral countryside to Silverton and on to Salem. Creeks descend the foothills to join the Molalla and Pudding rivers, which, in turn, flow into the broad Willamette.

Short detours from State 213 take motorists to Molalla, site of an outstanding rodeo; rustic Scotts Mills, an early Quaker settlement; and Mount Angel.

Molalla Buckeroo. One of the Northwest's oldest rodeos, the Molalla Buckeroo has been a feature of the town's July 4 celebration since 1913. The festivities include rodeo events and a parade. Fireworks follow the evening rodeo performance on the Fourth of July.

Bach and beer at Mount Angel. From the parking area of Mount Angel Abbey, the valley is a tapestry of green and golden fields stretching to the foothills. The Abbey Bach Festival, held in July, sells out early.

On the third weekend of September, Mount Angel turns into a Bavarian village during the town's 4-day Oktoberfest celebration. Dressed in traditional costumes, residents celebrate the community's German-Swiss ancestry with a biergarten, Bavarian-style foods and crafts, folk dancing, and strolling musicians.

Steam power at Brooks. Partisans of early-day farm machinery gather in Brooks on the last weekend of July and first weekend of August for Antique Powerland's "Great Oregon Steamup." Among the equipment that parades and performs are steam tractor engines, threshing machines, and gas tractors. Visitors also see blacksmithing, log sawing, and flour milling.

Flower fields brighten Willamette Valley. Fertile farmland and climatic conditions are ideal for growing flowering bulbs like these dahlias near Canby.

Oregon's capitol, faced with white marble, is topped by 24-foot statue of Oregon Pioneer. Sculptures flanking main entrance depict Lewis and Clark expedition and covered wagon.

Historic valley towns

South from Oregon City, State 99E links the historic valley towns of Canby, Aurora, and Woodburn as it traverses farmland east of the Willamette.

Canby's flower fields. One of Oregon's horticultural centers, Canby is a commercial growing area for many types of flowers—including dahlias, irises, daffodils, gladioli, pansies, lilies, and perennials—as well as shrubs and trees for wholesale and retail nurseries and evergreen seedlings for reforestation. In spring and summer you can see blooming flower fields from country roads.

Oregon's oldest railroad station, built in 1873, has been relocated to 888 N.E. 4th Avenue and restored; the Canby Depot Museum is open Saturday and Sunday from 1 to 4; in summer it is also open weekdays from 10 to 3.

From Canby, North Holly Street heads north to the Canby Ferry, crossing the Willamette (see page 56). In mid-August, Canby hosts the Clackamas County Fair—an old-fashioned county fair with modern trimmings.

Antiques in Aurora. Located 13 miles southwest of Oregon City, this small town was the site of the Aurora Colony, an unusual experiment in Christian communal living. Established here in 1856 by a group of German-American settlers, the nondenominational religious community thrived until 1883. Its citizens pursued interests in music, literature, and philosophy; the colony's craftsmen fashioned furniture and household articles that have become "Colony-style" collectors' items.

Antique buffs prowl Aurora's shops for 19th and early 20th century collectibles ranging from American and European furniture and glassware to jewelry and tools. Most antique shops are closed on Monday.

Informal tours of five restored Aurora Colony buildings are conducted from 10 to 4:30 Wednesday through Saturday (Tuesday through Saturday from June through August) and 1 to 4:30 Sunday. Colony buildings are closed in January. In the Ox Barn Museum at Second and Liberty streets, you can see examples of the furniture, household articles, and crafts familiar to members of the colony.

On the first Sunday after Easter, the Aurora Colony Historical Society serves a family-style sausage dinner at the Ox Barn Museum. All buildings are open during the day, and crafts people demonstrate the colony crafts. Other community celebrations include a strawberry social in June, Aurora Colony Days in August, a quilt show in October, and a Christmas festival in December. For information, call the Ox Barn Museum at (503) 678-5754.

Woodburn, past and present. Woodburn's pioneer father was Jesse Settlemier, who arrived here in 1863 with his bride. In 1889 he built a four-story showplace on Boones Ferry Road, now North Settlemier Avenue. Encircled by tall trees, the restored Settlemier house is a triumph of carpenter's artistry. It is open Sunday from 1 to 4 and for special events throughout the year.

A Chuck Wagon Breakfast is held on the Fourth of July. To honor the more than 2,000 Spanish-speaking residents who have settled near Woodburn, the town hosts a Mexican Fiesta on the first weekend in August. Agriculture is highlighted during the Oregon Farmfest on the second weekend of October.

In the early 1960s, Russian immigrants seeking religious freedom established a small colony of farms southeast of Woodburn. Known as the Old Believers, they dress in conservative garb and follow fundamentalist religious practices.

Herbert Hoover's boyhood home

Motorists traveling south of Portland on State 99W pass within a block of the boyhood home of former President Herbert Hoover.

After the death of his parents, the 10-year-old boy came to Newberg in 1884 to live with his aunt and uncle, Dr. and Mrs. Henry Minthorn. The Hoover-Minthorn House where he lived for 5 years is now a museum. Located at 115 South River Street, the two-story white frame house is furnished in the style of the 1880s; it has a manicured garden and a well near the back door. In Hoover's small bedroom you'll see some of his schoolboy treasures. The museum is open Wednesday through Sunday from 1 to 4 (closed January and holidays); group tours are by appointment only.

Newberg's Old Fashioned Festival in late July features art and entertainment in Memorial Park, a parade, an auction, athletic competitions, and other events.

Historic Champoeg

Seven miles southeast of Newberg off State Highway 219 is Champoeg (Sham-POO-ig), one of the most historically significant sites in the Pacific Northwest. Meetings held here in the early 1840s resulted in the formation of the Oregon provisional government.

Before fur trappers and settlers arrived, a large Calapooya Indian village was located at this riverside site. White men were attracted to its natural boat landing and the rich prairie land nearby. After retiring from Hudson's Bay Company, many trappers settled permanently near Champoeg to farm.

A decisive vote. By 1843, many settlers in the Willamette Valley felt the need of a civil government, though Hudson's Bay Company ruled the land at the time. At the Champoeg meeting, these men voted on whether to write their own constitution or continue under the rules of the British company. By a vote of 52 to 50, the Willamette settlers decided to write their own document.

The provisional government of Oregon—the first American commonwealth on the Pacific coast—was followed by territorial status in 1848 and statehood (for Oregon, not the entire territory) in 1859.

Champoeg became a thriving community in the 1850s, but in the winter of 1861–62, the Willamette's greatest flood swept away most of the town's buildings.

Champoeg today. Except on busy summer weekends, Champoeg State Park is a quiet place. You can study the historic monument, walk down to the river's edge, and wander through a garden of native trees and plants. Champoeg State Park has camping and picnicking areas and its own bicycle trail. In July the exciting story of Oregon's birth is dramatized in the outdoor amphitheater; for information, phone (503) 538-1800.

Near the entrance, the barnlike Visitor Center contains excellent exhibits depicting Champoeg's role in Oregon's history and government. It is open daily except major holidays from 9:30 to 5 (hours extended in summer); the center is closed weekends in winter.

Two other museums trace the history of the settlement. Adjacent to the park, the two-story clapboard Robert Newell residence is a restoration of a Champoeg house built in 1852. Inside the grounds, the Pioneer Mother's Memorial Cabin, a replica of a settler's log cabin, is furnished with period furniture and household items. Both of the private museums are open from noon to 5 Wednesday through Sunday (closed during December and January).

The rural charms of French Prairie

In pioneer days, the grassy undulating plain south of Champoeg was known as French Prairie, named for the French-Canadians who settled here—most of them former trappers. Bounded on the west and east by the Willamette and Pudding rivers and on the south by Salem, this fertile wedge became a wheat-growing area in the 1830s and '40s.

From Champoeg a 40-mile scenic loop, marked by *fleur-de-lis* signs, circles south through some of Oregon's oldest farming communities. The loop goes south through St. Paul and Fairfield, east through Gervais and Woodburn, and north along the Pudding River to Aurora. Some of the roads you'll travel were originally emigrant trails or early market and stage roads. Ask at the Champoeg Visitor Center for information on the route.

St. Paul, a National Historic Site, is noted for its 1846 church and the annual St. Paul Rodeo in July. Many early settlers are buried in the local cemetery.

Yamhill County byways

West of the Willamette, State 99W passes through Yamhill County's prosperous farming country. Roads wind through rolling hills covered by neat orchards of nut trees and fields planted with strawberries, wheat, grapes, beans, and other crops. Several wineries welcome visitors. Dundee is the center of the hazelnut industry.

Largest of the towns is McMinnville, on State Highway 18, dominated by Linfield College. Changing art exhibits hang at the McMinnville Art Gallery, which also offers art classes throughout the year. At McMinnville Airport, a Boeing KC-97 plane has been renovated as a restaurant. A major turkey-growing area, McMinnville honors the bird at a July Turkey-Rama barbecue and fair.

Works by Northwest artists and crafts people are featured at Bellevue's Lawrence Gallery, an arts center amid the fields about 9 miles west of McMinnville on State 18. More than 200 artists are represented here. Oregon wines are featured in the gallery's tasting room.

Nearly every community has its ties with valley history—old houses and stores, a grange or country school, perhaps a pioneer church or cemetery. Dayton has a number of 19th century buildings. Fort Yamhill blockhouse stands in the city park. The Yamhill County Historical Museum in Lafayette is housed in an 1890 church.

PEDAL ALONG OREGON'S BIKEWAYS

If you prefer touring on two wheels rather than four, climb on your bicycle and go for a ride on one of Oregon's bikeways. It's a relaxing way to see the countryside, and new cycling routes are freeing riders of the highway hassle.

In recent years, Oregon has taken a strong stand in favor of bike trails and footpaths. By law, 1 percent of state gasoline tax revenues goes for bikeway development and construction. Careful planning by trail designers, aided by strong community support, has resulted in an extensive network of bike lanes and trails.

Many pleasant cycling routes explore Willamette Valley back roads between Portland and Eugene. You can cycle leisurely along the Willamette and other streams or pedal along level roads through quiet farming country.

On a loop trip between Portland and Astoria, cyclists can follow the Columbia River route one way and the forest road through Mist and Jewell on the other.

Several state parks—among them Fort Stevens, Tryon Creek, Mary S. Young, Champoeg, Silver Falls, and Wallowa Lake—feature bike trails. The Eugene-Springfield area has more than 60 miles of bike lanes and trails.

One long-distance route parallels the Oregon Coast from Astoria to the California border. Many campgrounds are located along the coast; some have shower facilities. About 20 state parks have set aside undeveloped camping areas for use by cyclists and hikers.

Touring cyclists seeking a challenging route can take the cross-state trail. Beginning in Reedsport, it follows the Smith River Road to Eugene, continues up the McKenzie River Highway, and crosses the steep and winding McKenzie Pass (5,324 feet elevation). East of the Cascades it passes through Redmond and Prineville, crosses the plateaus and mountains of Central Oregon, cuts through Baker and south of the Wallowa Mountains, and reaches the Idaho border at Oxbow Dam (Copperfield).

For information on Oregon bicycle touring routes, write to the state's Tourism Division (address on page 9). Folders indicate varied Willamette Valley routings and elevation profiles, repair facilities, and campgrounds along long-distance routes.

Skier cuts across watery path of Canby ferry waiting to transport motorists and cyclists across river. Other ferries operate upriver at Wheatland and Buena Vista.

Apple picker near Albany harvests bags of bright fruit. Willamette Valley produces bountiful crops of fruits, nuts, vegetable crops, and lawn grass seed.

Among parks of special interest are Bald Peak State Park, northwest of Newberg off State 219, where you have wonderful views and can picnic beneath Douglas firs; Erratic Rock Wayside, 8 miles southwest of McMinnville, resting place of a massive boulder rafted here by a glacier during the Ice Age; and Yamhill Locks County Park, northwest of Dayton, on the Yamhill River. Maud Williamson State Park offers a pleasant spot to picnic near the Wheatland Ferry crossing (see page 56).

The Central Valley

The heart of the Willamette Valley boasts a rich and diversified agriculture. Country roads interrupt fields of row crops and berries, orchards of fruit and nut trees, pasture lands for dairy and beef cattle, and broad acreages where much of the nation's lawn grass seed is harvested.

Salem, the state capital, lies at the center of the valley. Other major towns are Corvallis, home of Oregon State University, and Albany, center of the grass seed industry and rare metals manufacturing.

Oregon's agriculture, industries, and natural resources are on display during the 10-day run of the Oregon State Fair, which climaxes on Labor Day weekend. The fairgrounds are located northeast of Salem's central district at 17th Street N.E. and Silverton Road.

Salem landmarks, old and new

Oregon's capital city marks the heart of the fertile valley some 50 miles south of the Columbia River. One of the state's oldest cities, Salem was settled by the Reverend Jason Lee and his small group of Methodist missionaries who arrived in the Willamette Valley in 1834. They established an Indian mission and founded the Oregon Institute (now Willamette University). The men of the mission were influential in the settlement and orderly development of the Oregon country by American citizens.

State capitol. Heading the list of Salem's attractions is the white marble capitol, topped by a 24-foot Pioneer statue covered in gold leaf. Marble sculptures flank the Court Street entrance, honoring the Lewis and Clark Expedition and the pioneers who traveled the Oregon Trail. In the rotunda, the polished bronze state seal gleams on the floor directly beneath the dome. Murals on the rotunda walls—and in the Senate and House chambers on the second floor—depict historic events in Oregon's early years.

Visitors can obtain maps and travel information about the state at the capitol visitor center at the rear of the rotunda. From Memorial Day until Labor Day, tours depart from here at frequent intervals to visit the Senate and House chambers and the Governor's office. The rest of the year, group tours are by appointment only, when the legislature is not in session. Hardy visitors can climb the 121 spiral steps of the tower.

Inviting park areas border the capitol. To the west is Willson Park, an attractively landscaped strip with a fountain. The Capitol Mall extends north of Court Street. An arboretum of labeled trees extends east of the capitol.

Civic Center. Salem's city offices and public library are located in a handsome creekside complex at 555 Liberty Street S.E.—a delight of modern architecture, landscaped plazas, fountains, sculpture, and art.

East of the city buildings, landscaped bike trails and footpaths follow Mill and Pringle creeks. A 5-block area along Trade Street has been transformed into the Pringle Park Plaza. Landscaping, walkways, and benches enhance the natural attraction of the Mill Race.

Reed Opera House. One landmark with a new lease on life is the old Reed Opera House, center of Salem's cultural and social life during the Victorian era. Built in 1871 at N.E. Court and Liberty streets, the four-story building now features specialty shops, restaurants, and offices.

Willamette University. A gracious tree-shaded campus and sturdy red brick buildings testify to the New England heritage of Willamette University's founders—Methodist missionaries who established the university in 1842. Located behind the capitol at 900 State Street, the university is known for its colleges of liberal arts, music, and law, and the graduate school of administration.

Bush Pasture Park. A tree- and grass-covered expanse near the heart of the city, Salem's favorite park was once the country estate of Asahel Bush, a Salem banker and newspaper publisher of the 1870s. The 89-acre park contains formal and natural wildflower gardens, picnic and sports areas, and hiking paths along Pringle Creek.

The Salem Art Association maintains the two-story Bush house at 600 Mission Street S.E. as a museum containing many of the family's original furnishings. Built in 1878, the elegant Victorian mansion has many innovations and utilitarian comforts unusual in the gaslight era. The house is open daily except Mondays from 10 to 5 May through September, from 10 to 4:30 the rest of the year.

Behind the house, the farm's barn is now the Bush Barn Art Center. Two exhibit galleries and a sales gallery feature the work of local and other Northwest artists and crafts people. Classes are presented the year round. The Art Center is open from 10 to 5 Tuesday through Friday, 1 to 5 Saturday and Sunday.

Each July the Salem Art Fair and Festival features works by more than 200 artists, as well as food booths and live entertainment, outdoors in the park.

Deepwood. Near the northeast corner of Bush Park at Mission and 12th streets S.E., Deepwood Estate contains four acres of formal gardens, informal displays, and natural wildflower gardens. Many weddings take place here. Built in 1894, the handsome Queen Anne–style house is noted for its hand-crafted woodwork and stained-glass windows. For visiting hours, phone (503) 363-1825.

Mission Mill Village. A 19th century textile mill and buildings associated with the early Methodist Mission draw visitors to Mission Mill Village at 1313 Mill Street S.E. Hours are 10 to 4:30 Tuesday through Saturday; from May to September, the Village is also open 1 to 4:30 Sunday. Salem's visitor information center is located near the entrance to the complex.

Restored buildings of the Thomas Kay Woolen Mill,

which operated here in the 1890s, now present the story of Oregon's pioneer textile industry. Also located here are the Jason Lee house and parsonage of the Methodist Mission, both built in 1841; the John D. Boon house, dating from 1847; and a pioneer church. Picnic tables are located near the mill stream. Shops featuring textile crafts, historic books, and fiber arts supplies are located in the village's Retail Store. For information on classes, tours, or special events, phone (503) 583-7012.

Other parks.   Among other local favorites is the Cascade Gateway Park, southeast of town on Turner Road, a 100-acre area oriented to family recreation.

Bordering the Willamette's west bank is Wallace Marine Park; you'll find picnic tables, a swimming area, boat ramp, and sports facilities. Minto-Brown Island draws hikers, joggers, and cyclists; this riverfront park has miles of trails and a wilderness preserve.

Enchanted Forest.   Families come here for fairytale fantasy and a bit of adventure—a haunted house, a model mining town, bobsled rides—in a woodland setting. Located 7 miles south of Salem near I-5, it is open daily from 9:30 to 6 from mid-March through September.

Waterfalls & an old mill

If the sight and sound of falling water revives your spirit, head for Silver Falls State Park. Located off State Highway 214 about 26 miles east of Salem and 15 miles south of Silverton, the park offers waterfalls in abundance. A 7-mile loop trail through Silver Creek Canyon passes 9 of the park's 14 waterfalls—5 of them plunging 100 feet or more. Spur trails allow hikers to shorten the route if desired. The park also has a 4-mile bike path and additional hiking and horse trails. A day lodge and picnic tables are located near the South Falls trailhead; campsites are also available.

Silver Creek flows north through the tree-shaded community of Silverton. Art galleries and antique shops here attract browsers. Historic exhibits have been assembled in the Silverton Country Museum, 428 South Water Street, and the adjacent 1904 Southern Pacific depot, which also houses the Silverton Chamber of Commerce. A covered bridge stands 4 miles northwest of town.

Stayton's historic woolen mill, founded in 1867, still manufactures woolen blankets, car robes, and yardage. Located about 17 miles southeast of Salem off State Highway 22, the Paris Woolen Mills is open to visitors daily except Sunday from 9 to 6 (the mill operates weekdays from 7 to 3). A retail store is adjacent to the mill.

Meandering Polk County byways

Quiet countryside and small towns mark rural roads southwest of Salem. Rickreall is known for its Christmas pageant. Dallas, the seat of Polk County, has an ivy-covered 1899 courthouse and the Muir & McDonald Tannery, which has been producing saddle and tooling leather since 1863; its small museum is open to the public.

Monmouth, home of Western Oregon State College, is also the site of the Paul Jensen Museum, 590 Church Street. Open 10 to 4 Tuesday through Saturday, it showcases art and artifacts of the Eskimo people.

Independence has renovated some of its historic downtown facades. A former church at South 3rd and B streets has been converted into the Heritage Museum, open afternoons Wednesday through Saturday.

Side roads branch west from State 223 to small logging settlements at the base of forested Coast Range slopes. South of Pedee, you'll pass the Ritner Creek covered bridge, a Polk County landmark since 1926.

Corvallis, home of Oregon State University

West of the Willamette, Corvallis marks the intersection of U.S. 20 and State 99W. It is the seat of Benton County and home of Oregon State University.

Downtown, take a look at the old Benton County Courthouse. Built in 1888, the classically simple main building and its clock tower contrast with a modern wing.

Headquarters for the community's art groups is the Corvallis Arts Center, housed in a renovated 1889 church building at 7th and Madison streets. The main gallery, marked by wood-beamed ceilings and arched windows, also serves as a theater and concert hall. Visitors browse through art exhibits and a sales-rental gallery from noon to 5 P.M. daily except Mondays.

South of U.S. 20, 75-acre Avery Park has picnic tables, bicycle and jogging trails, broad lawns, rose and rhododendron gardens, and children's play areas.

To Monmouth
Kings Valley
Scale in Miles
0   5   10
Paved Road
Unpaved Road
To Salem
River
South
Santiam River
99E
To Newport
20
Wren
CORVALLIS
Mary's Peak
Philomath
34
ALBANY
20
Willamette River
34
WILLAMETTE BYWAYS
Lebanon
To Waldport
Muddy Creek
River
Shedd
99E
99
WM. L. FINLEY NATL. WILDLIFE REFUGE
Bellfountain
Halsey
Brownsville
Calapooia
228
Crawfordsville
Sweet Home
Holley
20
River
Alpine
Monroe
Willamette
5
Harrisburg
N
To Triangle Lake
Cheshire
Long Tom River
Junction City
Marcola
Mohawk River
36
99
Coburg
Mohawk
To McKenzie Bridge
To Mapleton
Elmira
Fern Ridge Reservoir
ARMITAGE STATE PARK
McKenzie
105
Walterville
River
126
Veneta
126
EUGENE
SPRINGFIELD
126
To Lorane
To Cottage Grove

Oregon State University. Dominating and enriching the town is Oregon State University, established in 1868 and now home-away-from-home for some 15,200 students. Downtown, signs direct you to the 400-acre campus in the western part of town.

Visitors can obtain campus maps, courtesy parking permits, and information on campus tours at campus information centers. For a look at the heart of the university, drive west on Jefferson and park in the visitors' area east of Memorial Union.

Articles reflecting Oregon's natural history and human history are preserved and displayed at the Horner Museum, located in the basement of Gill Coliseum. Included in the exhibit are Oregon birds and mammals, minerals and fossils, Native American materials, and items from the pioneer and Victorian eras. The museum is open 10 to 5 Tuesday through Friday, noon to 4 Saturday, and 2 to 5 Sunday. From June through August, hours are 10 to 5 Monday through Friday, 2 to 5 Sunday.

Sports fans watch OSU teams compete against Pacific 10 Conference rivals and other top college squads. Football and track teams compete in 41,000-seat Parker Stadium, while basketball contests and special events are held in Gill Coliseum.

Benton County destinations. A favorite outing for picnickers, hikers, and campers is Mary's Peak, southwest of Corvallis off State 34 in Siuslaw National Forest. Highest peak in the Coast Range at 4,097 feet, it offers an inspiring panorama stretching from the Pacific to the Cascades. July is the prime month for wildflowers here.

In Philomath, 6 miles west of Corvallis, the Benton County Historical Museum occupies the New England-style brick building that once housed Philomath College.

South of Philomath in William L. Finley National Wildlife refuge, bird watchers can see valley wildlife and migratory birds. A refuge map and bird list is available weekdays at the refuge headquarters.

For information on Benton County covered bridges or wine touring, stop at the Corvallis Convention and Visitors Bureau, 420 N.W. 2nd Street.

Albany & its Timber Carnival

Bordering the Willamette's east bank, Albany sits 70 miles south of Portland at the hub of the valley's prime agricultural lands. The Calapooia River joins the Willamette along the town's northwest boundary.

Albany is best known for its World Championship Timber Carnival, a 4-day celebration saluting the Northwest timber industry. Burly loggers gather at Timber Linn Lake over the July 4th holiday to compete in championship log chopping, bucking, speed climbing, tree topping, log birling, ax throwing, and jousting. Spectators also enjoy a big parade and a fireworks display on the 4th. The Linn County Fair is held in Albany in mid-September; in November, Albany hosts one of the nation's largest Veterans Day parades.

City parks are scattered through town; favorite ones are the centrally located Swanson Park with its municipal swimming pool, Waverly Lake Park at Pacific Boulevard and Salem Road, and Monteith Riverpark and Bryant Park bordering the Willamette River.

Major highways have bypassed central Albany, leaving more than 350 residences and commercial buildings dating from the 1840s. Stop at the Albany Area Chamber of Commerce, 435 W. 1st Street, for brochures outlining a walking tour of downtown Albany and motoring trips to Oregon's remaining covered bridges.

Exploring Linn County back roads

The pastoral countryside east of Albany invites leisurely exploration of back roads and country settlements. Alongside small streams gurgling down from the foothills toward the Willamette, you'll discover historic settlements, covered bridges, and scenic picnic spots.

Take a look at Jefferson, once a river boat town on the South Santiam; Scio, gateway to a cluster of covered bridges; Lebanon, known for its strawberry festival; historic Brownsville; and Sweet Home, a favorite area for rockhounding and water sports.

Strawberry shortcake. Highlight of Lebanon's annual June Strawberry Festival is the world's largest shortcake—an 8-foot-tall pyramid using some 3,000 pounds of fresh strawberries. It is served to more than 16,000 festival guests after the Saturday parade.

Historic Brownsville. Founded in 1846, this town bordering State Highway 228 recaptures the past. Facades reminiscent of the 1890s blend businesses with the town's numerous fine old houses. The Linn County Historical Museum here is open Thursday through Saturday from 11 to 4, Sunday 1 to 5. You can also visit the restored Moyer House, an elegant mansion erected by one of the city's founders; it is open Saturday from 11 to 4, Sunday from 1 to 5.

Oregon's oldest continuing community festival— begun in 1887—is the Linn County Pioneer Picnic, celebrated here each June; festivities include a spelling bee, loggers' jamboree, and a tug of war across the river.

Rockhounding. Sweet Home hosts a rock and mineral show in late March, and Lebanon sponsors a Rockhounds' Pow Wow in late May. Carnelian agate, petrified wood, and Holley blue agate are dug in beds in the Holley–Sweet Home area near State 228. Tourist officials can direct you to good digging area.

Sweet Home. Housed in a former church, the East Linn Museum at 746 Long Street contains a model saddlery and blacksmith shop in addition to pioneer artifacts, which feature rock collecting and mining equipment and logging tools. Summer hours are 11 to 4 Tuesday through Saturday, 1 to 5 Sunday. From October to April, hours are 11 to 4 Thursday through Saturday, 1 to 5 Sunday.

Nine miles northeast of town at McDowell Creek County Park, you can picnic near scenic waterfalls.

Sweet Home is the gateway to recreation on the South Santiam River and its tributary reservoirs. Campgrounds and picnic areas border Foster and Green Peter reservoirs, both well used by water sports enthusiasts. In July the Sportsman's Holiday/Calapooia Round-up Rodeo features a logging contest and tube-a-thon race.

The Emerald Empire

Lane County calls itself the Emerald Empire—a spacious region stretching from the ocean beaches to the crest of the Cascades. Forests cover many valley foothills, and in a matter of minutes, Eugene and Springfield residents can journey to wooded glades far removed from urban bustle. Several wineries west of Eugene welcome visitors. Lumber mills and forest products industries dot the area. For information on regional attractions, contact the Eugene-Springfield Convention & Visitors Bureau, 305 W. 7th Avenue (P.O. Box 10286), Eugene, OR 97440.

Dominating the county is Eugene, the state's second largest city (104,000) and home of the University of Oregon. Neighboring Springfield adds another 40,000 to the metropolitan population.

Getting acquainted with Eugene

A landscaped pedestrian mall brightens the heart of Eugene's downtown business district. Trees, flowers, a fountain, benches, and children's play areas transform Willamette Street—between 7th and 11th avenues—and intersecting streets into an oasis for shoppers.

Eugene's status as a cultural center is enhanced with the widely acclaimed Hult Center for the Performing Arts, a downtown entertainment complex offering both touring performers and local artists in programs ranging from operas, ballet, and symphony to jazz and country music. June brings world-renowned artists to town for the Oregon Bach Festival here.

The area's primary suburban shopping complex is Valley River Center, bordering the Willamette River north of Eugene. Numerous stores and shops face an enclosed, climate-controlled mall.

You'll see joggers and cyclists everywhere, enjoying Eugene's extensive network of bikeways and traffic-free trails. A bikeways map is available weekdays from the Department of Public Works office, 858 Pearl Street. Canoeing is popular in summer; rentals are available.

Lean and tanned cowboys test their mettle against ornery rodeo stock during the Emerald Empire Roundup in July. Area residents gather for old-fashioned fun during the Lane County Fair in mid-August.

Downtown markets. The lively 5th Street Public Market, at 5th and High streets in the older part of the city, features 90 locally owned shops and restaurants offering an intriguing mix of handcrafted articles, foods, gifts, clothing, plants and flowers, books, wine, and other items. Shops are open from 10 to 6.

From April until Christmas, the area's crafts people and vendors offer a potpourri of hand-produced and home-grown wares at the Saturday Market; roving entertainers stroll amid the shoppers. The open-air bazaar is held from 10 to 5 Saturdays at 8th and Oak.

Outstanding parks. Eugene's river frontage and wooded slopes have been converted into superb parks. Put on your jogging shoes or climb aboard a bike to enjoy miles of traffic-free paths bordering the Willamette.

Curving along the Willamette's north bank is Alton Baker Park, reached from the city center by Ferry Street Bridge or by pedestrian-cyclist bridges across the Willamette. Many miles of bike paths wind through the park. Joggers enjoy a 4.2-mile European-style jogging trail and parcourse. Canoeists and kayakers paddle along a 3-mile canal that weaves peacefully through green fields and tall trees. In summer, music performances take place in an outdoor amphitheater.

Skinner's Butte Park borders the Willamette just north of Eugene's central business district. A replica of Eugene Skinner's cabin is situated on the slope facing the river. Picnic areas, playgrounds, bike paths, and foot trails make this an engaging destination. A road spirals up the forested butte to a view point overlooking the city. Roses peak in mid-June in George Owens Municipal Rose Gardens on North Jefferson Street.

Cyclists sample the best of Eugene's bikeways on the 5½-mile Greenway Loop along the river; it winds in and out of Alton Baker and Skinner's Butte parks.

The city's oldest park area is Hendricks Park, covering a large forested slope southeast of the University of Oregon. Masses of native rhododendrons and azaleas bloom here from May until early June. Rhododendrons are also featured at Greer Gardens, 1280 Goodpasture Island Road, where many hybrids have been developed.

Hikers who want to get away from the crowds find undeveloped parklands south of Eugene at Spencer Butte and at Mount Pisgah (Buford Recreation Area).

Museums and art. East of Alton Baker Park, the Willamette Science and Technology Center contains hands-on exhibits where visitors can peer through a solar telescope, read a seismograph monitoring geological activity in the Cascades, or learn more about light, sound, and other everyday phenomena. Located at 2300 Centennial Boulevard behind Autzen Stadium, the center is open daily except Monday from noon to 5 P.M. Shows are presented in the Planetarium Saturdays and Sundays at 1 and 3.

The Lane County Historical Museum mirrors 19th century life with exhibits of photographs, household and agricultural tools, and vehicles. Located at 740 W. 13th Avenue, the museum is open from 10 to 4 Tuesday through Friday, noon to 4 Saturday; library access is by appointment. Museum personnel can direct visitors to some of Eugene's fine pre-1900 houses.

The Maude I. Kerns Art Center at 1910 E. 15th Avenue sponsors local and traveling shows of contemporary art and crafts, classes, and special events. Hours are Tuesday through Saturday from 10 to 5. A sales-rental gallery and gift shops are located on the premises.

University of Oregon. Founded in 1876, the University of Oregon encompasses a 250-acre campus in the eastern part of Eugene. Enrollment is about 17,000.

The University of Oregon is a member of the Pacific 10 Conference. Autzen Stadium (football), located north of the Willamette, is connected to the campus by footbridge. Hayward Field (track), McArthur Court (basketball), and other sports areas are located in the southern part of the campus. Eugene's intense interest in track and field attracts top athletes to meets staged here.

Guided 1-hour campus tours depart weekdays at 10:30 and 2:30 from Oregon Hall at E. 13th and Agate. A

Sawdust flies as coed team crosscuts log in race against time. World Championship Timber Carnival takes place in Albany over July 4 holiday.

The Goose puffs up grade past Dorena Lake on run between Cottage Grove and Cascade foothills. Steam engine operates summer weekends only; diesel pulls train during the week.

Cyclists ride along bank of the Willamette in Eugene's Alton Baker Park. Greenway Loop is only part of 150-mile network of biking trails and lanes in and around the city.

guest parking lot is located here for visiting motorists. Campus maps are available at the information desk.

Center of student activity is the Erb Memorial Union (EMU) at E. 13th and University. A block northwest, vine-covered buildings mark the oldest part of the campus. Deady Hall, completed in 1876, housed the school's first classrooms. Other vintage buildings are Villard Hall (1885) and Friendly Hall (1893).

The Museum of Natural History is located on E. 15th, east of Agate Street. Open weekdays from 10 to 3, it features fascinating exhibits on Oregon's traditional native cultures, fossils, and environmental heritage.

North of the university library, the Museum of Art resides in a red brick, Moorish-inspired building. Famous for its Oriental art collection, the museum also displays works by contemporary Northwest, American, and Pacific artists. Open daily except Monday and Tuesday from noon to 5, the museum has a sales-rental gallery and a gift shop. Guided tours of the museum are available Sundays at 2 or by appointment.

Springfield, gateway to the McKenzie River

East of the Willamette, Springfield is a major forest products center and the gateway to the McKenzie River recreation area. Logging and the varied wood products industry dominate the local economy. Mills produce lumber, plywood, and veneer, and local manufacturers market products ranging from shingles and kraft paper to agricultural mulch and fencing. For information on summer plant tours, stop at the Springfield Area Chamber of Commerce, 223-H North A Street.

At 590 Main Street, the Springfield Museum is housed in a two-story brick building built in 1908 as a power-house. Permanent exhibits focus on the history of the

early mill town and Lane County's agriculture and timber industry; temporary exhibits highlight specialized aspects of these themes. Museum hours are 11 to 5 Wednesday through Saturday.

Tall trees shade the green lawns and picnic tables at Island Park along the broad Willamette at the western edge of Springfield's business district.

Spacious Willamalane Park contains a large indoor swimming pool, a children's play area, and tennis courts. During Springfield's annual Broiler Festival in early August, the scent of barbecued chicken wafts over the park as racks of poultry grill outdoors during the 2-day community celebration.

Scandinavian Festival in Junction City

Each August Junction City salutes its Scandinavian heritage and revives interest in its Nordic roots during a 4-day community-wide celebration. Many local residents are descendants of the Danish farmers and Norwegian, Swedish, and Finnish lumbermen who settled here decades ago. Participants dress in costume, prepare Scandinavian foods, demonstrate old-country handicrafts and folk dancing, and arrange cultural exhibits. Each day's festivities focus on a different country.

Originally planned as a railroad junction point, Junction City is now a busy farming center 13 miles north of Eugene and the point where State 99 forks into 99E and 99W to connect mid-valley towns east and west of the Willamette.

Covered bridges and riverside parks

Lane County is the heart of western Oregon's covered bridge country; 19 still stand. You'll find concentrations of the old bridges near State Highway 58 (south of Dexter and north of the highway on a Lowell-Fall Creek-Jasper route) and southeast of Cottage Grove. Others are scattered over the county. A brochure, "Oregon's Covered Bridges—Proudly Spanning the Years," shows their locations; it's available at local tourist offices.

Five miles north of Eugene on Coburg Road, Armitage State Park attracts picnickers and campers. Anglers can launch boats from the south bank of the McKenzie River or fish from shore.

Sailors and water-skiers take to the water at Fern Ridge Reservoir northwest of Eugene, site of many sailing competitions. A half dozen parks border the large impoundment on the Long Tom River. Along the west shore, motorists travel along a stretch of the old West Side Territorial Road—once a stage route—that winds through rolling farm country from Anlauf north to Monroe.

From Springfield, U.S. 126 heads east up the scenic McKenzie River, a favorite of trout anglers. Fishing guides maneuver oar-powered drift boats to holes where large trout lurk, or visitors can arrange to raft down the white-water stream. Parks and campgrounds border the river and its tributaries, and hiking trails lead deep into Willamette National Forest.

Southeast of Springfield, Fall Creek Road follows the reservoir's north shore to woodsy campgrounds. Hikers enjoy a creekside trail beginning at Dolly Varden Bridge

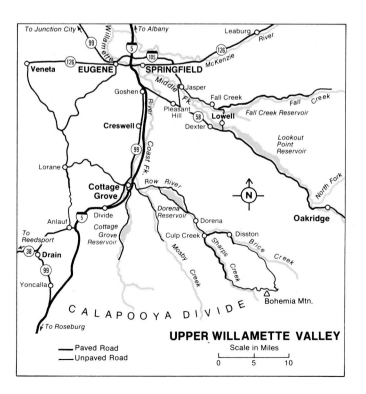

UPPER WILLAMETTE VALLEY

Paved Road
Unpaved Road

Scale in Miles
0   5   10

and a 1-mile nature trail that starts north of the parking area at Clark Creek Organizational Camp.

Cottage Grove salutes its past

South of Eugene, the town of Cottage Grove sits beside the Coast Fork of the Willamette just above its confluence with the Row (rhymes with cow) River. Southeast of town, parks border a pair of lakes—Cottage Grove Reservoir on the Coast Fork and Dorena Reservoir on the Row River. Families come here to picnic, camp, fish, and enjoy water sports.

Items from the area's pioneer and mining days are displayed in the Cottage Grove Historical Museum at Birch Avenue and H Street. The museum occupies an octagonally shaped former church built in 1897. Hours are 1 to 5 Wednesday through Sunday in summer, 1 to 4 on weekends the rest of the year.

Ride the "Goose."   On summer weekends the hissing and chugging of a steam-powered train still resounds in the Row River valley east of Cottage Grove. The Goose—short for Galloping Goose—got its nickname in pre–World War I days when it lurched and bucked over rough track, hauling loads of logs.

Passengers depart from the Village Green complex on a leisurely 2-hour, 35-mile round trip into the timber and mining country in the foothills of the Calapooya Mountains. Excursions depart daily from mid-June through Labor Day. A steam engine pulls the train on weekends, departing at 10 and 2; on weekdays, a diesel-powered train leaves daily at 2. Railroad articles from the steam era are on display in a railroad museum adjacent to the station.

The Bohemia Mines.   In the early 1860s, James "Bohemia" Johnson struck gold in the hills just southeast of Cottage Grove. On the third weekend of July, old mining traditions are revived for the 4-day Bohemia Mining Days, as the town commemorates this colorful era with a rodeo, parade, fast-draw contest, and guided tours of the Bohemia country.

The Bohemia mining district has been called the richest mining area in the western Cascades. Gold was discovered here first in 1858. New discoveries in the 1890s triggered a burst of shaft mining activity, which continued through the World War I period.

Narrow dirt roads, passable only from mid-June through October, climb the flanks of the Calapooya Mountains to the mines, where weathered buildings and half-hidden shafts mark the old mining sites. Before setting out on the all-day trip, check at the Cottage Grove Chamber of Commerce or Cottage Grove ranger station of Umpqua National Forest for information on roads and a map showing points of interest along the route.

The 70-mile mountain loop, known as the "Tour of the Golden Past," winds past more than a dozen mines, marked by rotting mine buildings and a maze of holes and shafts. You follow county and forest roads, but most of the historic mining claims themselves are on private land and are off limits to visitors. Overgrown bushes often hide dangerous shafts, and old timbers and equipment should not be trusted.

COVERED BRIDGES RECALL A QUIET ERA

Covered bridges add a nostalgic touch to the rural landscape of western Oregon. They recall a quieter day when horse-drawn buggies clip-clopped through the arched portals, the hoofbeats echoing in the dark, timbered interior. In the 1930s there were more than 300 covered bridges in Oregon; today, 53 remain, the largest concentration west of the Mississippi River.

Though designed for the era of horse and buggy transportation and Model Ts, many bridges still bear the traffic of everyday commerce on country routes. Some have been bypassed by newer spans, but preserved by local groups. The remaining bridges have become objects of affection, cherished even by persons who may never see them.

Oregon's first recorded covered bridge was built in 1851 at Oregon City. In the early days, builders felled big trees near the crossing, then shaped the timbers with adzes and broad axes at the site. Travelers were charged tolls to cross private bridges. Over the years, many covered spans were swept downstream by capricious flood waters.

Why covered bridges? Because the trusses and plank decking last considerably longer when protected from the weather. The sheltered timbers even strengthen with age. Portals were designed to match the contour of loads to be hauled through the bridge.

A new color brochure (see page 68) contains touring maps and a listing of Oregon's remaining covered bridges. For more information, contact the Covered Bridge Society of Oregon, P.O. Box 1804, Newport, OR 97365, phone (503) 265-2934 or 628-1906.

If you look at the bridges with a discerning eye, you'll note design differences varying from county to county. Portals may be rounded, square, or angled. Walls may be solid—except for slit windows just beneath the roof—or cut by eye-level "daylighting" windows, which enable drivers to glimpse oncoming traffic when the road ahead curves.

Open-sided, white bridges showing exposed trusses mark most of Linn County's bridges; a notable exception is the rebuilt Shimanek Bridge east of Scio with its barn red walls and attractive white trim. Many of Lane County's bridges have daylighting windows. Lincoln County's covered bridges can be recognized by their curved portals and flaring, windowless sidewalls.

Rafting the Rogue is just one way to enjoy this river of many moods that slices the state's southwestern corner. Designated a wild and scenic river, the Rogue attracts anglers, hikers, and white-water enthusiasts.

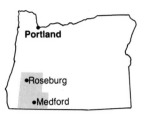

Portland

•Roseburg

•Medford

SOUTHWESTERN OREGON

Come here for Shakespeare, fishing, boat trips on the Rogue

Rimmed on the north by the Umpqua River and cradled between the Coast Range and the Cascade Mountains, the southwestern corner is one of Oregon's most enjoyable regions—a center of culture as well as outdoor recreation.

Whatever your interest, you can pursue it here. Ashland's famed Shakespearean Festival rates national acclaim, and art and music thrive in Jacksonville and other southern Oregon towns. You can learn about pioneer history or visit the Oregon Caves National Monument, an unusual geologic site on the slopes of the Siskiyous. Here you'll find two of the best fishing rivers in the world—the Umpqua and the Rogue. Heart of southwestern Oregon is the valley of the Rogue River, one of the wildest and most scenic canyons in the United States.

Interstate Highway 5 cuts a swath south from the Willamette Valley through Roseburg to Grants Pass, where it curves southeast toward Medford and Ashland. Much of this route closely parallels the Applegate Trail, a southern emigrant route blazed in 1846, that later became a territorial road linking California's capital city of Sacramento with the territorial capital of Oregon City. U.S. Highway 199 veers southwest from Grants Pass.

The Umpqua Valley

South of Cottage Grove, you leave the Willamette and its tributaries and enter the land of the Umpqua, renowned as one of the nation's outstanding fishing streams.

Now bypassed by the freeway, small communities—Oakland, Sutherlin, Wilbur, Winchester—are located east of the freeway along State 99, the old highway. Historic Oakland is a tidy gem, filled with turn-of-the-century structures. Pick up a map at the museum on Locust Street and take a self-guided walking tour, then drive west out Walnut Street to see the Rochester covered bridge. In Wilbur, take a look at the United Methodist Church, reputedly the oldest in continuous use in the state.

Winchester is the gateway to the North Umpqua Highway (State 138); many parks and campgrounds border the river (see page 92). At Winchester Dam you can watch through underwater windows as migrating salmon and steelhead climb the fish ladder.

Douglas County hosts a varied array of annual events. A sampling: In late April Glide's Wildflower Show displays some 350 southern Oregon species. Each spring white-water boaters race down the North Umpqua River from Steamboat to Glide. In June Roseburg hosts the Umpqua Valley Round-Up and a gathering of square dancers, and Oakland celebrates Old-Time Days.

Sutherlin holds a Timber Days festival each July. Events in August include Canyonville's Pioneer Days, Myrtle Creek's Summer Festival, and the Douglas County Fair in Roseburg. In September you can savor local melons at the Winston-Dillard Melon Festival or sample Oregon wines and German foods at Roseburg's Wine Festival.

Roseburg, timber town on the Umpqua

Now a town of 16,000, Roseburg got its start in 1851 when Aaron Rose and his family settled in the Umpqua Valley; their home became a travelers' stop along the old Oregon-California trail. Settlers arrived to farm the rich land, and the timbered hills reverberated with the sounds of ax and saw. Timber still dominates the local economy.

Umpqua Community College, bordering the North Umpqua River about 7 miles northeast of Roseburg, is the center of Douglas County's cultural and educational activities—including lectures, films, and community music, art, and theater programs.

A complex of strikingly modern wooden buildings east of I-5 preserves and displays the county's historical heritage. Exhibits at the Douglas County Museum indicate how the pioneers lived and worked; collected here too are Indian and fur trapper artifacts, pioneer agricultural tools, and early logging equipment. The museum is open Tuesday through Saturday from 10 to 4, Sunday from noon to 4; to reach it, take the Fairgrounds exit off I-5.

Works by local artists are exhibited at the Umpqua Valley Arts Center, 1624 W. Harvard Boulevard; you can visit weekdays from noon to 6 P.M. and weekends from noon to 4. For information on regional crafts and antiques, stop at the Roseburg Visitors and Convention Bureau, 410 S.E. Spruce Street. Visitors can tour the home of General Joseph Lane, Oregon's first territorial governor, 544 S.E. Douglas Street, on weekend afternoons from 1 to 5.

Riverside Park, a verdant picnic spot in downtown Roseburg (between the bridges), sparkles with spring displays of azaleas and rhododendrons.

Outside Roseburg, several Douglas County parks along the Umpqua entice you to picnic, camp, or fish from the shore. A half-dozen wineries east of I-5 offer daily self-guided tours and wine tasting (see page 77).

Drive amid wild animals

You can drive amid cheetahs, zebras, camels, and other exotic animals at Wildlife Safari, a 600-acre drive-through reserve in Winston, about 5 miles southwest of Roseburg. A brochure describes points along the route. Guided walking tours are available by reservation; phone (503) 679-6761.

The park contains some 600 birds and animals representing about 100 species from around the world. Animals you might see include hippos, African elephants, Barbary sheep, ostrich, Bengal tigers, and lions. Animals are most active during the cooler morning and evening hours.

Children can pet and feed young animals in the petting zoo. In the Safari Village you'll find a miniature train, seasonal live animal shows, and elephant rides.

To reach Wildlife Safari from I-5, take the Winston-Coos Bay exit and follow signs west on State Highway 42. Wildlife Safari is open all year; hours are 8:30 A.M. to 8 P.M. in summer, 9 A.M. to dusk the rest of the year.

Historic Wolf Creek Tavern

For more than a century, wayfarers have stopped at Wolf Creek Tavern. Believed to be Oregon's oldest hostelry, it has served travelers almost continuously since it first opened as a stagecoach station in the mid-19th century. Among celebrities reputed to have enjoyed the inn's hospitality were President Rutherford B. Hayes, writers Jack London and Sinclair Lewis, and actor Clark Gable.

Today the inn stands west of I-5 at exit 76, about 21 miles north of Grants Pass. A piazza decorates the long, two-story building. Acquired and restored by Oregon's state parks division, this historic roadside inn again welcomes travelers, offering meals and lodging. Furnishings in the inn's public rooms and eight guest chambers reflect eras from the 1870s through the 1930s, yet the building has modern amenities.

Six miles south of the tavern, Josephine County's only remaining covered bridge crosses Grave Creek east of I-5 just north of Sunny Valley. The creek's name derived from the grave of a young girl traveling with the Applegate party, who died and was buried near the stream.

The Siskiyou Mountains

South of Grants Pass, U.S. 199 curves southwest through the Siskiyou Mountains, site of Oregon's first gold discoveries, to reach the Pacific Ocean near Crescent City, California (see map, page 76). At Cave Junction, State Highway 46 branches east to Oregon Caves National Monument.

Gold was first discovered in Oregon in the spring of 1851 on Josephine Creek, a tributary of the Illinois River. A year later, prospectors hit pay dirt in the Illinois Valley along Democrat Gulch and Althouse Creek.

East of Selma is Lake Selmac, a trout-stocked, man-made lake in a wooded setting. Families camp, fish, and swim here. In summer, boat rentals, fishing supplies, horses, and bicycles are available at the lake resort.

Local events include a Siskiyou vineyards wine festival in Cave Junction in mid-June, a Fourth of July celebration at Lake Selmac, the Illinois Valley Wild Blackberry Festival in August, and a Labor Day Festival in Cave Junction.

UMPQUA WATERSHED
Scale in Miles
0   5   10

To Elkton
To Cottage Grove
Umpqua
Tyee
Oakland
Calapooya Creek
Sutherlin
Idleyld Park
Rock Cr.
To Steamboat
Umpqua
Umpqua River
Glide
SUSAN CREEK STATE PARK
Winchester
North Umpqua
Little River
Roseburg
N
Winston
North Myrtle Cr.
Dillard
South Myrtle Creek
To Coquille
South Umpqua
Myrtle Creek
Days Creek
River
Riddle
Cow Creek
Canyonville
Umpqua   Tiller
To Grants Pass
To Medford

Paved Road
Unpaved Road

The Illinois Valley

From headwaters high in the Siskiyous, two forks of the Illinois River flow north, merging near Cave Junction. Travelers can picnic near the confluence at Illinois River State Park. Wild blackberries grow along many roads.

The river continues northwest, carving a deep canyon on its journey toward the Rogue. Downstream from Selma, the turbulent Illinois is part of the Federally designated Wild and Scenic Rivers system; it's hard to navigate except in spring. A rough gravel road parallels the river west from Selma into Siskiyou National Forest. Trails parallel sections of the waterway.

Kerby's pioneer museum. During the early years of the gold rush, Kerbyville (now Kerby) was a mushrooming trading center crowded with tents and crude log shacks; in 1858 it became the Josephine County seat.

Pioneer days are recalled in the county-maintained Kerbyville Museum. Housed in a restored two-story merchant's dwelling of the 1870s, the museum is furnished with possessions from many local pioneer families.

An adjacent wing contains many outstanding exhibits, including a section of the old Waldo post office and collections of Indian artifacts and antique guns. Many displays relate to the mining era. You'll see early farming and mining equipment and a one-room log school built in 1898. The museum is open daily from 10 to 5, May through October.

Cave Junction. The main town along U.S. 199 is Cave Junction, gateway to the Oregon Caves.

South of town is the Woodland Wildlife Park, open daily from spring through fall; animals are trained here for films, stage, commercials, and other work.

Near O'Brien, the Rough and Ready Botanical Wayside preserves some of the area's unusual plants.

Oregon Caves National Monument

Deep in the Siskiyous, a spectacular underground cavern has been transformed by mineral deposits into a subterranean wonderland. Oregon Caves National Monument is 20 miles east of Cave Junction on State 46. The curving road climbs nearly 3,000 feet through conifer forest.

Though known as the Oregon Caves, it is a single cavern with a mazelike system of connected corridors and chambers. With a guide you walk through winding passageways into subtly lighted chambers bearing such descriptive names as Neptune's Grotto, Ghost Chamber, King's Palace, Banana Grove, and Paradise Lost. Some of the deposits are graceful, others are odd or fanciful. You'll see miniature stone waterfalls, limestone canopies, rock chandeliers, and fluted columns.

The cave was discovered in 1874 by Elijah Davidson while he was deer hunting with his dog Bruno. For many years few visitors made the difficult journey. After poet Joaquin Miller visited the site in 1907, he publicized the natural beauty of the "Marble Halls of Oregon" in his writings. In 1909 President William Howard Taft proclaimed it a national monument. The winding road to the caves was opened in 1922.

Guided tours. From May through September, guided trips depart frequently between 9 A.M. and 5 P.M.; from June 1 through September 10, hours are extended—8 A.M. to 7 P.M. In winter, trips depart at 10:30, 12:30, 2, and 3:30; more frequently if parties of 16 visitors assemble and guides are available. Children under 6 years are not permitted in the caves, but a child-care service is available.

Average time of a tour is 1¼ hours. It is a strenuous trip, not recommended for persons with heart or breathing problems or walking difficulties. During the tour participants walk, crouch, and climb through the cave's many marbled chambers, ducking low ceilings and dodging protruding stalactites. Metal steps and handrails ease passage in difficult stretches. Canes, crutches, tripods, and walking sticks are not permitted in the cave.

Wear good walking shoes and a warm jacket; average temperature inside the cave is 45°. It's drippy in spots (that's what builds up the formations).

Facilities. From June 15 through Labor Day, meals and lodging are available at the Chateau, a six-story wooden hotel rising in rustic grandeur from the floor of the canyon. Opened in 1934, the spacious lodge was constructed with huge wooden beams, peeled tree trunks, and local stone. A mountain creek gurgles through the dining room. In other seasons, only light refreshments are available at the monument.

Several commercial and Forest Service campgrounds are located along State 46, but no camping areas are located within the monument; the nearest area is Cave Creek Campground, 4 miles northwest.

Rugged Kalmiopsis Wilderness

Of primary interest to botanists, this Federal preserve harbors a number of rare plants and trees, including the *Kalmiopsis leachiana*, a small, low-growing, rhododendronlike shrub that is considered a relic of the pre–Ice Age.

Three main routes lead to the preserve's border. Best maintained is the Chetco River Road from the coast (see page 53). From U.S. 199, unpaved roads lead west from Selma and Kerby.

The Kalmiopsis Wilderness terrain is wild and rugged, and trails are extremely primitive. Hikers should plan to be completely self-sufficient. Poison oak and rattlesnakes abound, and yellow jackets and hornets are numerous. Persons planning to enter the wilderness should obtain detailed information from Siskiyou National Forest officials in Grants Pass, Cave Junction, or Brookings.

Rogue River Valley

Anglers and white-water boaters rave about the splendid Rogue River—that scenic ribbon cutting across Oregon's southwestern corner. From snowy Cascade slopes northwest of Crater Lake, it plunges on a 215-mile journey to the sea in a kaleidoscope of moods. You can enjoy it as a tumbling mountain stream, a quiet-flowing river deepening into pensive pools, or as crashing white-water rapids.

The Rogue is one of only a few Federally designated Wild and Scenic Rivers, and the only one entirely within Oregon. Greenery borders its banks for much of the route. Below Grave Creek, you can explore the ruggedly scenic canyon of the wild Rogue on white-water boat trips or on foot along a riverside hiking trail. Persons planning a trip along this section should obtain a copy of the Rogue River recreational map from Siskiyou National Forest officials or from the Bureau of Land Management office in Grants Pass.

Between Marial and Illahe, the Rogue flows through the 36,000-acre Wild Rogue Wilderness. Boaters wishing to make the trip through this section between Memorial Day weekend and Labor Day weekend must obtain a permit; for information on applications, contact the Galice Ranger Station, P. O. Box 113, Grants Pass, OR 97526.

The Rogue's runs of steelhead and salmon are legendary, but there's good rainbow trout fishing as well. You can fish by yourself along the bank or arrange for a guide and a drift boat. Fishing is best from September through May; summer days can be blistering hot in the canyon, when river waters warm to swimming temperatures. The best fishing in summer is along the upper river and its main tributaries, where anglers cast into deep holes and into smooth waters above and below riffles.

Most guided fishing and boat trips depart from the Grants Pass area. Write to the Grants Pass Visitor and Convention Bureau, P.O. Box 970, Grants Pass, OR 97526, for information on river guides, types of boat trips, and accommodations.

Grants Pass, gateway to the Rogue

River-oriented recreation dominates Grants Pass life; the Rogue flows through town, adding a pleasant ambience to the community.

Riverside Park, bordering the south bank of the Rogue, offers cheerful picnic spots with river views. Children clamber over playground equipment, and their elders head for the park's sports areas. During July and August, outdoor band concerts are performed here on Thursday evenings.

On Memorial Day weekend, the Boatnik Festival features a 35-mile white-water race from Grants Pass downriver to Hellgate Canyon and back—open to all comers—and a square-dance festival. In August local artists display their work at the Southern Oregon Art Show, and residents gather for the Josephine County Fair.

County parks and boat launching sites dot the river banks downstream from Grants Pass. You can follow the river as it heads northwest from town or turn west off I-5 toward Merlin to reach the Rogue above Hellgate Canyon.

Largest campground is at Indian Mary Park, 16 miles northwest of Grants Pass. Nestled in a curve of the river 2 miles below Hellgate Canyon, the attractive park overflows with camping families on weekends. Broad lawns slope down to the Rogue, where anglers cast their lines and children splash in sun-warmed water.

Gold was discovered on the Rogue in 1859; you'll see scars of hydraulic mining and occasional abandoned shafts and equipment. Galice was an early-day mining town, and dirt roads lead up nearby gulches to abandoned mines.

Grave Creek Bridge marks the start of the protected wild river section of the Rogue and its companion 39-mile hiking trail along the north bank. To sample this trail, pack a lunch and hike 2 miles downstream to Rainie Falls for superb views of the turbulent river as it drops 10 feet over large boulders. A BLM trail also follows the south bank from the bridge down to the falls.

Boaters and hikers can obtain a detailed trail and river guide to the Federally designated Wild and Scenic section of the Rogue River at the Siskiyou National Forest office in Grants Pass or the BLM district office in Medford.

Boat trips on the Rogue

The Rogue has a well-deserved reputation as a classic river run. Many white-water boaters confront its challenging rapids each summer. Day visitors can take jet-boat or raft trips between Grants Pass and Grave Creek Bridge. For more on Rogue boat trips, see page 52.

Jet-boat excursions.   From Grants Pass, 2-hour jet-boat trips speed downstream through pastoral country to Hellgate Canyon, a narrow deep cleft where rock walls rise some 250 feet above the water. Jet boats make the 36-mile round trip daily from mid-May through September. You can also combine the Hellgate Canyon trip with a country barbecue dinner.

A 5-hour round trip departs from Grants Pass from mid-May through Labor Day, traveling downstream to Grave Creek with a lunch stop at Galice.

Day rafting trips.   More adventurous souls can take half-day or full-day raft trips, either relaxing aboard a guided raft or maneuvering a row-it-yourself rental craft along the waterway. Peaceful, still waters alternate with exhilarating, tricky riffles. Full-day trips put in at Hog Creek Landing, just above Hellgate Canyon; Galice marks the midway stop, and the take-out point is Grave Creek Bridge.

White-water excursions.   From May through September, experienced local guides and numerous commercial operators conduct a variety of trips down the white-water Rogue by raft, wooden drift boat, and inflatable canoe. Most trips last 2 to 4 days.

Below Grave Creek Bridge, adventurers enter the formidable rock-studded Rogue canyon for a memorable wilderness journey. The river flows through towering canyons, splashes over riffles, and crashes in foaming fury over boulder-strewn cascades. In quieter stretches you absorb the canyon's beauty and listen to the stillness. Streams tumble in from side canyons. Wildflowers grow along the banks, and wild animals and birds inhabit the forest. At the end of the day's voyage, boaters splash in the river, cast fishing lines into shady pools, or try gold panning.

Some groups camp on sand and gravel bars along the river. Others stay in any of several rustic riverside lodges that offer comfortable beds and family-style cooking to anglers, hikers, and white-water boaters. Reservations are essential.

Odd to meet an ostrich in Oregon? Not if you're walking or driving through the 600-acre wildlife preserve in Winston. Drivers receive detailed brochures; guides lead walkers.

Costumed wench serves dinner at historic Wolf Creek Tavern, north of Grants Pass. Oregon's oldest hostelry, now restored and refurbished, dates back to 1857.

Hoisting light kayaks on their backs, Rogue River group portages around some dangerous white water.

Hiking the Rogue River Trail

For nearly 40 miles—from Grave Creek Bridge downstream to Illahe—the Rogue River churns a rugged, twisting route. An equally twisting trail, blazed by Indians and prospectors, follows the steep, timbered north shoulder of the canyon.

This is a trail for veteran hikers. Backpackers must carry provisions for the entire trip. Most hikers take 4 or 5 days to cover the distance, allowing time to enjoy the scenery and study trailside plants, wildlife, and geology.

Wear long pants and hiking boots and carry rain gear. Bring water purification tablets and a snakebite kit. Be alert for rattlesnakes and poison oak. Wood ticks are numerous in spring and summer. Primitive campsites are located along the trail between Grave Creek and Marial; downstream, hikers camp on or near river bars.

Early summer and early autumn offer the best hiking, when days are pleasantly warm and wildflowers or colorful foliage brighten the trail. Hot temperatures prevail in summer. Heavy winter rains often cause slides and bridge washouts. The Forest Service and Bureau of Land Management share trail maintenance; check on current conditions in Grants Pass before you depart.

Exploring the middle Rogue

Once the homeland of the Takelma Indians, the broad valley of the middle Rogue invites exploration. Local tourist offices in Jackson County can direct visitors to intriguing routes and attractions off the main roads.

The town of Rogue River is the site of a Rooster Crowing Contest each June; prizes go to owners of roosters crowing the most times in 30 minutes.

In Gold Hill the Old Oregon Historical Museum, located 2 miles up Sardine Creek Road off State Highway

234, contains items from the region's early years. Puzzling phenomena caused by magnetic force fields lure visitors to the nearby House of Mystery (also called the Oregon Vortex). Both attractions are closed in winter.

On the south bank, State 99 follows the route of the 1846 Applegate Party and later wagon trains. Open for year-round camping and riverside recreation, Valley of the Rogue State Park, 12 miles east of Grants Pass, is a favorite headquarters for many travelers while exploring southern Oregon.

Riverside parks dot the upper Rogue

From Medford, State Highway 62 follows the upper Rogue northward toward its source. At Eagle Point, historic Butte Creek Mill still stands on the banks of Little Butte Creek; its millstones first ground grain in 1872.

Small parks—most of them merely a few picnic tables and a boat ramp—dot the Rogue from Bear Creek upstream past Shady Cove to Lost Creek Dam, about 30 miles northeast of Medford. The dam marks the upriver migration limit for salmon and steelhead. Travelers are welcome at the state fish hatchery and visitor center just below the dam.

On the south shore of Lost Creek Reservoir, Joseph P. Stewart State Park is open for year-round camping, picnicking, fishing, hiking, and water sports.

Above Lost Creek Reservoir, the upper Rogue tumbles in the rushing torrents and cataracts of a mountain stream, carving its way through rocky canyons bordered in greenery. Motorists traveling along tree-lined State 62 to Crater Lake or Diamond Lake find numerous picnic areas and campgrounds. You can stretch your legs on a nature trail at Mammoth Pines; at Natural Bridge, where the Rogue vanishes into underground lava tubes; at rustic

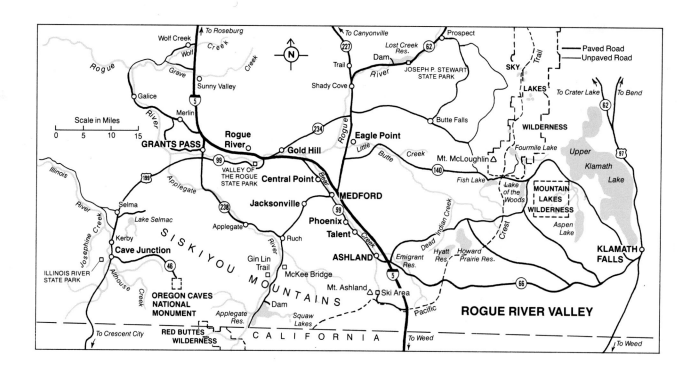

Union Creek Resort; and at the Rogue Gorge Viewpoint, where the river crashes through a narrow chasm.

Hikers enjoy the Upper Rogue River Trail, a 44-mile route that reveals the river's variety of moods and settings. It links Lost Creek Reservoir and the Pacific Crest Trail north of Crater Lake National Park. Autumn color is brilliant along the route. For trail and camping information, consult Rogue River National Forest officials in Medford or Prospect.

The Applegate Valley

Peaceful Applegate Valley's artery, State Highway 238, is the route for history buffs who enjoy investigating mining sites, old cemeteries, and back-country roads. The major destination is Jacksonville, a miners' boom town that refused to die. Today it's a thriving historic landmark and cultural center; its August music festival draws visitors from throughout the state.

Jacksonville, Oregon's first boom town

Richest and best known of the Siskiyou mining camps, Jacksonville mushroomed along Jackson Creek within weeks after gold was discovered late in 1851. Now a National Historic Landmark, this tree-shaded town lies 5 miles west of Medford on State 238.

In the 1850s and '60s, Jacksonville lived the fast-paced life of a lusty frontier mining town. Unlike most, it survived as a community when homesteading families settled in the Applegate Valley. Bypassed by both the railroad and the main highway, Jacksonville's importance was further diminished after the county seat was moved to Medford in 1927. It slumbered, nearly a ghost town, for more than 30 years until its resurgence began in the early 1950s.

Many of Jacksonville's 19th century wooden and brick structures have been restored, and about 80 historic buildings have been marked and dated. The old courthouse has been transformed into a historical museum. Several galleries and antique shops are housed in restored century-old buildings. Jacksonville celebrates its lively past each June on Pioneer Day.

A stroll through Jacksonville. Balustraded brick and frame buildings cut by narrow, high-arched entries and windows line Jacksonville's main street. Tall trees shade the side streets, where clapboard dwellings and steepled churches stand, having survived a pair of fires in the 1870s.

A former railway depot built in 1891 at Oregon and C streets serves as Jacksonville's visitor information center; the local Rogue River Valley Railway linked Jacksonville and Medford until 1925. Ask for a map leaflet showing the town's main points of interest.

Jacksonville's outstanding historical museum is housed in the monumental old Jackson County Courthouse on 5th Street, a block north of the business area.

WINEMAKERS INVITE YOU TO VISIT

A tour through an Oregon winery can be a casual, relaxed visit with a winemaker who loves tending his vineyards and making his wine.

Oregon wineries are small-scale operations with an air of informality that allows you a close look at the winemaking process, from the growing of grapes to the labeling of bottles. Your guide—who may be the winemaker himself—will show you wine presses, wooden aging barrels, perhaps a hand corking machine. Most wineries combine traditional methods with modern equipment. And when you get to the tasting room, you'll discover why Oregon wines are getting increased attention.

Oregonians made wine before Prohibition, but the winemaking revival didn't begin until 1961, when 20 acres were planted near Roseburg. Now hundreds of acres of vineyards are under cultivation.

Most of Oregon's table wine grapes are grown in the Willamette Valley in the north and the Umpqua Valley in the south, but numerous small vineyards are found throughout the western part of the state. Winemakers credit the even temperatures of the summer and autumn growing season with producing premium grapes; climate and growing factors resemble those of prime northern European growing areas.

About 50 Oregon wineries make dry table wines from vinifera grapes (varieties grown only for wine). Each winery has one or two wines it considers special—among them Riesling, Chardonnay, Gewürztraminer, Cabernet Sauvignon, and Pinot Noir. Other wineries specialize in fruit and berry wines.

Vintners and the wine-loving public gather to celebrate the grape at regional festivals. Many wineries also sponsor their own events during the year.

For a current directory of Oregon wineries, write to the Oregon Winegrowers Association, Box 6590, Portland, OR 97228-6590 and enclose a self-addressed #10 envelope with 39 cents postage attached. Member wineries are briefly described with wine specialties, winery hours, tours, and tasting facilities; some have picnic areas. Maps show routes to each winery, and regional maps offer wine touring suggestions.

Spotlights pierce the midsummer night, illuminating
Ashland's outdoor Elizabethan stage as Shakespeare's
plays come to life. Audience is bundled against the chill.

Built in 1883, the building contains one of the most extensive and fascinating historical displays in the state. Exhibits bring alive the daily life of Jacksonville's early residents—Indians, miners, gamblers, law men, Wells Fargo agents, teachers, circuit riders, farmers. You'll see pioneer firearms, 19th century money, and the vintage photographs and camera equipment of Peter Britt. The museum is open from 9 A.M. to 5 P.M. Monday through Saturday, noon to 5 Sunday (closed Mondays from Labor Day to Memorial Day).

One of Jacksonville's early settlers, Peter Britt was a Swiss immigrant who photographically recorded the history of Jackson County from 1853 to the early 1890s. His hobby was horticulture, and he planted many semitropical shrubs and trees in his garden on 1st Street south of California Street. The gardens are open to the public except during the Britt music festival period.

Another of Jacksonville's prominent early residents was Cornelius C. Beekman, the town's first Wells Fargo agent and banker. From 1863 to 1880, the Beekman Bank at the corner of 3rd and California streets was the most important financial institution in southern Oregon; about $31 million in gold dust crossed its counter to await safe transport by Wells Fargo. Furnishings remain much as they were in the 1860s; you'll see gold scales in a glass case.

The handsomely restored Beekman residence on Stage Road South is open for tours daily from 1 to 5 P.M. from Memorial Day through Labor Day.

The large brick United States Hotel on California Street once hosted President Rutherford B. Hayes and his party; a local bank now occupies the building.

The historic McCully House, built by a Jackson County physician in 1860 near 5th and California streets, has been completely restored and furnished with antiques. It is open to visitors in July and August from 10 A.M. to 5 P.M.

Jacksonville Inn, constructed in 1863, has been renovated as a hotel and restaurant; its eight rooms are furnished with antiques.

Jacksonville's Methodist-Episcopal church at 5th and D streets was built in 1854 with substantial contributions by local gamblers, among others. Four years later the Catholic church, at 4th and D streets, was built; the former Catholic rectory is open daily from 1 to 5 P.M. from Memorial Day to Labor Day.

The Presbyterian church at 6th and California streets was constructed in 1881 of native sugar pine. Its Gothic stained glass windows were imported from Italy.

Jacksonville cemetery. Headstones in the cemetery northwest of town provide vivid reminders of frontier hardships. To reach the cemetery, drive out E Street, cross Jackson Creek, and take the gravel road uphill.

Among the graves are victims of Indian attacks and smallpox, men who died of "lead poisoning" or hanging, even one killed by a grizzly bear. The cemetery contains graves of several prominent pioneers including Beekman, Britt, Indian fighter John Ross, and pioneer editor William Green T'Vault.

Britt Music Festival. Each summer Jacksonville hosts a series of outdoor music and performing arts events. Originated in 1963, the festival is one of the oldest and most renowned in the Pacific Northwest. Concerts feature classical, bluegrass, and jazz musicians; dance companies; and musical theater performances. For a schedule of events, write to Britt Festivals, Box 1124, Medford, OR 97501.

Many concert-goers relax on blankets and folding chairs, and picnic before the performances, which are presented in a natural amphitheater in the Britt gardens. Food, beverages, and rental pillows and seat backs are available.

Historic byways

If you want to explore some of the old mining sites, maps are available at the Jacksonville Museum for a nominal fee. Additional information on interesting back roads and destinations is available from the Jacksonville visitor information office or at the Rogue River National Forest ranger station south of Ruch.

If you take the road south from State 238 at Ruch, toward Applegate Dam and the headwaters of the Applegate River, you'll come to the inviting McKee Bridge picnic area, which features a picturesque 1917 covered bridge and a swimming hole.

A side road leads to Flumet Flat Campground and the start of the Gin Lin Trail, a ¾-mile self-guided Forest Service interpretive trail. It highlights the hydraulic mining operations of Chinese workers here in the 1880s. Mining boss Gin Lin and his laborers extracted more than $1 million in gold from the Applegate Valley.

In the upper valley, paved roads lead to picnic sites along the northwest shore of Applegate Lake and to French Gulch Campground; three other campgrounds can be reached only by boat or trail. Forest roads lead farther south toward the headwaters of the Applegate River and to Red Buttes Wilderness on the Oregon-California border.

You can taste locally-produced food products and wine at The Tasting Room just east of Jacksonville.

Medford and Ashland

Southern Oregon's largest city, Medford, and the Shakespearean center of Ashland lie south of the Rogue and north of the Siskiyou Range. They border Bear Creek, which begins north of Emigrant Reservoir and meanders northwest to join the Rogue near Central Point.

A narrow creekside park in Medford is one of a series under construction—collectively known as the Bear Creek Greenway—that will enhance the stream's natural assets and offer new possibilities for recreational use.

Rockhounds will enjoy a stop at the Crater Rock Museum in Central Point. Located at 2002 Scenic Avenue, it contains exhibits of cut and polished rocks and regional Indian arrowheads.

Pear orchards surround Medford

Partially framed by forested mountains, Medford lies in the center of vast pear orchards that cover the valley and climb the gently sloping foothills. Additional land is planted in apple, peach, and other fruit and nut trees. In mid-April, blossoming trees transform the valley, and Medford celebrates with a Pear Blossom Festival.

After the riches of the Jacksonville gold fields diminished, many prospectors settled in the fertile Bear Creek Valley. Medford prospered following the arrival of the railroad in the late 19th century, and in 1927 the Jackson County seat was moved here.

Now a town of about 39,000, Medford has benefited from wise city planning begun in its infancy. Mature native trees shade the town's wide streets, giving a parklike appearance. City and county buildings cluster along W. 8th Street near S. Oakdale Avenue. The imposing Jackson County Courthouse was completed in 1932. Mini Park, at the corner of East Main Street and Central Avenue, is a popular downtown gathering spot.

Bear Creek flows through Medford, bisecting the town. Cyclists and pedestrians enjoy a delightful bike and nature trail along the creek. The 4-mile bikeway begins at Barnett Road and extends north to Table Rock Road. A nature trail starts at Bear Creek Park.

Families relax and picnic along the stream's east bank in Bear Creek Park, near Highland Drive and Siskiyou Boulevard. In summer, outdoor concerts are held here and tennis players rally on lighted tennis courts.

South of town on State 99, travelers can stop at Harry and David's Bear Creek Store, near the headquarters of the mail-order fruit and food business that started here in 1934. The complex includes a gift shop, restaurant, and country produce market. Nearby is a Jackson & Perkins' test and display rose garden, in bloom from May to October.

For information on regional attractions and back-country destinations, inquire at the Medford Visitors & Convention Bureau, 304 S. Central Avenue.

Theater dominates Ashland activities

Known throughout the nation for its outstanding Shakespearean Festival, Ashland is a charming town of 15,000 tucked into a mountain-ringed bowl. Green slopes climb steeply into the Siskiyou's wooded foothills. Southern Oregon State College is located at the south end of town. Swedenburg House Museum, on the campus, is a branch of the Southern Oregon Historical Society with exhibit galleries and a research center. Schneider Museum of Art features contemporary art.

A classic example of community pride and cooperation, the Oregon Shakespearean Festival has grown from a small community event to a nationally recognized repertory theater. The Elizabethan atmosphere spills over into the community, where some downtown facades and shops have adopted an old-English motif. Many turn-of-the-century buildings also have been preserved. A stroll around the historic Railroad District on A Street recalls the era when Ashland was a thriving railroad town. The center of activity is the Plaza, near the theater complex. A walking tour brochure is available at the information center.

The town's jewel is 99-acre Lithia Park, a greenway extending from the business district about a mile up Ashland Creek. An integral part of the community, it is the site of community picnics and outdoor concerts and classes. Families enjoy its lawns and picnic areas, duck ponds, children's playground, nature trails, tennis courts, band shell, and other features.

Ashland celebrates an old-fashioned Fourth of July with a parade and events in Lithia Park. From Thanksgiving through New Year's Day, Ashland celebrates the 12 Days of Christmas with a variety of festive events.

Oregon's famous Shakespearean Festival

In 1935 a small group of Ashland residents decided to present a Shakespeare play as part of a 3-day Fourth of July celebration. That original venture has grown until it now encompasses three theaters and a season extending from late February through October, with both matinee and evening performances throughout the season. For schedule and ticket information, write to Shakespeare, Box 158, Ashland, OR 97520; box office phone is (503) 482-4331. Some performances sell out far in advance.

In summer Shakespeare is performed on the outdoor Elizabethan stage, patterned after the Fortune Theater of 17th century London. Plays are staged in the lively, human, often bawdy manner of the era with elaborate costuming, little scenery, and Elizabethan-style music.

Costumed dancers and troubadours entertain in the courtyard before outdoor performances, setting the Renaissance mood. Since evenings can be quite cool, knowledgeable spectators bring coats, heavy jackets, and lap robes. Rental cushions ease the hardness of the seats.

Throughout the repertory season, plays drawn from all theatrical periods are performed in two indoor theaters: the 600-seat Angus Bowmer and the intimate 140-seat Black Swan.

Special events with an Elizabethan theme dot the summer calendar. The exhibit center, a museum of the Festival's history at Main and S. Pioneer streets, features displays depicting production details of a current play and a room where visitors can try on costumes; the center is open on performance days from 10 A.M. to 4 P.M.

The educational repertory theater also offers backstage tours, talks by members of the staff and company, concerts, movies, and college-level workshop classes.

Atop Mount Ashland

Located 18 miles south of Ashland in the Siskiyou Range, Mount Ashland is an inviting destination for festivalgoers or skiers. The paved road ends at the ski area, but a good graveled road continues along the Siskiyou crest.

Picnickers can stop at Mount Ashland Campground about 2 miles below the summit or follow the steep rocky road that climbs the final mile to the summit picnic area and view point. Summer wildflowers bloom along mountain roads and in the meadows in July.

If driving remote gravel mountain roads doesn't faze you, consider the 75-mile Mount Ashland Loop that winds along the summit of the Siskiyous. Wildflowers and mountain panoramas make this a memorable trip. The mountain road is generally open from early July to mid-October; it is usually well marked, but motorists should inquire at Rogue River National Forest offices in

Medford or Ashland for detailed directions and current road conditions.

From Thanksgiving into April the skiers take over. Mount Ashland's ski area has a low-key, cozy charm. Two chairlifts and three surface tows transport skiers to 22 runs on the 7,533-foot peak. The day lodge contains a cafeteria and cheery lounge; other facilities include a ski shop with rental equipment and a ski school. Night skiing is available Thursday, Friday, and Saturday evenings from 4 to 10. For information on bus service to Mt. Ashland from Medford and Ashland, phone (503) 482-8948.

Water sports on reservoir lakes

Sailing and fishing enthusiasts head for three large reservoir lakes east of Ashland. County parks are located at Emigrant and Howard Prairie reservoirs; Hyatt Reservoir has a BLM recreation area.

Located 5 miles southeast of Ashland off State Highway 66 is Emigrant Reservoir. Boat ramps, campgrounds, and picnic areas combined with good fishing, swimming, and a 270-foot water slide make this lake a family favorite.

Howard Prairie Reservoir lies 22 miles northeast of Ashland by way of Dead Indian Road. Tucked between mountain ridges, the 6-mile-long lake covers a former meadow surrounded by pines and fir trees. Four county parks border its western shore. Fishing supplies and boat rentals are available at the lake marina. In summer, sailboats and canoes glide across the lake and water-skiers sweep in foaming arcs at its south end. Several regattas are held here each year.

Continue 5 miles southwest of Howard Prairie to Hyatt Reservoir (or you can reach it by spur road from State 66). It has a year-round resort, boat rentals, and camping and picnic areas. In winter, families go snowmobiling, cross-country skiing, and sledding near the lake—and ice skate on it when conditions permit.

Mountain Lakes

South of Crater Lake, the Cascades are a wonderland of mountain lakes—some large, many small—sprinkled along the alpine crest and slopes. A few large lakes have highway access and simple resort amenities, but most are in remote areas accessible only by trail.

Most visitors explore this high country in July and August, but it's delightful during the long, unhurried days of early autumn when days are warm, nights are crisp, and crowds have departed. In winter, skiers and snowmobilers enjoy the forest and lakeside trails.

State Highway 140 is the main route between Medford on I-5 and Klamath Falls on U.S. Highway 97. Farther south, State 66 is a winding, 65-mile scenic drive linking Ashland and Klamath Falls.

A trio of popular lakes

When residents of southern Oregon head for the mountains, the destination is often one of three Cascade lakes—Fish Lake, Lake of the Woods, or Fourmile Lake. Each has at least one public campground and a small resort where visitors can obtain supplies, fishing tackle, and boats.

State 140 climbs east from State 62 through Rogue River National Forest to Fish Lake. East of the summit, it passes Lake of the Woods and descends through Winema National Forest to Klamath Falls. Side roads north of State 140 lead to Fourmile Lake.

Fishing for rainbow and eastern brook trout is the primary activity at Fish Lake, at the foot of 9,495-foot Mount McLoughlin. A resort lodge (closed weekdays in winter) and rental cabins provide accommodations.

Southeast of the peak, summer homes, youth camps, and campgrounds border the shore of Lake of the Woods. The resort operates all year; the dining room is open daily in summer, and Wednesday through Sunday from October through May. Fishing and water sports are popular in summer, and trails fan out to many destinations.

Forest roads lead north of State 140 to Fourmile Lake, most remote of the three large lakes. Anglers fish for rainbow trout and kokanee salmon here. From the campground, hikers depart on the Pacific Crest Trail.

Uncrowded trails draw cross-country skiers and snowmobilers in winter. When Lake of the Woods and Fish Lake freeze solidly, anglers fish through the ice, and there's ice skating, as well.

Sky Lakes Wilderness

Straddling the crest of the Cascades south of Crater Lake National Park, the Sky Lakes Wilderness abounds with lakes and scenic trails. This lake-studded high plateau is jointly administered by Rogue River and Winema National forests; trail information is available at Forest Service offices in Medford, Butte Falls, and Klamath Falls.

More than 200 shallow lakes and ponds are scattered across the timbered glacial basins. Rocky ridges and sharp peaks break the terrain. The Pacific Crest Trail winds through the Wilderness, and other trails connect the lakes. Hiking routes are open from July through October.

Water is abundant in the southern part of the area, but hikers should carry water when traveling north of Ranger Spring, across the pumice area known as the Oregon Desert. Bring mosquito repellent, warm clothing, and rain gear; sudden rain or snow storms can occur at any time of year.

Mountain Lakes Wilderness

One of Oregon's original wilderness areas, the Mountain Lakes Wilderness is a 6-mile-square tract some 20 miles northwest of Klamath Falls.

Known for its rugged topography and dozens of high lakes, it is reached by primitive roads and forest trails south of State 140. Most of the area lies above 6,600 feet elevation. Trails are generally blocked by snow until late June, and weather turns brisk by September.

Core of the wilderness is a large glacial cirque surrounded by eight peaks, all topping 7,700 feet; highest is 8,208-foot Aspen Butte. A loop trail enables hikers and horseback riders to visit the main trout-stocked lakes. Trail information is available at the Winema National Forest office, 2819 Dahlia Street, Klamath Falls.

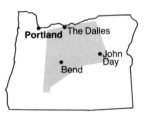

CENTRAL OREGON

This sunny land stretches from snowy peaks across a vast plateau

Oregon's backbone is the Cascade Range, a chain of massive dormant volcanoes dividing the state. The Cascades marked the final rugged barrier for early travelers.

Towering above the lesser mountains, the lofty and serene peaks we see today belie their violent origin. Formed by outpourings of lava and fiery volcanic eruptions, their slopes gouged by glaciers, these snowy cones now rest, their slopes carpeted by vast forests.

From the pine-clad eastern slopes of the Cascades, a spacious, sun-drenched, high plateau stretches halfway across the state to the Blue Mountains. Two main rivers—the Deschutes and the John Day—and their tributaries carve scenic canyons through the plateau as they wind northward toward the Columbia.

Central Oregon still kindles memories of the Old West. Indians roamed these lands, fur trappers and pioneer scouts explored the valleys and canyons, and sheepmen and cattlemen battled for grazing rights. Occasional ghost towns and tumble-down buildings testify to the hard life on the windswept prairie.

A Vast Mountain Playground

Oregonians and visitors flock to the magnificent Cascades for year-round mountain recreation. Campers, hikers, anglers, boaters, mountain climbers, horseback riders, hunters, and skiers choose from dozens of destinations on the forested flanks of the Cascades. You can explore the moist, lush river valleys off the western slope; the drier, open pine country east of the mountains; or the alpine wilderness along the Cascade crest.

In spring, tender shoots of new growth and early wildflowers adorn forest roads. Summer brings the temptations of the high country—shady forest trails, tumbling mountain streams, and blossom-filled alpine meadows. Autumn splashes the foothills and valleys with vibrant shades of gold and scarlet. Winter snows cloak the trees, and ski slopes glisten in the frosty sun.

Most of the land is administered by the Forest Service. Officials of the various national forests—Mount Hood, Willamette, Deschutes, Umpqua, Rogue River, and Winema—provide information on campgrounds and trails, and suggestions for forest recreation within their territories. Maps of each national forest can be purchased at Forest Service offices for $1 per map.

Hiking the Cascade crest

Experienced hikers enjoy the challenging trek along a skyline trail that traverses the forests and peaks of Oregon's Cascades for more than 400 miles. Providing a well-signed route through the high country, the Pacific Crest National Scenic Trail extends approximately 2,400 miles from the Canadian border to Mexico, linking the high mountain routes of Washington, Oregon, and California.

Oregon's 420-mile portion of the route begins at the Columbia River Highway near Cascade Locks and winds south along paths first followed by animals and later by Indians, who gathered olallie (huckleberries) on the mountain slopes to dry for their winter food supply. Snowy peaks loom in spectacular panoramas along the route, and side trails lead to trout-filled mountain lakes. The trail crosses the California border east of Copco Lake.

Most backpackers take about a month to complete the entire Oregon portion of the trail. However, trans-

Rugged crags of Mount Jefferson loom above wilderness camp at Scout Lake, just north of peak. Mountaineers practice climbing skills here, and anglers fish for trout in alpine lakes.

Cascade highways and forest roads provide access to this primitive country, making it feasible for hikers and riders to plan shorter trips on sections of the trail.

In most years, the best hiking period is between mid-July and September, though portions of the trail may be passable in early July and early October. Trail elevations range from 4,000 to 7,100 feet. Snowy patches often remain on northern exposures until August. Mosquitoes can be a problem in some regions. Hikers must be prepared for great variations in weather, for the temperature may drop suddenly from 80° or 90° to below freezing; midsummer snowstorms occur occasionally. Running streams are plentiful, particularly on the western slope.

Forest Service personnel provide up-to-date information on trail conditions and outfitters who conduct riding and pack trips into the mountains. Topographic maps are available from the U.S. Geological Survey, Denver Federal Center, Denver, CO 80202.

Crossing the Cascades

Portions of today's trans-Cascade highways still follow old Indian trails, emigrant routes, and pioneer wagon roads across the mountains.

From north to south, motorists cross the Cascades on the Mount Hood Highway (U.S. Highway 26); the Santiam Highway (U.S. Highway 20); the old McKenzie Pass scenic route (State Highway 242, closed in winter); the Willamette Pass Highway (State Highway 58); and the North Umpqua Highway (State Highway 138).

In the southern Cascades, State Highways 62, 140, and 66 link southwestern Oregon towns with U.S. Highway 97.

Mount Hood Highway

Traveling southeast from Portland, the Mount Hood Highway climbs through Douglas fir forests to Mount

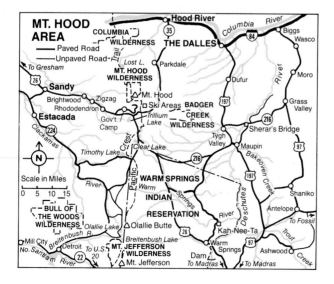

Hood. Much of the route parallels the Barlow Road, the pioneer wagon route across the mountains.

A favorite drive of Portlanders—particularly if they are entertaining out-of-state visitors—is the Mount Hood Loop. From Mount Hood the circuit continues north along State Highway 35 through the Hood River Valley and returns to Portland along the famous Columbia River Highway.

Monarch of the Oregon Cascades, snow-capped Mount Hood towers over its empire. The 11,235-foot peak dominates Mount Hood National Forest, which spreads over more than a million acres from the Columbia River south to Mount Jefferson.

Once a landmark for pioneers seeking the green valleys west of the mountains, today Mount Hood is probably the most accessible peak in the Cascades. Skiers throng to its slopes, climbers ascend its glaciers, and hikers tramp its trails. The mountain's northwestern slopes have been preserved as Mount Hood Wilderness. Four additional areas of Mount Hood National Forest also have been granted wilderness status.

Timberline Lodge, an artisans' showcase

High on the south slope of Mount Hood perches Timberline Lodge, a unique showcase of Oregon arts and crafts. Built during the depression days of the 1930s, the lodge was an ambitious WPA project that utilized the state's native materials and the diverse skills of Oregon artisans. Timberline Lodge was dedicated by President Franklin D. Roosevelt in 1937. The building is now on the National Register of Historic Places. Open year round, it offers accommodations, meals, and other services to Mount Hood visitors.

A small museum on the lodge's lower level provides a good introduction to the building's architecture and art. Carpenters and metal workers, painters and stonecutters, woodcarvers, and weavers all contributed to the construction and furnishing of the great lodge. Three themes are emphasized: the pioneers, the Indian influence, and Oregon plants and wildlife.

So overwhelming is the building's distinctive rugged architecture that visitors often miss its carefully executed details. Each piece of furniture, each lamp and lamp shade, each door hinge was hand-crafted especially for the building. Elaborate woodcarvings, painted murals, intricate mosaics of wood or stone, and numerous original paintings contribute to the art heritage of the lodge. The stonework of the hexagonal fireplace, the pegged oak floors, and the massive exposed beams of the lobby testify to the talents of many artisans.

Across the road, Wy'East Day Lodge is a showcase of 1980s Northwest crafts as well as a place for skiers to eat, to warm up, and to rent equipment.

Ski trails traverse Mount Hood

Winter sports fans approach Mount Hood with enthusiasm. The exciting freedom of its slopes, a dependable snowfall (averaging 17 feet), and a concentration of excellent ski facilities little more than an hour's drive from Portland attract a profusion of skiers, from beginners to experts.

If there's enough snow, ski areas open by Thanksgiving weekend. Facilities around Government Camp usually shut down in March, but there's good downhill skiing until mid-April at Timberline.

Advanced skiers head for the mountain's three major areas: Timberline Lodge, Mount Hood Meadows, and Mirror Mountain Ski Area. Skiers choose from more than 100 miles of challenging downhill runs—including a 5-mile course from Mount Hood's upper slopes—and numerous ski touring trails. Several areas offer nighttime downhill skiing. Day lodges serve skiers at all three areas.

From Timberline Lodge at 6,000 feet, skiers take the Magic Mile up to the 7,000-foot level; four double chair lifts operate during the winter season. A variety of runs and trails descend below the lodge to 5,000 feet.

Families enjoy the gentler slopes and children's play areas at Summit Ski Area and Snowbunny Lodge, both near Government Camp, and Cooper Spur ski area on the northeastern slope. Snowshoe hikers and cross-country skiers traverse the countryside on miles of uncrowded trails.

Summer activities on the mountain

When snow melts at the lower elevations, skiers head for Mount Hood's upper slopes. Climbers look toward the mountain's glaciers, and hikers take to the trails.

Summer skiing. The 1¼-mile Palmer double chairlift transports skiers from the top of the Magic Mile lift on to the Palmer Snow Field at 8,700 feet elevation, where a succession of afternoon thaws and nighttime freezes creates good corn snow conditions for those skiers who are reluctant to pack away their equipment. Summer racing schools share the slopes with recreational skiers in June and early July.

During the summer when weather permits, non-skiers can ride the Magic Mile chairlift from Timberline Lodge to the upper slopes. Rising 1,000 feet in elevation during the 1⅛ mile ride, you look over the peaks, valleys, and forests of the Cascade Range.

Mountaineering. Several thousand people climb Mount Hood annually. Novice climbers with guides and rented equipment can reach the summit in spring and early summer, but only experienced mountaineers should attempt to scale the peak in winter, as weather conditions can change quickly at high altitudes. Mountaineering clubs and schools provide instruction for those new to the sport.

Many climbers leave from Timberline Lodge, ascending the south slope; other groups depart from Cloud Cap Inn or Tilly Jane Forest Camp to climb the more difficult north face. The best climbing period is March to mid-July. Mountaineers usually start about midnight, making the climb in the cool morning hours before the sun softens the snow. The round trip takes 10 to 14 hours, depending on the route taken. Climbers should register before departure and check out on return at Timberline Lodge, Cooper Spur, or the Parkdale Ranger Station.

Alpine Slide. From mid-May through Labor Day, summer visitors can combine a scenic lift ride at Mirror Mountain Ski Area with a thrilling descent on the Alpine Slide.

WINTER FUN IN THE MOUNTAINS

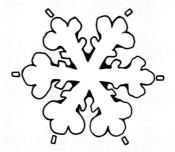

Snow and ice transform the Cascade forests into a winter fantasy. Conifers are cloaked in dazzling snow, and lakes gleam blue in the valleys.

You can schuss down wide, open slopes high above timberline or plot your route across miles of untracked snow. At Mount Bachelor and Mount Hood, chairlifts transport skiers to the highest slopes, extending good downhill skiing well into summer. Cross-country skiers and snowshoers follow marked and groomed trails near many ski areas or strike out for magnificent backcountry touring. Some routes are restricted to nonmotorized travel. Marked snowmobile trails often follow unplowed forest roads.

Ice fishing draws midwinter anglers to some southern Oregon mountain lakes, and dog sled racing has become part of the winter fun for an increasing number of enthusiasts. On race days, dozens of drivers and their dog teams gather for a weekend of racing at Beaver Marsh, Sisters, or Diamond Lake.

Skiers can rent boots and other equipment at ski area rental shops or at sporting goods stores in towns near the mountains (check the telephone directory Yellow Pages).

For a list of the state's ski areas and their facilities, contact the state's tourism office in Salem (see page 9). Regional and district offices of the U.S. Forest Service can provide detailed information on cross-country and snowmobile routes within their areas. Always check the weather report before starting out.

Snowplows keep the main roads clear. Winter travelers in mountain areas should carry chains; they may be needed at any time.

From mid-November through April you'll need a "sno-park" permit to park in many lots plowed for winter sports use. About 60 mountain parking areas—including most ski areas—are included in the system. Lots are policed rigorously and violators are fined. Washington snow passes are honored in Oregon snow areas.

Non-transferable permits can be purchased for the season or by the day. Permits and a list of sno-park lots are available at most ski resorts, from ski and sports shops, or from the state Motor Vehicles Division, Salem, OR 97314. Permits will indicate your vehicle license plate number; one-day permits also give the date of intended use.

Alpenglow tints top of Mount Hood behind snow-packed Timberline Lodge. This grand wooden showplace, built in the 1930s, offers accommodations for winter skiers and summer hikers.

Flowing from icy springs north of Black Butte, Metolius River twists and turns through tall pines and smooth meadows on its way to Lake Billy Chinook.

Hours are 10:30 to 7:30 weekdays, 9:30 to 7:30 weekends and holidays. From Labor Day to mid-October, the slide operates weekends only from 9:30 to 6:30.

Wilderness hiking

Mount Hood National Forest trails provide forest and alpine scenery to delight any hiker. You'll find no shortage of destinations for day hikes, weekend trips, or longer excursions. Forest rangers can suggest routes of varying lengths along rivers and streams, through wooded valleys, or to waterfalls, hot springs, or backcountry lakes. High trails may be blocked by snow until late June or July. Alpine wildflowers carpet mountain meadows in July and August.

Several wilderness preserves set aside scenic regions near the peak. The Columbia Wilderness is briefly described on page 32.

Mount Hood Wilderness. Encircling Mount Hood is the Timberline Trail, a rugged 37½-mile alpine mountain path. On the north side of the mountain, it cuts through Mount Hood Wilderness; on the western slope, it links up with a section of the Pacific Crest Trail, then follows Ramona Creek up to its falls.

Seldom an easy route to hike, the Timberline Trail offers an awesome variety of scenery—steep, exposed slopes; glacier-fed streams; dense conifer forests; wildflower-strewn meadows. Most hikers cover only a section of the Timberline Trail at a time, entering and leaving by one of a dozen side trails.

Salmon Huckleberry Wilderness. Located south of Zigzag off U.S. 26, this wilderness includes the headwaters of Eagle Creek and the Salmon River. Trails crisscross the area. The Salmon River Trail heads upriver to a series of waterfalls, which plunge into the river below the trail. Other favorite routes include the Eagle Creek, Wildcat Mountain, Huckleberry Mountain, and Hunchback trails. A half-dozen Forest Service campgrounds are located at the edge of the wilderness.

Bull of the Woods Wilderness. Hikers still come upon old shafts and rusting equipment in this region, reminders that this was once an active mining area. Steep, mountainous slopes are cut by fast-moving streams, which are the major headwaters of the Collawash, Breitenbush, and Little North Fork Santiam rivers. More than a dozen isolated lakes are scattered here.

Jointly administered by Mount Hood and Willamette National forests, the Bull of the Woods Wilderness can be reached by forest roads from State 224 (south of Bagby Hot Springs) or from State 22 and the Breitenbush River Road (north of Elk Lake).

Badger Creek Wilderness. Southeast of Mount Hood, this region is reached by forest roads east of State 35. Trails lead to the summit of 6,525-foot Lookout Mountain, which commands a panorama of the Cascade Range and the high desert country to the east. Steep slopes and glacial features dominate the upper miles of Badger Creek. Best known of the area's hiking routes is the Badger Creek Trail, which follows the stream down from Badger Lake toward Tygh Valley and the Deschutes River.

Along Santiam Routes

From the central Willamette Valley, highways follow the North and South Santiam rivers upstream into the Cascades, joining near Santiam Pass. Before entering Willamette National Forest, the roads pass reservoirs—popular for water sports—and forest campgrounds.

From Santiam routes you can hike into Mount Jefferson Wilderness and other preserves, go skiing at Hoodoo Bowl, or cast your fishing line into the famed Metolius River.

The North Santiam

Southeast of Salem, State 22 follows the North Santiam River east and south into the Cascades to a highway junction with U.S. 20.

Detroit Lake. Boaters head for this reservoir, about 46 miles east of Salem. Tackle, supplies, and boat rentals are available in Detroit. State and Forest Service campgrounds await travelers; Piety Island Campground, on a knobby island in the middle of the lake, can be reached only by boat.

Ollalie Lake Scenic Area. More than 100 solitary mountain lakes and ponds are tucked away amid rocky buttes and virgin forests in the Olallie Lake Scenic Area north of Mount Jefferson Wilderness. About 22 miles square, it rests atop the crest of the Cascades in the southernmost section of Mount Hood National Forest. From Detroit on State 22, the Breitenbush River Road branches northeast to the lakes; inquire at the Detroit Ranger Station about road conditions.

A half-dozen forest campgrounds are located near the twisting dirt road that connects the main lakes—Olallie, Monon, Horseshoe, and Breitenbush. At the north end of Olallie Lake, a small summer resort has groceries, fishing tackle, cabins, and rowboat rentals. No motorboats are permitted on the lakes.

Trails lead from the camps to literally dozens of backcountry tarns where you can fish for brook, rainbow, and cutthroat trout. From Breitenbush Lake Campground, the Pacific Crest Trail bears south into Mount Jefferson Wilderness.

Mount Jefferson Wilderness

In the shadows of 10,497-foot Mount Jefferson stretch over 111,000 acres of alpine wilderness—tranquil lakes, swift streams, mountain meadows, and dense conifer forests. On the eastern slope, narrow lava flows follow Jefferson and Cabot creeks. Willamette and Deschutes National forests administer the wilderness jointly.

From State 22 forest roads climb eastward to trailheads near the wilderness border. East of the Santiam summit, roads north of Suttle Lake lead to east-side trails.

Hikers relish more than 150 miles of trails, including a 36-mile stretch of the Pacific Crest Trail. You pass waterfalls and small lakes shimmering like scattered jewels, cross rushing creeks on rustic bridges, and traverse snowfields shaded by evergreens or glistening in the sun. Many of the area's 150 lakes, clustered in rocky basins or lake-studded valleys, are trout fishing favorites.

From mid-July through mid-September, experienced mountaineers pit their climbing skills against both Mount Jefferson and Three Fingered Jack, whose three rock needles thrust up against the skyline.

Along the South Santiam

East of Albany, U.S. 20 parallels the South Santiam River, climbing through Willamette National Forest as did its predecessor, the Santiam Wagon Road—a pioneer toll road that crossed the Cascades just north of Mount Washington.

At the Sweet Home Ranger Station, you can inquire about nearby campgrounds or picnic sites and interesting hikes. Here, too, you can learn about two small preserves—Middle Santiam Wilderness and Menagerie Wilderness—recently established near Santiam streams.

In the Cascade foothills, two dams—Foster and Green Peter—hold the Middle and South Santiam waters in check. Reservoir lakes behind the dams are well used by water sports enthusiasts. Recreation facilities are found along the north side of the lakes.

At Cascadia State Park, once a mineral springs resort, the river flows through a narrow, rocky gorge beside U.S. 20. Campers and picnickers can fish or splash in the river or hike nearby trails. East of Cascadia, trails at Trout Creek and Fernview campgrounds lead north from the highway into Menagerie Wilderness; climbers practice mountaineering techniques on rock pinnacles here.

Just west of its junction with State 22, the Santiam Highway crosses a lava field and passes near Sawyer's Cave, formed by a volcanic gas bubble in the crust as it cooled. A small sign on the south side of the highway marks the route to the cave. It's refreshingly cool on a hot summer day; a sheet of ice usually covers the cave's floor.

Hoodoo Ski Bowl.

When winter snows arrive, activity quickens at Hoodoo Ski Bowl, just west of the Santiam Pass, about 88 miles southeast of Salem. Activities center around two day lodges, a cafeteria, a ski shop, and a new nordic center. From December to mid-April, the area is open Tuesday through Sunday, on holidays, and daily during Christmas and spring vacations.

Three double chairlifts take skiers up Hoodoo's broad, open slopes. Beginners' areas are located near the lodge. Cross-country skiers and snowshoers enjoy marked loop trails east of the downhill area; unmarked routes lead north from a highway sno-park into Mount Jefferson Wilderness. Marked snowmobile trails loop south of U.S. 20 and the ski area. A Forest Service brochure is available.

The eastern slope.

The Pacific Crest Trail crosses U.S. 20 just west of Santiam Pass; hikers head north into Mount Jefferson Wilderness or south toward Mount Washington. On the eastern flank of the Cascades, the highway cuts through Deschutes National Forest, passing high above Blue Lake, cradled in its deep volcanic basin below Mount Washington. A year-round resort, Blue Lake is the departure point for summer pack trips and trail rides and winter ski touring.

U.S. 20 skims along the north shore of popular Suttle Lake, glimpsed through tall pines. Families enjoy its campgrounds and a lakeside hiking trail. At its eastern end are a picnic area, swimming beach, and playground; water-skiers practice at the western end.

Another favorite is small Scout Lake, just south of Suttle Lake. Campsites and picnic areas overlook the water; firs and pines grow near the shore. Wide gravel beaches slope gently into the water, which warms enough for summer swimming. Trails border the lake shore.

Vacationing in the Metolius country

Northeast of the Santiam Pass, the Metolius River is famed for superb and challenging fly fishing. Bubbling from icy springs north of Black Butte, it races northward past the community of Camp Sherman, following a twisting course through ponderosa pines and parklike meadows. Fed by numerous springs and creeks, it passes several forest camps on its way to join Lake Billy Chinook and the Deschutes River.

Resort accommodations and cabins are available, and in summer you can go horseback riding. The Metolius River Road loops north of Camp Sherman along the stream; at Lower Bridge Campground, cross the river and return on the west side of the stream. Forest roads lead west to campgrounds at Jack and Round lakes and to trailheads near the border of Mount Jefferson Wilderness.

For close-up views of the Metolius, take a walk along the river trail that begins at Lower Canyon Creek Campground and follows the river downstream to a state fish hatchery at Wizard Falls and Candle Creek Forest Camp.

Highways converge at Sisters

Once Indian trails met near the site of Sisters; now the Santiam Pass and McKenzie Pass highways join here, forming the town's main street before forking again toward Redmond and Bend. Remodeled stores reflect an old-fashioned western town, complete with false fronts, verandas, and hitching posts. Campers, anglers, hikers, and hunters use Sisters as a convenient supply point. In mid-June, visitors gather for the popular Sisters Rodeo, one of the state's best small rodeos.

Just west of town along State 242, you can see dozens of llamas grazing in a pasture backed by mountains; some are used as pack animals on back-country excursions. Southeast of town off U.S. 20, Sisters State Park straddles Squaw Creek amid pines and junipers.

Up the McKenzie

From Springfield, State Highway 126 heads eastward, hugging the banks of the McKenzie River for more than 40 miles. Boating is a way of life on the river, and most of the people who live along the McKenzie are as much at home on the water as they are on the road beside it.

River guides conduct visiting anglers to promising fishing holes hidden in this famous trout stream Chinook salmon and steelhead migrate upstream in May and June. You can also arrange rafting trips along white-water stretches of the river; for information on boat trips and fishing guides, check with the Springfield Area Chamber of Commerce or the McKenzie River Chamber of Commerce in Blue River.

Below Vida you pass the Goodpasture covered bridge, a landmark on this stretch of the river. Two more of the distinctive bridges are located south of the highway near Rainbow and McKenzie Bridge.

Above the town of Blue River, dams harness the waters of the Blue River and the McKenzie's South Fork. You'll find campgrounds and boat ramps beside both Blue River and Cougar reservoirs. Water levels are lowered in summer to provide storage for the flood season; by late summer, it's often difficult to launch boats.

The wooded hillsides, fish-filled lakes, and rugged terrain of Willamette National Forest offer endless recreation opportunities. Ranger stations in Blue River and McKenzie Bridge can provide information. Aufderheide Drive branches south from State 126 east of Blue River; it follows the McKenzie's South Fork, skirting Cougar Reservoir and passing several small riverside campgrounds. Numerous trails lead into the mountains toward the western boundary of the Three Sisters Wilderness. On the western slope of the Cascades, hikers tramp through tall forests of fir and hemlock, past vine maple, and along rushing streams and high ridges.

The Clear Lake cutoff

About 5 miles east of McKenzie Bridge, State 126 veers sharply northward along the upper McKenzie toward the Santiam Highway. No towns disturb this forest route. Lovely in any season, it is especially enjoyable when white dogwood blossoms herald spring; masses of pink rhododendrons bloom in late June; or bright gold and scarlet foliage add vibrant touches of autumn color.

Waterfalls. During the past 3,000 years, several lava flows from Cascade volcanoes blocked the ancient bed of the McKenzie, creating Clear Lake, Beaver Marsh, and several waterfalls. Portions of the highway cut through the black lava. Short trails lead to 70-foot Koosah Falls, where you gaze down the McKenzie canyon from a view point near the waterfall, and Sahalie Falls, which plunges 100 feet over a rim into a clear pool edged by ferns and moss-covered rocks.

Clear Lake. A geological curiosity, Clear Lake lies high in the Cascades 4 miles south of U.S. 20. One of the clearest and coldest of Oregon's mountain lakes, it preserves within its calm waters an old and unusual forest inundated when lava dammed the McKenzie centuries ago. Tree snags beneath the surface are visible to boaters. In summer you can rent rowboats at the lake resort, or you can launch your own canoe or kayak; motorboats are prohibited. Visitors picnic along the shore and camp in Coldwater Cove Campground.

McKenzie River Trail. Hikers can follow the sparkling waters of the upper McKenzie along the McKenzie River National Recreation Trail. Beginning east of McKenzie Bridge, the 27-mile route traverses part of the Cascade lava beds, skirts Koosah and Sahalie waterfalls, and ends near the McKenzie River headwaters at Clear Lake. It is accessible from several points along State 126; campgrounds are located near the highway and trail. Maps are available at Forest Service offices in Eugene or McKenzie Bridge.

Mount Washington Wilderness

Spanning the Cascade summit between the Santiam and McKenzie highways, the wilderness surrounding Mount Washington offers strenuous challenges to hikers and mountain climbers.

Dominating the region is the austere peak, topped by a craggy pinnacle, its steep volcanic flanks deeply carved by glaciers. South of the mountain, great floods of black lava have spilled across the slopes, leaving huge jagged boulders. Cinder cones and islands of trees dot lava flows.

Travel in this formidable and desolate area is limited to hikers and pack animals. The Pacific Crest Trail provides the main access, entering the wilderness on its northern border near Big Lake and, on its southern, at the McKenzie Pass west of Dee Wright Observatory. North of State 242, hikers set out from Scott Lake Campground.

One of the most popular rock climbs in Oregon, the ascent of 7,802-foot Mount Washington should be undertaken only under qualified leadership and with proper equipment. The final climb of the pinnacle is through rock chimneys and up sheer walls.

The old McKenzie Highway

For 37 miles State 242 curves up and over Oregon's highest east-west pass. Not a road for hurrying, the scenic route across 5,324-foot McKenzie Pass winds through Douglas fir forests, traverses the state's largest lava beds, edges two wilderness areas, and offers superb views of some of the Cascades' mightiest giants. At the first heavy snowfall, the McKenzie Pass is closed for the winter.

East of its junction with State 126, the McKenzie Pass Highway cuts a narrow corridor through dense fir forests, then climbs in steep, twisting hairpin turns up Deadhorse Grade, appropriately named when this was a wagon road across the mountains. Short spur roads and trails lead to forest camps, waterfalls, and high mountain lakes.

You drive through miles of lava country, so desolate it once served as a training ground for moon-bound astronauts. At the summit, Dee Wright Observatory is built atop the lava. You can look through 11 windows in the stone tower and see 11 different mountain peaks.

At the base of the observatory, a paved, ½-mile loop trail leads you safely into the field of jumbled lava; signs along the trail explain geological features of this volcanic wonderland.

Three Sisters Wilderness

Stretching south from the old McKenzie Highway, the vast Three Sisters Wilderness rides the crest of the central Oregon Cascades. During the past few thousand years, considerable volcanic activity has occurred in this region. Hikers see volcanic mountains and cinder cones, lava flows, obsidian creeks, and lava-dammed lakes.

Winding for 50 miles along the skyline, the Pacific Crest Trail links hiking paths from western and eastern slopes, trails that weave through volcanic fields and grassy meadows to craggy peaks and tree-rimmed lakes.

From the north the main entry points are Frog Camp and Lava Camp Lake, both near State 242. On the west, Aufderheide Drive leads up the McKenzie's south fork to trails up French Pete Valley and Olallie Meadows, up Rebel Creek, and along Roaring River Ridge. Hikers and equestrians climb the southeastern slopes on trails originating at lakes along the Cascade Lakes Highway.

Before beginning a trip, check trail conditions at the nearest ranger station—in Blue River or McKenzie Bridge (for west side trails) or in Bend or Sisters (for east side routes).

The southern part of the wilderness is an angler's paradise with more than 300 lakes strewn across the mountains. For mountaineers, the Three Sisters are among the most popular of Oregon's major peaks. All top 10,000 feet elevation. Most formidable of the three is North Sister; South Sister has become the favorite climb.

Across the Willamette Pass

Angling southeast from Eugene, the Willamette Pass Highway (State 58) parallels the Middle Fork of the Willamette River to Oakridge, then follows Salt Creek toward the summit.

Dams now control the upper waters of the Willamette and its main tributaries, which formerly flooded parts of the Willamette Valley with depressing regularity. Dexter and Lookout Point reservoirs, on the Middle Fork some 20 miles from Eugene, are popular destinations for water sports enthusiasts. Further upstream is Hills Creek Dam and Reservoir, 3 miles south of Oakridge. Forest Service campgrounds provide overnight facilities. Near Oakridge the Middle Fork of the Willamette is enlarged by four additional streams—the river's North Fork, and Salmon, Salt, and Hills Creeks—draining a vast watershed.

Forest roads converge at Oakridge, 43 miles southeast of Eugene in the Cascade foothills. Each spring Oakridge hosts a community-wide Tree Planting Festival, reforesting the hills with Douglas fir seedlings. In Green Waters City Park beside the river, residents and travelers enjoy picnic and sports facilities and a nature trail.

For information on roads and trails, suggestions on recreation activities, and trail maps, check with officials of Willamette or Deschutes National forests.

Exploring forest back roads

If you enjoy backcountry exploration, you'll find roads branching off State 58 to a number of destinations.

The North Fork of the Willamette River flows past the old mill town of Westfir, where you can see a covered bridge; fly fishermen cast in these waters for rainbow and cutthroat trout. Aufderheide Drive follows the North Fork northeast to link up with State 126 east of Blue River. From Oakridge, the Salmon Creek Road leads northeast to Salmon Creek Falls and up toward its Cascade headwaters.

South of the highway, forest roads follow the Middle Fork of the Willamette and Hills Creek. Campgrounds are located along the Middle Fork road, which ends deep in the mountains south of Diamond Peak. Portions of this route follow the 1864 Oregon Central Military Wagon Road and the earlier emigrant route across the summit. A primitive road branches 3 miles south to Opal and Timpanogas lakes.

Year-round recreation

No matter what the season, forest lands off State 58, near the summit of Willamette Pass, offer opportunities for outdoor fun.

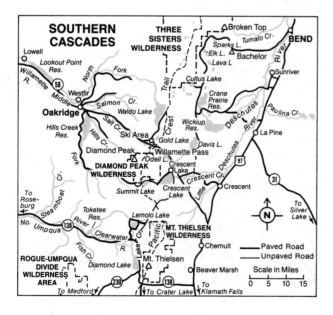

Rider picks his way through lava rock on Skyline Trail in Three Sisters Wilderness. In background are Three Fingered Jack and Mount Jefferson.

Phantom Ship rock appears to ride the waves of Crater Lake, deepest body of water in the U.S. Lake was created thousands of years ago when Mount Mazama blew its top.

Salt Creek Falls. Just west of the Willamette Pass, motorists glimpse Salt Creek Falls, half screened by tall conifers, south of the highway. Easy trails lead from the parking area to the top of the waterfall, or down into its misty bowl.

Waldo Lake Wilderness. Eighteen miles east of Oakridge, a paved road leads north off State 58 to Waldo Lake. Three campgrounds dot the lake's eastern shore, but the north and west sides survive in a primitive state, accessible only by boat or trail. Solitude-loving anglers fish from rowboats, and canoeists explore the lake's coves. A loop trail circles the 6-mile-long lake, and other paths lead north and west into the wilderness to small scattered lakes.

Gold Lake, south of Waldo, is also accessible by road. Angling is limited to fly fishing.

Diamond Peak Wilderness. South of State 58, another wilderness straddles the Cascade crest around 8,744-foot Diamond Peak. Formed during the volcanic period and later deeply carved by glaciers, the peak is often climbed by mountaineers. In the northern part of the wilderness, the steep precipices of 7,100-foot Mount Yoran also offer fine rock climbing practice.

The Pacific Crest Trail enters the wilderness west of Odell Lake, continuing southwest past Summit Lake. Access to the western slopes of the wilderness are from the Hemlock Butte Road; eastern slopes are reached from forest roads west of Crescent and Summit lakes (part of an old pioneer route across the mountains).

Dozens of small lakes, gouged by moving glaciers, surround Diamond Peak. Most are reached only by cross-country hiking. Lakes deep enough to support fish are stocked regularly, but you may have to share lakeside locations with hungry mosquitos.

High Cascade lakes. On the eastern side of the mountains, State 58 cuts through Deschutes National Forest. The highway skirts the northeast shore of Odell Lake and passes east of Crescent and Summit lakes. All three offer lakeside campgrounds and boat ramps and are crowded in summer.

Odell and Crescent lakes have rustic resorts where visitors can purchase supplies, arrange accommodations, and rent boats. Summit Lake lies west of Crescent Lake on a forest road. Other forest roads lead north of State 58 to Davis Lake; campsites and boat ramps are located along the shore.

Winter fun. From December to March, families from the Eugene-Springfield area drive to the Willamette Pass Ski Area for a day of skiing. A day lodge, a ski shop, and new chairlifts attract downhill skiers; lessons are available. The area operates Wednesday through Sunday, with night skiing on Friday and Saturday.

When snow blocks forest routes, the Waldo Lake road becomes a marked, 13-mile snowmobile trail. From the Gold Lake Sno-Park, marked cross-country trails lead north of the highway around Gold Lake and the Rosary Lakes, and south around the western end of Odell Lake. Other trails begin near Crescent Lake. Check with Forest Service officials for a trail map. Warming shelters are located at Gold Lake, South Waldo Lake, and Westview.

Along the Umpqua

Named for the Umpqua Indians who once roamed these hills, Umpqua National Forest stretches from the summit of the Cascades down the timbered western slopes toward Roseburg. Twisting through the forest, tumbling over rocky ledges, and plunging in misty waterfalls are the North and South Umpqua rivers and their tributaries.

The North Umpqua River is regarded as one of the state's best fishing streams (see page 71). Thirty miles of the river—from Rock Creek upstream to the Soda Springs power plant—are open to fly fishing only. Steamboat Creek and its tributaries are closed to all fishing.

Tucked away deep in the rugged forests northeast of Crater Lake is Rogue-Umpqua Divide Wilderness, which protects the headwaters of the South Umpqua River. Access is from forest routes off the South Umpqua River Road or west of State 230.

North Umpqua Highway

Winding beside the North Umpqua and Clearwater rivers for more than 50 miles, State 138 offers a water-level route from I-5 to Diamond Lake, Crater Lake National Park, and U.S. 97. Campgrounds border the river—some nestled in thick forests with wild rhododendrons and ferns, others open to the sky in sparsely wooded areas. Trails parallel sections of the river, offering access for hikers and anglers, and lead to bubbling springs and secluded waterfalls. Information is available from Umpqua National Forest officials in Roseburg, Glide, Idleyld Park, and (summer only) Diamond Lake.

State 138 meets the North Umpqua River about 16 miles northeast of Roseburg at Glide, where the annual spring wildflower show is a local tradition. Not far from the Glide Ranger Station, the North Umpqua and Little rivers collide head-on; near the view point, many of the forest plants have been labeled. The drive up Little River offers scenic diversions at any time of year.

Boulder Creek Wilderness. From Boulder Flat Campground, 50 miles east of Roseburg, a trail follows Boulder Creek north from State 138 into Boulder Creek Wilderness. Old-growth ponderosa pine and unusual rock monoliths and outcroppings are found along Boulder Creek; in season, salmon and steelhead come here to spawn.

Lemolo Lake. Paved roads lead north from State 138 to encircle Lemolo Lake, a reservoir near the North Umpqua's headwaters. Campgrounds dot the lake shore, and a rustic resort offers accommodations and facilities year round.

Summer visitors enjoy lake fishing, swimming, and water-skiing. Hikers head upstream to high country lakes in Mount Thielsen Wilderness or down the steep canyon to 169-foot Lemolo Falls. In winter, Lemolo Lake is a center for ski touring and snowmobiling.

Vacationing at Diamond Lake

Below Mount Thielsen's jagged pinnacle and somber green slopes spread the blue waters of Diamond Lake.

Located just north of Crater Lake National Park, Diamond Lake is a family favorite. Campgrounds and picnic areas dot its shore, and a resort on the lake's east side offers accommodations and meals throughout the year.

In summer, the Diamond Lake Information Center can provide recreation suggestions. Sandy beaches attract swimmers and sunbathers, while anglers cast their lines both from boat and shore. Boat rentals are available at the Diamond Lake Resort. From June to September, you can obtain trail horses and pack animals for horseback riding on forest trails.

Wilderness hiking.   Diamond Lake is a convenient departure point for hikers heading east into the Oregon Cascades Recreation Area and, farther east, the Mount Thielsen Wilderness.

Created by 1984 legislation, the 55,000-acre Mount Thielsen Wilderness spans the Cascade crest between Diamond Peak Wilderness to the north and Crater Lake National Park to the south. Forming the area's backbone is an ancient volcanic ridge dominated by 9,182-foot Mount Thielsen, the "lightning rod of the Cascades."

The Pacific Crest Trail traverses the length of the wilderness, passing close to Lake Lucile and Maidu Lake near the northern boundary, and Tipsoo Peak and Howlock Mountain farther south. The wilderness is administered jointly by Umpqua, Deschutes, and Winema national forests.

Oregon Cascades Recreation Area borders the wilderness to the west. It includes portions of the Willamette, Umpqua, and Deschutes national forests. Snowmobiles are permitted in some areas.

Winter fun.   Winter brings hardy skiers, snowshoers, and snowmobilers to enjoy marked trails in the southern Cascades. Access is generally from State 138 or State 230 near Diamond Lake; Forest Service officials can provide information. When the lake freezes over, anglers fish through the ice. Snowcats transport downhill skiers from Diamond Lake Resort to the slopes of Mount Bailey 9 miles away.

Crater Lake National Park

In a state filled with spectacular scenery, Crater Lake ranks in a class by itself. A sapphire jewel set in encircling cliffs, it is the deepest lake in the United States—1,932 feet—and seventh deepest in the world. Its surface is approximately 6,176 feet above sea level, and rugged rock walls tower as much as 2,000 feet above the water.

Figures mean little as you gaze at the lake. Its moods change with the light, the weather, and the season. Whether you first see its deep blue waters reflecting a mirrorlike panorama of cliffs and clouds, shimmering like molten silver on a midsummer afternoon, or framed by a snow-powdered rim, it's a sight you'll long remember.

Oregon's only national park, Crater Lake lies in the caldera of a collapsed volcano. Discovered in 1853 by a prospector searching for a rumored lost mine, the unique lake became a national park in 1902.

CRATER LAKE FILLS A VOLCANIC BOWL

Thousands of years ago, Mount Mazama was a 12,000-foot volcano, one in the chain of snowy Cascade giants. Built up by repeated flows of molten lava, it towered high above its neighbors. Glaciers carved ravines on its higher slopes, and dense forests covered the lower flanks.

Then about 6,800 years ago, Mount Mazama blew its top. Earthquakes shook the mountain. In a series of climactic eruptions, gases and steam burst upward, blocking out the sun. Frothy, red-hot pumice spewed forth, filling the valleys and covering the land for miles around.

Mazama's great cone became a huge shell covering an empty chamber. Shaken by the volcanic forces and deprived of underground support, the peak collapsed with a thundering roar. When the skies finally cleared, the mountaintop was gone. In its place was a vast bowl, more than 6 miles across and 4,000 feet deep. Later volcanic activity inside the caldera formed the cinder cone now known as Wizard Island.

Over the centuries, rain and melting snow accumulated in the caldera, forming a deep, intensely blue lake. Amazingly pure, the water supports little aquatic life.

Along entrance routes to the park, forests grow where volcanic debris once poured down the mountainsides. Creeks have cut deep canyons through beds of pumice, ash, and cinders.

In summer, rangers at Crater Lake National Park conduct an extensive interpretive program to help visitors understand and enjoy the park's unique setting and its varied plant and animal life. Sinnott Memorial view point offers a panorama of Crater Lake; park rangers present short talks here on the geological origin of the lake. Throughout the year, you can view natural history exhibits in the visitor center near park headquarters.

Visitors can experience the park in a variety of ways: motoring around the lake on the Rim Drive, hiking along nature trails or to view points, or cruising on the lake.

Snows transform the park into a winter wonderland. Motorists can drive to the view point at Rim Village, but other roads and trails belong to hardy cross-country skiers and snowshoers.

Crooked River carves a swath through Smith Rock State Park. Climbers' reward for ascent of Monkey Face rock formation is a sweeping view across the plateau to the Cascades.

In search of salmon, men from Warm Springs reservation deftly dip long-handled nets into swirling waters of Deschutes River.

Visiting the park

Crater Lake National Park is open the year around, but full services and accommodations are available only in summer.

The all-year entrance is State Highway 62, cutting across the southern part of the park. Along the route, forests grow where volcanic debris once poured down the mountainsides. Creeks have cut deep canyons through beds of pumice, ash, and cinders.

From State 138, the north entrance road crosses a pumice desert to the lake's northern rim. Snow closes this route to motorists from about mid-October until late June.

A new visitor center in Munson Valley, near the park headquarters, is open daily from 8 to 5. Visitors can learn about the park's natural history from interpretive exhibits and audio-visual programs. Maps and publications are available.

Perched on the rim overlooking the lake, Crater Lake Lodge is open from June 15 to September 10. A dining room and cocktail lounge overlook the lake. Rustic cabins are also available.

Rim Village is a picnicking and day use area. Visitors find a cafeteria and gift shop here, where picnic supplies, film, souvenirs, and other small items can be purchased. It is open daily the year around (from 10 to 4 during the winter).

Park campgrounds are located near the south entrance and on the road to the Pinnacles. Weather permitting, campgrounds remain open from mid-June until late September. No campsites can be reserved. Dogs and cats must be kept on a leash or in vehicles at all times; animals are not permitted in buildings or on park trails.

Enjoying yourself at Crater Lake

After viewing Crater Lake from the rim, take time to enjoy more of the park. Rangers conduct an extensive summer program for visitors; check posted schedules for guided hikes, evening programs, and other events.

Early in your visit, stop at the Sinnott Memorial, near Rim Village overlooking the lake. Landmarks are identified here, and rangers give short talks on the geologic origin of the lake (usually scheduled hourly in summer from 9 A.M. to 6 P.M.).

Rim Drive. A favorite excursion is the Rim Drive, a 33-mile loop around the lake rim. In summer a small sightseeing bus makes the trip daily, departing from Crater Lake Lodge and stopping at several points high above the water. If you prefer, make the drive in your own car. Take along a picnic and break your circuit with one or more side jaunts. Snow closes the road in winter.

Down to the lake. For a boat trip on Crater Lake, you must hike down the Cleetwood Trail, a 1-mile switchback path descending steeply from the north rim to the water. In summer sightseeing boats leave from Cleetwood Cove for 2-hour trips around the lake (check the bulletin board at the top of the trail for the current schedule). A park naturalist usually goes along to point out geological features. The boat makes a brief stop at Wizard Island and passes near Phantom Ship rock.

Nature trails. Several self-guided nature trails invite you to learn more about park plants and animals. Wildflowers bloom throughout the park in July and early August. Hikers often see wildlife along the trails, especially in early morning. Jays and Clarks nutcrackers scold in harsh tones from the trees, and chipmunks and golden-mantled ground squirrels scramble among the rocks. Occasionally, hikers spot a grazing deer or a prowling bear in the woods.

View points. From Rim Village, the 1½-mile Discovery Point Trail heads north along the rim to the point where prospector John Wesley Hillman first saw the lake in 1853. The trail to Garfield Peak begins behind the lodge, climbing east along the rim wall to the peak some 1,900 feet above the water.

On the south rim, a 6-mile road branches southeast from Kerr Notch to the Pinnacles; these needlelike pumice spires rise 200 feet out of Wheeler Creek Canyon. An easy, 10-minute walk from Rim Drive leads through hemlock forest and a wildflower meadow to Sun Notch for a spectacular view of Phantom Ship.

Trails also lead to mountaintop fire lookouts atop Mount Scott and The Watchman.

Winter at Crater Lake. Snow and ice cast a magic spell over the park. As you drive between high snowbanks, firs and hemlocks appear quilted in dazzling white. Snowy cliffs rim the indigo lake. Tire chains may be needed at any time.

For information on activities, stop at park headquarters daily from 8 to 5 or phone (503) 594-2211. Marked cross-country trails traverse the park. Visitors can rent equipment at Rim Village and thaw out in the cafeteria daily from 10 to 4.

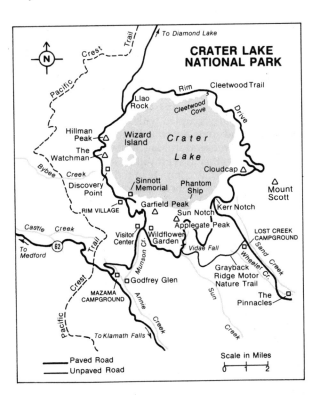

Along the Deschutes

A complex and scenic waterway, the Deschutes River dominates central Oregon. More than 150 years ago, French-Canadian trappers named it *Rivière des Chutes* (River of the Falls).

It bubbles from underground springs in the southern Cascades and tumbles northward, cutting through ponderosa pine forests and lava flows. In its central section, the Deschutes is joined by the Metolius and Crooked rivers, their waters expanding in a pair of deep reservoirs. It plunges another 100 miles northward through deep, basalt-rimmed canyons to the Columbia.

Anglers know the Deschutes well; this splendid river offers some of the finest trout, steelhead, and salmon fishing in the state. When Chinook salmon move upriver in spring and steelhead migrate upstream in autumn, every riffle and bar has its cluster of anglers.

In recent years, white water boaters have taken up the challenge of the Deschutes rapids. Guides and commercial outfitters conduct fishing and float trips; river excursions start below Pelton Dam.

The lower river

The Deschutes canyon has a grandeur and raw magnificence best experienced from the water. At times the rugged, rocky gorge walls close in; at other points they broaden to border grass-fringed flatlands. Occasional trees and clumps of grass dot the shore. Rattlesnakes gravitate toward the water, so be alert. Summer days can be quite hot in the canyon, but mornings are fresh and sparkling, and in evening, strong winds cool the canyon.

Downriver from Maupin, a road off U.S. Highway 197 provides access to 25 miles of the river; it passes Sherar's Bridge on State Highway 216, a traditional Indian fishing site and location of a pioneer toll bridge. Stop at the BLM district office in Prineville for information about riverside campgrounds and boat ramps.

All-Indian Rodeo.   In cattle states like Oregon, many Indian cowboys are occupied with daily tasks of the corral and range, and some are equally fine rodeo performers. On the third weekend in May, Indian cowboys from all over the West gather in Tygh Valley, 34 miles south of The Dalles on U.S. 197, to compete in rodeo events and enjoy Indian dance performances and other activities. In late August Tygh Valley hosts the Wasco County Fair.

Frontier towns.   The Old West lingers on in Shaniko, a scattering of weathered buildings in the middle of a grassland plateau along U.S. 97. Seventy-five years ago Shaniko was in its prime—central Oregon's sole railroad terminus, center of a sheep raising and wool shipping industry, and headquarters for railroad construction workers building a new line up the Deschutes.

The most impressive building in this one-time railroad town is the two-story brick Shaniko Hotel, built in 1900. Shaniko's other buildings, and its sidewalks, are constructed of wood. Efforts have been made to preserve historical vehicles and articles of bygone days.

State Highway 218 cuts southeast from Shaniko to Antelope, another one-time stage station and rip-roaring frontier town. Poplar and locust trees shade the remaining buildings here and in Ashwood, 20 miles south by gravel road. Both towns thrived around the turn of the century but today are virtually deserted.

Visit an Indian reservation

Visitors are welcome on the Warm Springs Indian Reservation. You can unroll your sleeping bag inside a tepee or relax in a comfortable lodge, ride horseback over sagebrush-covered hills, savor Indian foods such as baked salmon and wild huckleberries, and attend tribal festivities.

The Confederated Tribes of the Warm Springs Indian Reservation have developed a handsome vacation resort —Kah-Nee-Ta—along the Warm Springs River. To reach it, drive northwest of Madras on U.S. 26 to the community of Warm Springs, then continue 11 miles south.

Families with young children often choose to stay in one of several dozen tepees clustered near the meandering river or in a *nee-sha* (cottage). Campgrounds and trailer hookups are also available. High above the river valley, a hilltop lodge–convention center blends with the red rock and semiarid landscape.

Natural hot springs warm the swimming pool, and a golf course extends along the river. Hiking, horseback riding, tennis, and cycling are other diversions; daily or seasonal reservation fishing permits are available during the fishing season. Special activities at Kah-Nee-Ta may include Indian storytelling, dance performances, crafts, or outdoor salmon bakes.

Major events on the reservation include the Root Feast in the spring, Pi-Ume-Sha Pow Wow and Rodeo in June, Fun Day on July 4, and the Huckleberry Feast in late summer. For exact dates, check with the Madras Chamber of Commerce.

Madras, farming & recreation center

East of the Cascades, settlement proceeded slowly during the mid-19th century. After Indian problems were resolved in 1855 and the first trans-Cascade road was completed in 1862, homesteaders soon followed.

Madras, hub and county seat of sun-drenched Jefferson County, owes its agricultural prosperity to the railroad, which arrived in 1911, and the development of irrigation projects in the late 1930s. Peppermint, potatoes, and grass seed are grown on some 50,000 irrigated acres.

A town of about 2,200, Madras is a center for rockhounding, fishing, boating, and hunting. Water-skiers flock to the two large reservoirs impounded behind Pelton and Round Butte dams on the Deschutes. Anglers fish the big lakes or nearby rivers, and hunters bag deer and game birds. At Rimrock Springs Wildlife Management Area, 9 miles south off U.S. 20, viewing platforms and a 1½-mile loop trail bring you close to wildlife.

Rockhounds gather in Madras during the Rockhound Pow Wow in July. If you're in town in late October, you can watch working cowboys at the Oregon Horse Cutting Association annual show.

Cove Palisades State Park

Ten miles west of Madras, the waters of the Deschutes River have been impounded behind a pair of dams. For centuries, the Deschutes and its main tributaries, the Crooked River and the Metolius River, have cut through many layers of lava, leaving the banded rim rocks and sheer walls exposed to view.

These towering vertical cliffs provide a spectacular setting for two popular water recreation areas: Lake Billy Chinook, with narrow watery fingers stretching back from Round Butte into the three river canyons; and Lake Simtustus, confined behind Pelton Dam.

Central Oregon's most popular state park, Cove Palisades borders the southeastern shore of Lake Billy Chinook near the confluence of the Crooked and Deschutes rivers. The park has shaded campgrounds, picnic and swimming areas, boat ramps, and a marina (on the Crooked River arm) where summer visitors can rent boats and obtain supplies. From late April through September, houseboats can be rented at 3 Rivers Marina on the Metolius arm. Lake fishing is outstanding from bank or boat. In summer, a naturalist conducts guided walks and evening programs.

A road descends the canyon's east side to the water (boaters can launch their craft here) and north to an observation building overlooking Round Butte Dam.

The Crooked River Valley

Southeast of Lake Billy Chinook, the Crooked River carves its unique signature across the central Oregon landscape—twisting and cutting through narrow canyons, meandering across wide valleys, and swelling into a reservoir lake behind Prineville Dam.

Fur trappers and frontier scouts passed through this country in the early 19th century. Ogden Scenic Wayside, overlooking an awesome stretch of the Crooked River Gorge 8 miles north of Redmond, honors Peter Skene Ogden, a Hudson's Bay Company fur trader who explored this area in 1825–26.

Another splendid view point is Smith Rock State Park, 10 miles northeast of Redmond, where the Crooked River cuts a curving 300-foot-high canyon through colorful sedimentary rock. Thrusting high above the river, Smith Rock commands a view of flat farm lands and lava plains for miles around.

Prineville.   As a young town in the Old West, Prineville saw Indian raids, range wars between cattlemen and sheepmen, and vigilante justice. Homesteaders struggled to exist on these windswept desert grasslands. Between Madras and Prineville you can see a few windmills that pumped water for early 20th century farmers.

Prineville, with its population of 6,100, is the largest town and only incorporated one in sparsely settled Crook County. Livestock raising, lumbering, and mining are the county's principal industries.

Take a look at the handsome old Crook County Courthouse and its clock tower, surrounded by green Pioneer Park. Bowman Museum at 3rd and Main streets has historical articles of Prineville and Crook County.

The city is also proud of its City of Prineville Railroad, the only city-owned railway in the United States. Built in 1918, the 18-mile-long railroad links Prineville to the main north-south line.

In May, the Central Oregon Timber Festival attracts contestants from all over the West. Regional artists display and sell their work at the Central Oregon Art Festival in Pioneer Park each July. The outstanding Crooked River Roundup, part of the Rodeo Cowboys Association (RCA) rodeo circuit, comes in mid-July; pari-mutuel racing is an added attraction. Ranchers and farm families gather for the Crook County Fair in August.

Rockhounding country.   Central Oregon offers probably the most concentrated beds of semiprecious gemstones in the state, though rockhounds find minerals and fossils in all parts of Oregon.

Rockhounds can dig for agate, limb casts, agatized jasper, petrified wood, and thundereggs on more than 600 acres of Rockhound Pow Wow Association mining claims on public lands; several commercial beds are also available for digging. Stop at the Chamber of Commerce office, 390 North Fairview, for a map and information on digging areas. Rockhounds gather in Prineville in June for a Rockhound Pow Wow.

Excursions from Prineville.   Located 17 miles southeast of Prineville, Prineville Reservoir backs up behind a dam on the Crooked River. A state park along the reservoir's north shore attracts anglers and water sports enthusiasts. It offers campsites and picnic areas spread over the juniper-studded hillside, a boat ramp and dock, a bathhouse and swimming area. Anglers fish for bass, rainbow trout, and catfish. Boat rentals, tackle, and supplies are available at a small resort on the south shore.

One of the best side trips is the all-day excursion along upper Crooked River to Paulina and Big Summit Prairie. Four miles east of Paulina, turn north to Wolf Creek Campground. Forest Road 42 follows the creek, then veers west past the pastoral prairie, where cattle graze placidly. You return to U.S. 26 east of Ochoco Lake.

The tiny community of Powell Butte, 12 miles southwest of Prineville on State 126, hosts visitors from all over Oregon on the first Saturday of November. Local families stage the Lord's Acre Sale and Barbecue, an old-fashioned fundraising social to benefit the community church.

Wilderness preserves.   Three wilderness preserves were established in Ochoco National Forest in 1984; for information, contact the headquarters office in Prineville or district rangers in Prineville or Paulina.

Mill Creek Wilderness lies northeast of Prineville; drive east on U.S. 26 to Ochoco Reservoir, then north on Mill Creek Road for 11 miles to Wildcat Campground. Bridge Creek Wilderness is 37 miles east of Prineville, reached by U.S. 26 and Forest Road 22. Black Canyon Wilderness is located 11 miles south of Dayville off Forest Road 47.

In Redmond— reindeer & a rock garden

Redmond, a town of about 6,500 at the junction of U.S. 97 and U.S. 126, is a Deschutes vacation center in the heart of juniper and sagebrush country. Lumbering, cattle

Bulldogging stirs excitement at Spray's rodeo. Object is to grasp the steer's horns, twist the neck, and throw him with head and legs facing the same direction.

Cloud-dappled sky intensifies hues of Painted Hills west of Mitchell. Bands of color in dome-shaped hills mark age and variety of composition.

It's hard to keep your eye on the ball on this resort course in central Oregon. Fairway, surrounded by trees in autumnal attire, looks out toward Cascades.

ranching, dairy farming, and agriculture support the local economy. The Deschutes County Fair is staged here in late July, featuring traditional rodeo events, horse racing, and a buckaroo breakfast.

Redmond Air Center at Roberts Field, 2 miles east of town, is the regional U.S. Forest Service base for a variety of activities, including training smokejumpers, the hardy firefighters who parachute to the scene of remote forest fires. In summer, visitors can watch training activities, including practice jumps from towers. Telephone (503) 548-5071 to arrange a visit to the facility.

Two miles west of Redmond on U.S. 126, you pass Operation Santa Claus, a reindeer ranch. During the Christmas season reindeer are away for appearances, but visitors are welcome to stop at other times of the year.

Cline Falls State Park borders the Deschutes River 4 miles west of Redmond on State 126. This pleasant picnickers' oasis has tables scattered amid the juniper and willow trees along the river bank. Children can explore the grassy shore; anglers fish for rainbow trout.

Petersen Rock Gardens, 7 miles southwest of Redmond, is known for its whimsical rock structures. When his rock collection grew beyond manageable size, Rasmus Petersen transformed his rocks into agate mansions, lava bridges, obsidian castles, and traditional rock gardens.

Land of Lakes & Lava

East of the Cascades, central Oregon is prime vacation country, enhanced by a sunny dry climate, thick pine forests, scenic mountain lakes, and opportunities for year-round outdoor recreation. For information on attractions and accommodations, contact the Bend Chamber of Commerce, 164 N.W. Hawthorne, Bend, OR 97701, phone (503) 382-3221; or the Central Oregon Recreation Association, P.O. Box 230, Bend, OR 97709, phone (503) 389-8799.

Ancient volcanoes have left dramatic imprints on the land, allowing geologists to trace the story of major eruptions such as those of Mazama and Newberry. Fascinating exhibits offer a chance to learn more about the geology and natural history of the region.

Pause awhile at Bend

Since pioneer days, Bend has been a place where travelers paused to rest and refresh themselves. Its site at the crossroads of U.S. 97 and U.S. 20 still makes it a logical stopping point. A fast-growing town of 36,000, Bend borders the Deschutes River, which flows through town. The town hosts a Cascade Festival of Music each June.

Exhibits of Indian artifacts and pioneer memorabilia can be seen Thursday through Sunday afternoons at the Deschutes Historical Center, on Idaho Street between Wall and Bond.

Downtown parks. Tall ponderosa pines and gnarled junipers shade sloping lawns at Drake Park, which borders a wide, placid stretch of the river as it curves near the heart of town. Families relax on the grass, paddle in canoes, or feed the resident ducks and swans that share the stream with migrant waterfowl.

Downstream is smaller Pioneer Park, landscaped with lawns and flower beds. East of U.S. 97, Juniper Park contains a pool, sports facilities, and a playground.

For a spectacular panorama of nine snow-capped Cascade peaks, drive to the top of Pilot Butte, a 599-foot-high symmetrical cinder cone a few blocks east of town.

Other riverside parks. Anglers and picnickers enjoy Robert W. Sawyer Park beside the Deschutes just north of Bend. Another pleasant spot beside the river is Tumalo State Park, 5 miles northwest of Bend just off U.S. 20. Five miles west of town you can picnic along sparkling Tumalo Creek at Shevlin Park, a large forest reserve.

Southwest of Bend, forest camps border the upper Deschutes; most have boat ramps. The river cuts through lava flows at Pringle, Benham, and Dillon Falls, cascading through narrow chutes. La Pine Recreation Area, in a river bend west of U.S. 97, is one of the largest riverside camping areas.

Visit an observatory

Pine Mountain Observatory, a University of Oregon astronomy research facility near the summit of 6,395-foot Pine Mountain, welcomes visitors from mid-afternoon to dusk the year around. Call (503) 382-8331 after 3 P.M. for information (night-owl astronomers sleep late).

On clear days, the site affords fine views of the Cascades and plateau. Visitors can talk with astronomers, who answer questions and describe the observatory's research and operation. When schedules permit, visitors gaze at the sky at dusk through the 32-inch telescope, largest in the Pacific Northwest. Research work begins 1 hour after dark. To reach the observatory, take U.S. 20 southeast from Bend for 25 miles; just east of Millican, turn south and continue driving for 9 miles.

The High Desert Museum

Located 6 miles south of Bend on U.S. 97, the High Desert Museum is a "living museum" featuring the plants, animals, birds, and cultural history of the arid Intermountain West. It is open daily except major holidays from 9 A.M. to 4 P.M. (to 5 P.M. June through September).

Live birds-of-prey programs and river otter feedings are presented daily. A waterway flows through the developed part of the site, culminating in the otter exhibit, where visitors watch the animals from both above and below water level. A "Desert Wasteland" exhibit contains snakes, lizards, and toads. Other natural history exhibits illustrate the high desert's ecological zones and man's relationship to the land.

Slide shows and videotape shows are presented in the Orientation Center. Visitors participate in some exhibits, especially the popular "please touch" area that contains animal pelts and bones, artifacts, and other items. The museum shop stocks nature-related books, toys, and other items. For more information, contact the museum at 59800 S. Highway 97, Bend, OR 97702, or telephone (503) 382-4754.

Ski on Bachelor's challenging slopes

Oregon's foremost ski resort, Mount Bachelor Ski Area clusters along the northern slope of 9,065-foot Bachelor Butte (also called Mount Bachelor) about 22 miles west of Bend. Dry powder snow, sunny days, and 3,100 vertical feet of challenging slopes attract skiers and racers from all over the world.

Skiing activity begins in mid-November and continues until July. Ten chairlifts transport skiers above the timberline for superb downhill and slalom runs. The newest addition is the "Lift to the Top," which goes to the mountain's upper slopes. (Non-skiers may ride the lift from May through Labor Day.) Beginners have their own electric rope tow. Cross-country skiers can follow more than 30 miles of groomed trails of varying lengths or glide over miles of untracked countryside. Guided ski touring is also available. Snowmobilers have more than 100 miles of groomed snowmobile trails and open terrain routes.

Four alpine day lodges and one nordic day lodge cater to skiers with food service, warming rooms, ski shops, equipment rentals, and day-care service. Lessons and ski packages are available. Ski races are held several times each season, and in summer a racing camp attracts young skiers. In winter, buses shuttle skiers from Bend and Sunriver accommodations to the slopes.

The Cascade Lakes Highway

Stretching along the eastern slopes of the Cascade Range, Deschutes National Forest encompasses a 1½-million-acre preserve. One of the loveliest parts of the Deschutes country is the Cascade Lakes region west of Bend. A paved, 100-mile scenic loop road arcs through fragrant ponderosa pines to some of the state's best boating, fishing, hiking, and camping. The route usually opens in early June and closes with the first heavy snow.

The Cascade Lakes Highway (also known as Century Drive) climbs southwest from Bend over the 6,000-foot-high north shoulder of Bachelor, curves south to Crane Prairie Reservoir, and cuts east to return to U.S. 97 near La Pine. Constantly in view are some of the state's highest peaks. Many tree-rimmed lakes lie along the route.

More than 30 Forest Service campgrounds dot the shores of these jewel-like lakes and the clear, cold streams nearby. Rustic resorts are located at Elk, Cultus, and South Twin lakes. For recreation information, stop at the Forest Service office, 1656 Highway 20 East, in Bend, or at district offices in Sisters and Crescent.

Fishing and water sports. Fishing is superb in most of the lakes and tributary streams. Some waters have boat speed limits or restrictions on trolling or the use of motorized boats. Some lakes and streams are restricted to fly fishing only.

You can sail, canoe, or swim in chilly lake waters. Water-skiers head for Cultus Lake. Several lakes have marinas where visitors can rent boats and obtain tackle. Boat ramps are located near many campgrounds.

Hiking trails. Numerous trails cut across the forested slopes to small, backcountry lakes and into the alpine country of the Three Sisters Wilderness. Pack and saddle animals are available. At some lakes, mosquitoes can be pesky in summer, so bring insect repellent. Wildflowers bloom in alpine meadows and rocky crevices in July and August. Climbers and amateur geologists explore the region's volcanic terrain; an accessible lava flow borders the northeastern shore of Davis Lake.

Osprey sanctuary. Perched atop ghostly snags at Crane Prairie Reservoir, ospreys breed and raise their young. The fish-eating hawks nest in this wildlife sanctuary from April to September, protected from tree-climbing predators by the flooded reservoir. Bald eagles, blue herons, deer, and other animals also inhabit this area. Bring your binoculars and look for the ospreys from an observation point near Quinn River Campground. In July and August, you can sometimes spot fledglings in their nests.

Lava Lands— a volcanic wonderland

Ancient Mount Newberry was the center of a volcanic region scattered for some 70 miles over the Deschutes country east of the Three Sisters. Lava eruptions varied from frothy pumice and molten rivers to tiny cinders and glassy fields of obsidian.

Some of the most interesting volcanic activity occurred during relatively recent geologic times—within the past few thousand years—and has been little altered by weathering or erosion.

Lava Lands Visitor Center. The fiery volcanoes that shaped this area provide the theme for Lava Lands Visitor Center 11 miles south of Bend on U.S. 97. Blending into the pines just south of Lava Butte, the Forest Service center interprets the fascinating story of volcanism in the Cascades (including the Mount St. Helens eruption). The center is open daily from May through September.

Animated displays simulate volcanic activity and interpret the Cascades' violent geologic history. Visitors learn how eruptions formed the lava flows, cinder cones, underground tubes, and buckled buttes and ridges, and how physical features illustrate the series of events that

LAKE AND LAVA COUNTRY

— Paved Road
— Unpaved Road
Scale in Miles
0   5   10   15

transformed this countryside. A relief map locates points of interest.

Naturalists direct visitors to self-guided trails near the center to see first-hand the effects of rampaging nature. These interpretive trails lead over a lava flow, through pine forest, and around the top of Lava Butte.

Lava Butte.   North of the visitor center, a paved road spirals up Lava Butte, one of many miniature volcanoes in the Deschutes country. It hurled volcanic cinders into the air, gradually building up a cinder cone more than 500 feet high. A self-guided trail circles the crater rim.

From the observation area atop Lava Butte, visitors have a fine view of the Cascades. You gaze over a massive black apron of lava that streamed northwest from the volcano. Fingers of molten lava spilled into the Deschutes channel, blocking the river's flow. Eventually, it cut a new river channel, forming several waterfalls as it cascaded over the lava (see page 99).

Lava River Cave.   About 1½ miles south of the Visitor Center off U.S. 97, Lava River Cave marks the ancient course of a liquid rock river. Visitors may explore the cave on self-guided tours from mid-May through mid-September. Check at the Lava Lands Visitor Center for more information on touring the lava tube.

Thousands of years ago, a hot stream of lava broke out of the Mount Newberry foothills, leaving a long underground tunnel that extends nearly a mile through now-solid rock. Visitors rent lanterns at a nominal charge, then descend stairs into the cave to explore. The tube averages about 35 feet in width, but in places it widens to 50 feet and reaches a height of 58 feet. Walls and ceiling are marked by the lava stream, and in spots iciclelike projections of lava hang above your head.

Lava Cast Forest.   Some 6,000 years ago molten lava from Mount Newberry poured into a living pine forest, forming "stone trees"—lava casts around upright trees. Other trees were knocked over and encased in horizontal, pipelike casts. Eventually the charred trees inside died and rotted away, leaving a forest of hollow lava tubes extending above the surface of the flow. The imprint of pine bark is visible on the inner wall of some casts.

To reach Lava Cast Forest, drive about 14 miles south of Bend on U.S. 97 and turn east on Forest Road 9720 opposite the entrance to Sunriver. The cinder road continues 9 miles, ending near a small picnic area among trees (no water). A paved loop trail meanders for nearly a mile through the jagged lava fields.

Newberry's massive caldera.   Ancient Mount Newberry was a massive fire mountain, around 12,000 feet high and some 25 miles in diameter at its base—the most imposing peak east of the Cascades. Lava drained from the volcano through faults and fissures, and the walls supporting its broad dome weakened. The giant shield volcano then collapsed within itself, leaving a crater 4 to 5 miles in diameter.

Newberry Crater now cradles a pair of scenic lakes noted for their excellent fishing. To reach Paulina and East lakes, drive south of Bend on U.S. 97 for about 24 miles, then turn east on paved County Road 21, which leads about 13 miles to the lakes. Forest camps, rustic resort accommodations, boat rentals, and supplies are available at both lakes.

Just west of Paulina Lake, the waters of Paulina Creek tumble from a semicircular rim into the canyon.

South of the main road near Paulina Lake, molten rock from within Mount Newberry creates a large obsidian flow, one of the most extensive fields of black volcanic glass in the world. A ½-mile interpretive trail winds through the area. For generations, Indians chiseled arrowheads and spear points from obsidian found here.

In summer you can drive up an unpaved road to the summit of 7,984-foot Paulina Peak, renowned for its magnificent view of the crater, Cascades, and plateau.

Lava and ice caves.   Many interesting lava tubes, some of them ice-choked, are found throughout the area. Inquire at the Deschutes National Forest office in Bend to see if any are currently open to visitors (summer only).

Dress warmly for cave exploring; a jacket and comfortable walking shoes are essential. Don't explore alone and, as a precaution, tell someone your destination.

Outdoor fun at Sunriver

The resort of Sunriver borders the winding Deschutes River 15 miles southwest of Bend. A lodge and residential areas face a pine-fringed meadow and, beyond, a sweep of snowy Cascade peaks and dark green forests.

At Sunriver, bicycles and electric carts are more popular than automobiles; paved trails link all parts of the complex. Sunriver also has its own airstrip. Activity focuses around the lodge; a small shopping mall is located nearby.

Life at Sunriver is oriented toward the outdoors—fishing in nearby lakes or along the Deschutes, boating or canoeing on the river, horseback riding and cycling on a web of pathways. You can play tennis, golf on two 18-hole courses, swim in an outdoor pool, or stroll a nature trail—all without leaving Sunriver. The resort has its own nature center; a resident naturalist conducts programs and leads field trips. Guest artists and crafts people conduct summer classes. In winter, snowshoe and ski touring enthusiasts probe the countryside, while downhill skiers enjoy powder snow at Mount Bachelor. Ski packages are available. Horse-drawn sleigh rides are also popular.

Wheat Country

The serpentine gash of the John Day River cuts through central Oregon's vast wheat lands. To the west, between the Deschutes and John Day rivers, lies Sherman County. To the east, stretching some 45 miles south from the Columbia, expansive fields of ripening wheat cover the rolling hills of Gilliam, Morrow, and western Umatilla counties.

State Highways 19 and 207 are the main north-south roads connecting I-84 and U.S. 26. Together with intersecting routes, they cut across the ruts of the Oregon Trail, traverse the wheat plateau, and provide access to quiet farm communities. Farther south in Wheeler County, the scenery changes to the sagebrush-strewn hills and rocky gorges of the central plateau.

For some 300 miles, the John Day River curves and twists across central Oregon's northern plateau—watering broad fields and pasture lands, carving through ancient rock formations, snaking between lonely hills.

From Service Creek Bridge, at the junction of State 19 and State 207, downstream to Tumwater Falls, a 147-mile stretch of the lower river is a state-designated scenic waterway. The 31 miles of the John Day between Thirtymile Creek and East Ferry Canyon is river essentially untouched by man. Trickling creeks and narrow side gulches lead into the steep-walled river canyon. Few roads and fewer communities touch the lower river; it must be explored by boat. Day float trips can be arranged in Fossil. Longer river excursions cover up to 40 miles.

Greenery amid the wheat fields

Gilliam County's main thoroughfare is State 19, cutting south from Arlington on I-84 to Condon, the Gilliam County seat. About 7 miles south of Arlington, a sign marks the highway crossing of the Oregon Trail.

Condon lies in the heart of the Columbia Basin wheat lands. Mature trees shade its pleasant city park—site of a big July 4 celebration that includes a patriotic program, parade, rodeo, and fireworks.

From Condon, State Highway 206 cuts 41 miles northwest to Wasco and 43 miles east to Heppner. You can picnic beside the John Day River at J.S. Burres State Park, 25 miles northwest of Condon.

Once the trading center for surrounding ranchers, Lonerock now is virtually deserted. Only a few families live in this once-thriving community 20 miles southeast of Condon. From above, it looks like a small New England village, its buildings clustering around a steepled church and imposing two-story school.

Along Willow Creek to Heppner

If you drive along State Highway 74 south from the Columbia, you get insight into the gradual transition of wheat and cattle country towns from thriving farm centers to lonely outposts. For more than 55 miles, the road parallels Willow Creek to Heppner.

Homesteaders settled along Willow Creek, and in horse-and-buggy days, farmers and ranchers drove into town from miles around for social gatherings. But as their energy, money, and water gave out, many settlers departed. Today only a few small communities break the vast golden wheat fields; Ione and Lexington survive as friendly country towns.

Sheltered by high domelike foothills, Heppner occupies a site on the valley floor of Willow Creek. A community of about 1,400, Heppner is the largest town on the northern plateau and the hub of Morrow County. Take a look at the sturdy courthouse, built of local stone. Items used by pioneer settlers are displayed in a museum adjacent to the city library. A flood-control dam creates Willow Creek Lake, popular for boating, swimming, and fishing. Ordinarily a slow-paced community, Heppner bursts with grassroots vitality during its St. Patrick's Day celebration

in March and the Morrow County Fair and Rodeo each August.

Twenty miles southwest of Heppner on State 207, a sea of wheat isolates lonely Hardman. In its heyday, this farm town served the scattered families of the upper Rock Creek Valley; when they could no longer make a living, however, the homesteaders drifted away. A few families still live here, but most of the town's weathered buildings stand empty, drowsing in the sun.

South of Hardman, the wide plateau dips sharply as you enter Rock Creek Canyon; the stream separates the wheat growing region from range land to the south.

The John Day Valley

Between the wheat lands and U.S. 26, you come upon a succession of startling contours—jagged peaks etched against blue sky, pinnacled upthrusts of solid rock, gashes carved through multicolored volcanic formations, dome-shaped hills brilliant with banded strata. A profound stillness hangs over the land.

Imbedded in these buckled hills are fossils dating back more than 40 million years to the time when alluvial plains covered this region. Parts of this area have been set aside as John Day Fossil Beds National Monument.

East of the fossil country, the upper John Day River drains the western slopes of the Blue Mountains and irrigates a broad valley planted with alfalfa and rimmed by folded, barren hills. To the southeast, the Strawberry Mountains form a rugged backdrop.

The discovery of gold on Whiskey Flat in 1862 triggered a rush of prospectors who, during the following decade, panned some $30 million in gold from local streams. Today's gold is in cattle ranching. Broad-brimmed hats and cowboy boots are everyday wear for sun-tanned ranchers. Livestock have the right-of-way on roads.

Fossils & a ghost town

A few miles south of Condon you leave rolling wheat fields. Travelers on State 19 enjoy a pair of wayside parks north and south of Fossil.

The town of Fossil marks the intersection of State 19 and State 218. Giant cottonwood trees shade the square and belfried Wheeler County Courthouse. For information on local history and geology, visit the museum (open Wednesday through Saturday in summer). A car museum also is open to the public. Visitors can dig for fossils in the sedimentary banks behind the high school.

State 19 continues another 20 miles south through pine forests and canyons to meet the John Day River at Service Creek. One of Oregon's more interesting ghost towns stands about 6 miles south on State 207 and ½ mile east down a country lane. Tall Lombardy poplars shade Richmond's abandoned buildings along the curving road. Once the town had its own literary and dramatic society; now sagebrush overruns the site.

State 207 ends at Mitchell, where it meets U.S. 26. In the old-fashioned general store here, shoppers can pur-

Late evening light casts a mellow glow on the old railroad station in the ghost town of Shaniko. In its prime the city was a wool shipping center.

Combine stands ready to shear shimmering wheat fields near Heppner, one of the few small communities that invade the vast golden hills.

chase everything from groceries and work clothes to carpenters' tools and fishing lures.

Cattle country & fruit orchards

From Service Creek, State 19 curves eastward, closely following the John Day River through Spray and Kimberly. Scenery varies from orderly fields and fruit orchards (where "you pick" signs welcome you in harvest season) to colorful red rock formations and brown hills spotted with pine and juniper. At Kimberly a pleasant side road branches east along the North Fork of the river. Travelers pass through the small cattlemen's towns of Monument, a cozy riverside settlement with an interesting general store and buildings dating back to stagecoach days, and Hamilton before meeting U.S. 395 at Long Creek.

John Day Fossil Beds National Monument

Established in 1974, John Day Fossil Beds National Monument includes three widely separated units northwest of the town of John Day. Fossil collecting or digging is prohibited. Visitors can see fossil displays and obtain information and natural history publications on the area at monument headquarters, 420 West Main Street, John Day. Staff members are on duty daily in summer, weekdays only the rest of the year.

Sheep Rock section.   Largest of the monument's three areas, this unit borders the river for some 7 miles. It begins 8 miles north of Dayville on U.S. 26 and continues north along State 19. Near the junction of the two highways, the John Day River winds through Picture Gorge, an awesome defile cut through high basalt cliffs.

Farther north on State 19, a prominent landmark is basalt-capped Sheep Rock, striped by horizontal bands of

pale green and buff. From an overlook, travelers gaze toward contorted hills rising above the valley.

The old three-story Cant Ranch homestead is maintained as a visitor center containing exhibits on local geology and ranching. Trees provide a welcome bit of shade. The center is open daily in spring and summer, weekends only the rest of the year.

Two trails lead into the colorful badlands of Blue Basin. Exhibits explain the geologic features. Fossil replicas have been placed along one of the trails.

Painted Hills.   Varying in hue with the changing light, these vividly streaked, domelike hills and ridges exude an austere beauty. In early morning the banded buttes present an awesome vista; the first rays of light bring out pastel shadings that gradually deepen to vivid shades of rust, pink, buff, green, gold, and charcoal. Moisture intensifies the color.

To reach the site, drive 4 miles west of Mitchell on U.S. 26, and turn north on the paved, 6-mile road that follows Bridge Creek to the base of the hills. Several Russian olive trees shade a few tables along Bridge Creek (rest rooms, drinking water). Stop at the visitor contact station, then drive to the overlook. One short trail starts here; another leads to colorful formations at Painted Cove. Stay on the trails; even footprints leave lasting scars.

Clarno unit.   Northernmost of the three areas, this part of the monument is located along State 218 about 20 miles west of Fossil. Picnic tables are scattered among small junipers at the base of eroded palisades about 2 miles east of the river (restrooms, drinking water).

West of the picnic area, a ½-mile self-guiding geology trail loops through an area where subtropical plants and animals flourished in primeval times. Another short hike leads to Clarno Arch and the base of the palisades.

John Day, legendary cattle town

Located in the center of sprawling Grant County, the town of John Day marks the intersection of highways U.S. 26 and U.S. 395. Appearing larger than its 1,900 population, John Day is the supply center for valley ranchers. Memories of the Old West are revived each spring during the annual cattle drive; large herds are driven along the town's main street as the animals move from winter pasture to greener fields north of town.

Visitors can get information about the region and see an excellent fossil collection at the Grant County Chamber of Commerce, 710 S. Canyon Boulevard.

A link with mining days is the Kam Wah Chung Building, adjacent to the city park, which has been restored as a museum. Built in 1866 as a trading post on The Dalles Military Road, the old stone landmark served as a general store, pharmacy, and doctor's office catering to the Chinese community until the early 1940s. Filled with Chinese memorabilia, the museum is open May through October daily except Friday. Hours are 8 to noon and 1 to 4 weekdays; 1 to 4 on Saturday and Sunday.

Kam Wah Chung Days, a festival celebrating the Chinese heritage in Grant County, is held each September in John Day. Events include a Chinese parade, lion dancers, fireworks, and booths and exhibits.

JOHN DAY COUNTRY

Scale in Miles
0 5 10 15
Paved Road
Unpaved Road

Gold fever on Canyon Creek

After gold was discovered on Whiskey Flat in 1862, prospectors streamed into the region and a mining camp sprang up along Canyon Creek. At the peak of activity, 10,000 miners and camp followers crowded into town. Millions of dollars in gold dust and nuggets were taken from the creek during the 1860s. Later miners scarred the canyon walls with hydraulic mining operations.

Several of Canyon City's original buildings still stand on the banks above Canyon Creek. Life is quieter these days, but in early June the town hosts the lively '62 Days Celebration, featuring a variety of old-time events.

The excellent Oliver Historical Museum beside U.S. 395 contains relics of the gold mining era and pioneer days, Indian and Chinese artifacts, and specialized exhibits on rocks, guns, and the regional livestock industry. The museum is open from April through October; hours are 9 to 3 Tuesday through Saturday, daily in July and August. Near the museum are the old Greenhorn city jail and the Joaquin Miller cabin.

DeWitt Museum, 13 miles east of John Day in Prairie City, has an interesting collection of mining relics dating from the 1860s, along with other memorabilia.

Strawberry Mountain Wilderness

Rising in striking contrast to the irrigated John Day Valley and semiarid plateau, the rocky peaks of the Strawberry Range dominate the country southeast of John Day. Travelers can obtain information at Malheur National Forest offices in John Day or Prairie City.

A narrow ridge of jagged peaks, the small but rugged range is topped by 9,038-foot Strawberry Mountain, highest point between the Cascades and the Wallowas. The wilderness encompasses tree-filled canyons, five mountain lakes, and several high peaks. Forest roads lead from Prairie City and Seneca to trailheads.

About 150 miles of trails lace the area; an 18-mile loop trail links Strawberry Mountain and all five lakes. Though the lakes are open to year-round trout fishing, snow limits access much of the year. You can hike here from early July through October; horseback riding and hunting are also popular. In July and August wildflowers splash riotous color across meadows and hillsides. You may see mule deer, elk, and bear; a small herd of bighorn sheep roams the western part of the wilderness.

Monument Rock Wilderness

Thirty miles east of John Day, this new wilderness exemplifies the Blue Mountains; it includes headwaters of the Little Malheur River and the upper reaches of the South Fork of Burnt River. Information is available at Malheur National Forest offices in John Day or Prairie City or at Wallowa-Whitman National Forest offices in Baker or Unity. Forest roads lead southeast from Prairie City and southwest from Unity to trailheads and to a viewpoint at Table Rock forest lookout.

From June through October, hikers and horseback riders can follow about 15 miles of trails through large stands of old-growth timber covering a variety of forest types. Trout fishing is best in early summer. In winter, cross-country skiers enjoy the wilderness terrain.

FOSSILS UNLOCK GEOLOGIC HISTORY

About 30 million years ago, giant pigs, saber-toothed cats, rhinoceroses, and three-toed horses roamed the subtropical forests of eastern Oregon. Erupting volcanoes spit out clouds of ashes, trapping and smothering these prehistoric animals. Later eruptions sealed these animals and the primeval plants in rock, making them fossilized pieces in Oregon's paleontological puzzle.

These fossil beds constitute the John Day Fossil Beds National Monument, a 14,000-acre preserve in Grant and Wheeler counties. It encompasses one of the most outstanding natural depositories of prehistoric fossils on the North American continent.

The geologic unraveling of this country began more than a century ago when Thomas Condon, minister and paleontologist, saw fossils brought to The Dalles by a cavalry officer returning from an expedition. Condon soon explored the John Day country himself, uncovering plant and animal fossils dating back to eras when the dry hills were covered with lush subtropical forest. The fossil beds became the training ground for some of America's early paleontologists.

Palms, redwood, magnolia, ginkgo, cinnamon, and fig trees once flourished here. Rhinos, tapirs, crocodiles, and four-toed horses inhabited the area covered by the Clarno Formation, created from eruptions during the Eocene epoch more than 40 million years ago.

In overlying layers of alluvium and volcanic ash—known as the John Day Formation—Condon found fossil remains of camels, giant pigs, saber-toothed cats, tapirs, and three-toed horses. Then followed the Picture Gorge Basalt flows, topped by the relatively recent fossil-bearing Mascall and Rattlesnake formations. For millions of years, the John Day River and its tributaries cut through the accumulated layers, exposing fossilized skeletons of Cenozoic animals and plants and carving out the steep cliffs.

Casual fossil hunting is not permitted within the Monument. Trained paleontologists continue to remove and study fossils in order to piece together information on ancient animals and their environment.

Examples of the fossils have found their way into museums all over the country. In Oregon you can see major collections at the University of Oregon's Natural History Museum in Eugene and at the Oregon Museum of Science and Industry in Portland.

Trail crew penetrates heart of the Wallowa Mountains in Eagle Cap Wilderness. Rugged terrain permits only hikers and riders to enter this alpine wonderland.

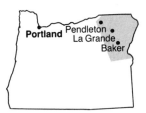

NORTHEASTERN MOUNTAINS

Trace the pioneers' route along the legendary Oregon Trail

Interstate Highway 84 angles across Oregon's scenic northeast corner, paralleling the historic Oregon Trail from the Columbia River to the Snake. The highway connects the region's largest towns—Pendleton, La Grande, and Baker. Here, splendid mountains tower above broad, prosperous valleys. The awesome Grand Canyon of the Snake River forms the state's northeastern boundary.

In this prime recreation country, the Blue and Wallowa mountains entice outdoor enthusiasts to explore backcountry trails on foot and horseback, fish in remote lakes and streams, ski on powder snow, and hunt for deer, elk, and game birds. You can enjoy exciting rodeos, stay at guest ranches, or visit old mining sites to relive the area's gold rush days.

Along Pioneer Trails

From the Columbia River, I-84 cuts southeast toward Pendleton. Hermiston, north of the highway at the junction of U.S. Highway 395 and State Highway 207, is the business hub of the lower Umatilla Basin. The town is a watermelon-growing center, and heart of the region's potato harvest. A major part of the potato crop is processed into French fries and potato flakes at plants in Hermiston and Boardman.

Birdwatchers view migratory waterfowl in spring and autumn at Cold Springs National Wildlife Refuge, 6 miles east of Hermiston, and at the McKay Creek National Wildlife Refuge, just south of Pendleton.

For a leisurely change of pace from highway travel, take the road south of I-84 that winds through Echo along the Umatilla River toward Pendleton. The Echo Historical Museum, open Saturday and Sunday afternoons from April to October, contains pioneer memorabilia. Ruts left by wagon trains traveling the Oregon Trail (see page 113) are still visible, particularly around Wells Springs, south of Boardman.

Pendleton, a town with a western air

Backed by the Blue Mountains, Pendleton is the center of northeastern Oregon's wheat-producing region. Most roads leading to Pendleton cut through vast, rolling wheat fields, magnificently golden as they ripen under hot summer sun. The Umatilla River flows westward through the center of town on its way to join the Columbia.

Pendleton is a town with a western flavor. Expect to see plenty of wide-brimmed hats and cowboy boots. The Umatilla Indian Reservation begins just east of town. Learn more about the Indian culture and eastern Oregon's early days at the Vert Museum, S.W. Dorion Avenue at 4th. Pendleton celebrates this era with an event-filled Pendleton Rendezvous in early July and the renowned Pendleton Round-Up each autumn.

Round-Up time. For 4 days every September, Pendleton's usually quiet, elm-shaded streets resound with the rhythm of hoofbeats and the jingle of Indian trappings. One of the major western rodeos, the Pendleton Round-Up got its start in 1910 when ranchers and farmers of the Umatilla Valley gathered to celebrate the harvest.

Each day begins with a hearty cowboy breakfast in Stillman Park and ends with the historic Happy Canyon Pageant. Some of the nation's best rodeo riders compete daily in calf roping, saddle bronc riding, bulldogging, bareback riding, steer roping, and Brahma bull riding. Members of Indian tribes from throughout the Northwest set up a tepee village along the Umatilla River, adjacent to the rodeo grounds; visitors are welcome to stroll through the encampment. The Indians compete in tribal ceremonial dancing and participate in the evening pageant.

A highlight of the Pendleton Round-Up is the lively, colorful Westward Ho parade. You'll see costumed characters depicting pioneers, trappers, and prospectors; mounted Indians in full regalia; pack trains, stagecoaches, and Mormon carts; and ox teams pulling freight wagons. For more information, contact the Round-Up Association, P.O. Box 609, Pendleton, OR 97801.

Behind the scenes. Western memorabilia are displayed in the Round-Up Hall of Fame under the south grandstand on the Round-Up grounds, S.W. Court at 13th (tours by appointment weekdays; phone (503) 276-2553).

Visitors can tour the Pendleton Woolen Mills on weekdays to see wool processed and woven into blankets and fabrics.

The Walla Walla Valley

From Pendleton, State Highway 11 curves northeast toward Milton-Freewater and the Walla Walla Valley.

High on a northwestern flank of the Blue Mountains, just below the Washington state line, the waters of the Walla Walla River begin their journey toward the Columbia. Forest hiking trails follow both the North and South forks of the river, which converge just east of Milton-Freewater.

Located about 5 miles south of the state border, Milton-Freewater is the agricultural center of the upper Walla Walla Valley. Peas are a major crop; fruit orchards—apples, prunes, and cherries—and grain fields cover many acres as well. Local fruits and vegetables are sold in season at roadside produce stands.

To learn about life on a homestead, visit Frazier House Museum in the south part of town, located off State 11 near the river at 14th Avenue and Chestnut Street. Farther

south, Marie Dorion Historical Park honors an Indian pioneer woman who journeyed overland with her family in 1811 with the Astor Expedition; she was the first woman to cross the plains and settle in Oregon.

The northern Blue Mountains

State Highway 204 crosses the northern Blue Mountains east of Pendleton, following an old short cut from the Oregon Trail to the Walla Walla Valley. Stagecoaches and other early-day travelers stopped at the small settlement of Tollgate, 3 miles west of Spout Springs, to pay a toll. In Weston, pioneer household goods from Oregon Trail and homesteading days are exhibited in the Weston Museum.

Campgrounds are located along State 204 at Langdon Lake and off the highway in Umatilla National Forest. Several border the river and North Fork Umatilla Wilderness; the Umatilla Forks Campground has a nature trail.

From Tollgate, scenic forest roads follow the ridge of the Blue Mountains northeast to Troy. Forest Service campgrounds are located at Jubilee Lake, 12 miles northeast of the Tollgate junction, and at springs along the route. From Timothy Springs Campground, a trail follows the South Fork of the Wenaha River for nearly 30 miles. Other trails also provide access from Forest Road 62 into the Oregon portion of the Wenaha-Tucannon Wilderness.

Spout Springs. Skiing lasts from late November to mid-April at Spout Springs, located about 45 miles northeast of Pendleton on State 204. The ski area features dry snow, a large ski school with instruction in both downhill and cross-country skiing, complete equipment rentals, and limited overnight accommodations. Two double chairlifts, T-bars, and a rope tow move skiers to ten runs.

North Fork Umatilla Wilderness. Already popular with anglers, hikers, horseback riders, and hunters, this wilderness is located southwest of State 204 near Tollgate and Spout Springs. Trails enter the wilderness from Umatilla Forks and Buck Creek campgrounds on the western border. Deer and elk roam the region, and fishing is excellent. For information, stop at Umatilla National Forest headquarters, 2517 S.W. Hailey, in Pendleton.

Wenaha-Tucannon Wilderness. Rugged ridges and steep canyons typify the Wenaha-Tucannon Wilderness, spanning the Oregon-Washington border in the northern reaches of Umatilla National Forest.

Remote and roadless, the area attracts hikers, anglers, and hunters. Streams have cut deep canyons into the table lands, leaving heavily timbered areas such as Moore Flat and Grizzly Bear Ridge along the Wenaha River canyon. Scattered stands of evergreens—primarily Douglas fir and white fir—shield wildlife.

La Grande, hub of the Grande Ronde Valley

Surrounded by thriving farms and livestock ranches, La Grande spreads across the broad, rich valley of the Grande Ronde River. Located here is Eastern Oregon State College, the only 4-year institution of higher education east

WALLA WALLA
WASHINGTON
To Lewiston
Walla   Walla
Milton-Freewater
Wenaha River
Troy
Flora
Weston   Tollgate
Ski Area
River
PENDLETON   UMATILLA
Umatilla   River
204
Grande Ronde
Wallowa
3
INDIAN
RES.
Minam   82
Elgin
Wallowa
Lostine
EMIGRANT
SPRINGS
STATE PARK
Oregon
Trail
Mount
Emily
Minam
Lostine
River
Enterprise
Joseph
84
LA GRANDE
To Baker
River
River
WALLOWA LAKE
STATE PARK

— Paved Road
— Unpaved Road
- - - Oregon Trail

Scale in Miles
0 5 10 15

NORTHEASTERN OREGON

of the Cascades. The college maintains an Oregon Trail interpretive exhibit on the edge of the campus.

In October the college community, local residents, and regional crafts people join in a joyous Oktoberfest combining traditional college homecoming events with the fun of a Bavarian beer fest.

From La Grande, highways branch north and west into the Blue Mountains and eastward to the Wallowas. A winding mountain road north of town climbs 10 miles to the summit of 6,064-foot Mount Emily, where you have a splendid view from 3,000 feet above the wide Grande Ronde Valley and meandering river.

State Highway 203 makes a deep curve southeast through Union along Catherine Creek to Medical Springs. Union boasts some fine old brick buildings, and Catherine Creek State Park offers campsites and picnic tables.

The Grande Ronde Valley

The drive northeast through the wheat fields of the broad Grande Ronde Valley leads to Elgin, a farming and lumbering center. The Elgin Stampede draws visitors each July for the Northwest Champion Horse Pulling Contest. The Eastern Oregon Timber Carnival attracts contestants from as far away as New Zealand in June.

Two-day float trips on the Grande Ronde River usually start at the mouth of the Wallowa River at Rondowa, northeast of Elgin, and continue downstream to Troy.

For information on river trips, inquire at the La Grande-Union County Chamber of Commerce office. High water in the spring and early summer makes the trip easier; later, rubber rafts must be pulled part of the way. Good camping spots are located at the mouths of Bear Creek and Elbow Creek.

Into the Wallowas

From La Grande, State Highway 82 makes a 70-mile curve eastward to Joseph, gateway to the Wallowa (first two syllables rhyme with *allow*) Mountains. Exciting canyon vistas and roadside stretches of the Wallowa, Minam, and Lostine rivers make this a beautiful route.

Renowned for the grandeur of its alpine scenery, the compact and rugged Wallowa range offers superlative mountain recreation—hiking, horseback riding, stream and lake fishing, hunting, rock climbing, and, in winter, skiing and other winter sports. Nearby, rafting parties float down the challenging Snake River through Hells Canyon, or explore the easier Grande Ronde and Minam rivers.

For information on the region's recreational activities, events, guides and packers, and scenic backcountry tours, contact the Wallowa County Chamber of Commerce, P.O. Box 427, Enterprise, OR 97828.

The last great Indian war

The Wallowa Valley was the ancestral home of the Nez Perce Indians, who called it the "valley of the winding water." A treaty negotiated by the U.S. government in 1855 stipulated that the Wallowa country be included in lands to be kept by the Nez Perce. However, over the next 20 years settlers arrived and pressured the government to reduce the Indian lands.

In 1875 President Ulysses Grant opened the Wallowa Valley to settlers, and in 1877 the government ordered the Nez Perce out of their valley and onto a reservation.

With their families, livestock, and all packable possessions, Young Chief Joseph and his people crossed the swollen Snake River and joined other Nez Perce in Idaho. Hostilities between several braves and white settlers led to the epic 1700-mile retreat of the Nez Perce, during which they repeatedly battled and defeated numerically superior military troops before finally being subdued just a few miles from Canada.

The town of Joseph and Chief Joseph Mountain, rising west of Wallowa Lake, honor the young Nez Perce leader. His father, Old Chief Joseph, is buried in the Indian cemetery at the north end of Wallowa Lake, where a monument stands in his memory.

Wallowa towns
retain a frontier flavor

Towns in this remote corner of the state exude western atmosphere. This is horse country—several outfitters have pack and riding stock available for hire. You can obtain a list at local Forest Service offices or the Wallowa County Chamber of Commerce office in Enterprise.

Tucked away in the mountains are several guest ranches where horses are available for day sightseeing and fishing trips. The Wallowa Valley is a prime starting point for hiking, fishing excursions, pack trips, and llama trekking into the Eagle Cap Wilderness.

In the Wallowa Valley you can enjoy events with an old-time folksy flavor. Enterprise hosts a Western Arts Festival in late April. Summer events are highlighted by Wallowa's old-fashioned Fourth of July celebration, with a parade, community picnic, and dancing; Lostine's Sidewalk Flea Market; an old-time fiddlers contest in Enterprise; and the event-filled Chief Joseph Days celebration and rodeo in Joseph.

In September, Enterprise hosts the lively Hells Canyon Mule Days, with a parade, mule races, speed mule shoeing, a western dance and other events; at Wallowa Lake, a 3-day Bavarian-style Alpenfest plans events for the whole family.

Joseph. On your way to Wallowa Lake, stop in Joseph to visit the Wallowa County Museum, open daily from the end of May through mid-September. The museum is housed in a renovated 1888 bank building, the site of a famous robbery, that displays many hand-crafted architectural details typical of that era. Exhibits feature Nez Perce and Wallowa Valley pioneer relics.

Flora. Travelers motoring south to the Wallowas from Washington on State Highway 3 pass near the once-prosperous farming community of Flora, now almost a ghost town. Oregon's northeasternmost settlement, Flora lies 2 miles west of State 3, about 35 miles north of Enterprise. Many of its weather-beaten buildings stand empty and deserted on the open meadow, scoured to a silvery sheen by silt-laden winds. Wildflowers carpet the grassy fields in spring.

Relaxing at Wallowa Lake

Nestled at the foot of steep, forested mountains at the upper end of the Wallowa Valley is Wallowa Lake, the region's most popular recreation site. Scooped out by a glacier during the Ice Age, the lake basin is still rimmed on east and west by lateral moraines; at the north end of the lake, the glacier's terminal moraine became a natural dam collecting the lake's clear, deep waters. A manmade dam installed to control water for irrigation enhances the effect.

Nearly 5 miles long, Wallowa Lake attracts many water sports enthusiasts. A resort and state park are located at the south end of the lake.

Wallowa Lake State Park. A popular family vacation destination, the park has a large campground and two picnic areas. A boat launching ramp, bathhouse, dock, and swimming beach are located along the southwestern shore.

Many visitors spend their days on the water—boating, water-skiing, or fishing for rainbow trout or kokanee (landlocked sockeye salmon). Boats, canoes, water bikes, and other water sports equipment can be rented in summer. You can walk a park nature trail or pedal along a bicycle path. Hikers, horseback riders, and llama packers ascend graded trails high into the Wallowa Mountains; horses are available for day rides or longer trips.

Sightseeing flights over the Wallowa Mountains and Hells Canyon can be arranged at the Enterprise, Joseph, and Baker airports.

Gondola ride up Mount Howard. From a terminal near the lake's southeast corner, blue gondola cars climb silently to the summit of 8,250-foot Mount Howard. On the 15-minute ride, passengers ascend 3,700 vertical feet, sur-veying the rugged peaks and green canyons of the Wallowa Mountains, Wallowa Lake, the fields of the Wallowa Valley, and the canyon country. To the east lie Idaho's Seven Devils Mountains. The Wallowa Lake Tramway operates from 10 P.M. to 4 P.M. weekends only from mid-May to early June, then daily in summer. For more information, phone (503) 432-5331.

Snacks and beverages are available at the upper terminal. Two miles of nature trails meander through meadows and into groves of alpine fir, juniper, and whitebark pine. View points overlook the mountains and canyons. Often you'll see elk and deer browsing in the meadows.

Winter sports. Families enjoy downhill skiing at the Ferguson Ridge ski area, 10 miles southeast of Joseph; cross-country skiing is also available in several areas. At Salt Creek Summit, on the western edge of Hells Canyon National Recreation Area, about 60 miles of groomed trails await snowmobilers.

Eagle Cap Wilderness, heart of the Wallowas

Some of Oregon's finest mountain country lies in the heart of the Wallowas within the boundaries of 361,000-acre Eagle Cap Wilderness. Rugged granite peaks rise to nearly 10,000 feet above delightful alpine meadows and thick forests.

Swift-flowing rivers—among them the Minam, Eagle, Lostine, Wallowa, and Imnaha—radiate from Eagle Cap peak, cutting deep canyons through the mountain range and nearby plateaus. The Minam River, untouched by any road for most of its 45-mile length, has been designated a state scenic waterway. About 60 jewel-like lakes nestle at the base of steep slopes or hide in basins.

Exploring the high country. You can drive up several scenic canyons to forest campgrounds on the edge of the wilderness, but no road penetrates to the high lakes. This paradise is reserved for hikers and horseback riders. Trails are dusty across the mountainous terrain.

Check for current information on trail conditions and any fire restrictions at the district offices of the Wallowa-Whitman National Forest in Enterprise or in Joseph (or in other main towns).

Saddle and pack animals are available for short rides, day excursions, or long pack trips. If you prefer, a guide will pack you in and out, leaving you free to fish and explore the high country within range of your camp.

High trails are usually blocked until late June or July, and patches of snow often remain the year around on the high peaks. From mid-July to mid-August, alpine wildflowers brighten stream beds and other moist areas.

Trout fishing is generally good or excellent in the lakes. Mountain goats roam the high country between Sacajawea Peak and the Matterhorn, and bighorn sheep inhabit the Hurricane Divide to the west. Campers frequently see deer, elk, and smaller animals.

Though most visitors come in July and August, the pleasant sunny days of Indian summer are especially enjoyable, often lingering well into October. Bring along some warm clothing, for evenings are brisk in the high

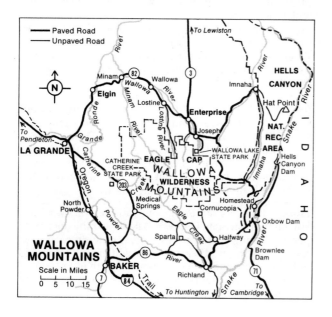

WALLOWA MOUNTAINS

Hopping through hoops requires nimble feet and an expert sense of timing. Ceremonial dances add to the excitement during the Pendleton Round-up in September.

Children explore weathered remnant at Whitney. Almost lost among tall grass and weeds, this ghost town near Sumpter was a major logging center in late 1800s.

Uplifting gondola ride gives passengers a bird's-eye view of Wallowa Lake and surrounding valley. Tram soars over 4,000 feet to Mount Howard's summit.

country and you might encounter a brief storm in any season.

On the trail.   Scenic routes lead up the rivers radiating from this alpine wilderness, offering hikers and riders more than 480 miles of trails. Because of the area's open terrain, cross-country travel is easy, and visitors can reach areas unapproachable by trail.

Trails and destinations that lead from Wallowa Lake and Lostine Canyon in the northern part are heavily traveled, but trails departing from the south and east sides of the wilderness offer travelers an opportunity to avoid the crowds. You can camp in many spectacular U-shaped valleys or ridgetops for an enjoyable wilderness experience; lake shore areas are usually congested.

Along the Snake River

More than 200 miles of Oregon's northeastern border is formed by the Snake River, which swells into large reservoirs and narrows as it tumbles and surges through Hells Canyon. Three hydroelectric dams—Brownlee, Oxbow, and Hells Canyon—transform water power into electricity; guided tours through the generating plants are available on request. For information on guides and packers, river trips, and scenic tours, consult tourist offices in Enterprise or Baker. Additional information on Hells Canyon National Recreation Area is available in Oregon at the headquarters office in Enterprise or at the Wallowa-Whitman National Forest office in Baker.

Hells Canyon
National Recreation Area

Hells Canyon is the scenic highlight of the 1,000-mile-long Snake River as it erodes a natural boundary between northeastern Oregon and Idaho. North America's deepest gorge, the mile-deep canyon is awesome and fascinating as it plunges between basaltic strata and high mountains.

The generations of Indians who camped on the riverside benches and deltas covered some of the rock faces with carvings and paintings. Yet until the late 1800s, the deep, swift river and torturous mountains formed a barrier to non-Indian exploration of the West. Homesteaders built cabins on some of the larger terraces.

The 652,000-acre Hells Canyon National Recreation Area was established in 1975; about 216,000 of the acres in Oregon and Idaho are being managed as Hells Canyon Wilderness by the U.S. Forest Service. The 67-mile section from Hells Canyon Dam downstream to Wallowa-Whitman National Forest northern boundary is now part of the Federal Wild and Scenic Rivers System, and no new dams will be constructed in the scenic canyon of the middle Snake River.

To Hat Point & Imnaha Canyon

Steep, narrow gravel roads lead to a variety of scenic destinations. If you prefer just to enjoy the view, inquire at the Wallowa County Chamber of Commerce office in Enterprise about sightseeing tours. Motorists should obtain current road information, fill the car's gas tank before setting out and take along drinking water and a picnic lunch.

Hat Point.   A 30-mile paved road heads northeast from Joseph to Imnaha. Here the Hat Point route narrows to a rough, single-lane, unimproved forest road that climbs steadily, with occasional turnouts, up the steep and dusty flank of Grizzly Ridge. About 24 miles southeast of Imnaha you arrive at Hat Point lookout on the canyon rim.

More than a mile below, the Snake River winds ribbonlike through the narrowest and deepest gash on the North American continent—a chasm averaging 5,500 feet in depth for about 40 miles. The Seven Devils Mountains loom on the Idaho side of the river; to the west and south you see the snow-tipped Wallowas.

Imnaha Canyon.   Two routes lead south from the Joseph-Imnaha road into the forest, to campgrounds and fishing sites along the upper Imnaha River and in the southern part of Hells Canyon National Recreation Area.

Eight miles east of Joseph, Forest Road 39 heads up Little Sheep Creek; paved most of the way, it meets State Highway 86 east of the community of Halfway. Or take the gravel road from Imnaha south along the Imnaha River; it meets the paved route at Gumboot Creek.

Boat trips on the Snake River

Awesome cliffs constrict the Snake through stretches of the 31-mile wild river section, which extends from Hells Canyon Dam downstream to Pittsburg Landing. Farther north the 36-mile scenic river corridor opens into rolling hills sparsely marked by abandoned homesteads. The easiest way to enjoy the river and canyon is by boat.

Permits are required for all boating on the Wild and Scenic Snake River from the Friday preceding Memorial Day weekend through September 15. For information on reservations and permits, phone (208) 743-2297.

Float trips.   River runners launch oar-powered rubber rafts and wooden dories in the Snake below Hells Canyon Dam and float north past the Imnaha and Salmon rivers to the Grande Ronde, about 85 miles away.

Rapids give way to placid pools that invite swimming. Water is highest and fastest on spring trips, when the canyon is at its greenest and pleasantly cool. Vegetation ranges from cool green ferns to bright cactus blossoms. In side canyons and on ridges you can discover ancient petroglyphs, Indian caves, and old mines.

Temperatures soar in summer, but the water is warm enough for swimming, and you can float alongside the boat in calm water. Autumn provides cooler weather and excellent fishing.

Jet boat trips.   Travelers can also arrange 1-day round-trip jet boat trips downstream from Hells Canyon Dam to Wild Sheep Rapids or upstream from Lewiston, Idaho, to Johnson Bar or Granite Creek Rapid. The mail boat makes regular trips upstream from Lewiston. Fierce rapids hamper motor navigation on the 3-mile section between Wild Sheep Rapids and Granite Creek.

Hiking Hells Canyon trails

For a different look at this rugged countryside and the Snake River Canyon, buckle on a backpack and strike out on foot. Nearly 1,000 miles of trails traverse this region. Hiking routes in the Oregon portion of Hells Canyon National Recreation Area are supervised by Forest Service personnel assigned to the Wallowa-Whitman National Forest. Information on trail conditions and regulations and a list of outfitter guides can be obtained at offices in Enterprise and Joseph. In Idaho, information is available at Forest Service offices in Lewiston and Riggins.

Rugged backpackers get a fresh perspective on the river from a trail winding high above the river's churning waters. Hikers should carry a collapsible plastic water container and a small fuel stove, since sources of drinking water are few and wood is scarce. Campfires are not permitted between July 1 and September 15 in the Snake River corridor. Poison oak is abundant in some areas, and rattlesnakes are common; hikers should carry a snake bite kit. A topographic map is helpful.

The Nee-Me-Poo (or Nez Perce) Trail, now a designated National Recreation Trail, follows part of the route taken by Chief Joseph and members of the Nez Perce tribe during their 1877 exodus from the Wallowa Valley toward Canada (see page 109).

Ghost towns & forest camps

State 86 curves along the southern foothills of the Wallowas between Baker and the Snake River. For much of the way, it parallels the Powder River.

Prospectors once mined these valleys. Only a few remnants mark the once-flourishing gold camp of Sparta, 5 miles north of State 86, but hillsides show the scars of abandoned diggings. A roaring boom town in the 1860s, Sparta produced more than $2 million in gold.

For more than 60 years—until 1941—the mines of Cornucopia produced gold totaling $16 million. Remains of the town are located about 11 miles north of Halfway off State 86. Heavy winter snows have taken their toll, but some sagging, dilapidated buildings remain. A few summer residences have been built nearby. A 6,300-foot mine adit provided access to 36 miles of underground workings in gold-bearing veins. In recent years, rising gold prices have caused renewed mining interest in this once-prosperous area.

An unpaved forest road from Halfway west toward Medical Springs leads to campgrounds along Eagle Creek. Abandoned logging roads make fine hiking trails. At Cornucopia Pack Station, visitors can arrange for riding horses or pack trips into the southern part of Eagle Cap Wilderness (see page 110).

Northeast of Halfway at Homestead, 4 miles north of Oxbow Dam, the old Iron Dyke Mine camp is again in operation. Between 1916 and 1928, it produced sizable amounts of copper, gold, and silver.

Riverside campgrounds

Roads parallel sections of the Snake River, providing access to boaters, fishers, and hunters. Communities are

TREKKING ALONG THE OREGON TRAIL

Travelers who speed along Interstate Highway 84 through northeastern Oregon are never far from the route of the fabled Oregon Trail, the overland route of emigrants journeying west to the fertile Willamette Valley. Traveling in long wagon trains, thousands of pioneers made the arduous 2,000-mile journey in search of a better life in the West.

The mass migration began as a trickle in the spring of 1841, when a wagon train of 69 pioneers headed west, following routes discovered by trappers and pathfinders. Each year the number of emigrants increased, peaking at 55,000 in 1850. Pioneers traveled by wagon train to Oregon through the 1870s, and travelers continued to arrive by wagon until the 1890s. Some 350,000 pioneers traveled the ruts of the Oregon Trail.

Leaving Independence, Missouri, at the first sign of spring, the wagon trains arrived at Old Fort Boise on the Snake River in late summer or early autumn. Another weary month and 400 difficult miles of travel still lay ahead.

Wagons were loaded with family possessions, along with provisions for the long journey and the first year in the Pacific Northwest. Most family members trudged beside the plodding oxen; a lucky few had saddle horses.

Straining oxen pulled the creaking wagons across dusty plains and up steep slopes; today, a modern freeway reduces that month's journey to a few hours. Where pioneers camped or stopped to water their stock, state parks and rest areas now offer conveniences to motorists.

Yet time and the elements have not erased all signs of the route. Ruts carved by the narrow wheels of heavily loaded wagons still run for miles across parts of northeast and central Oregon. South of Mount Hood on Laurel Hill, trees retain deep gashes made by ropes used to slow the wagons' descent on the Barlow Road.

Interpretive displays in four state parks and seven rest areas along I-84 recount life on the trail in the words of the people who experienced it, point out details of terrain, and discuss the route's impact on Oregon and on the nation. Roadside markers relate historic details.

Write to the state's tourism division office (address on page 9) for a brochure on the Oregon Trail. It maps the route in relation to today's towns and highways, notes the location of interpretive displays, and describes the hazardous trip of the pioneers toward the Willamette Valley. You can see pioneer relics in local museums along the route and at the Oregon Historical Center in Portland.

Skier sways between snow-laden trees on slope of Blue Mountains at Anthony Lakes, one of the Northwest's highest ski areas. Take your choice of packed or powder snow from November to May.

Boaters beach rafts and kayaks along rocky shore of Snake River in hauntingly beautiful Hells Canyon. In spring hills are green and water high. Region is roadless; only trails cross the rugged landscape.

small and scattered; you'll see many abandoned houses.

Idaho Power Company maintains four reservoir parks (three of them on the Idaho shore of the Snake). Access to these parks is from State 86. All four campgrounds have trailer spaces with electric hookups, picnic tables, boat ramps, and drinking water; tent campsites are available at Woodhead Park, behind Brownlee Dam. You'll find docks on the east shore of reservoirs behind Oxbow and Brownlee dams.

Camping and picnicking facilities, boat ramps, and access to Brownlee Reservoir are also available at Hewitt County Park, east of Richland.

Brownlee Dam creates a 50-mile lake from a wild, treeless section of the Snake. From Richland on State 86, an all-weather road hugs the Oregon bank south for 38 miles to Huntington on I-84. Along this sparsely settled route you'll see a few ranches and fewer private fishing cabins, but most of the time not even a fence—only the road, hills, and river. Sunflowers grow along the river bank in summer. From spring to autumn, this is good birdwatching country. Bald eagles frequent the river area in late winter.

At Farewell Bend State Park, south of Huntington off I-84, travelers find campsites, picnic tables, a swimming area, and boat launching facilities.

The Lure of Gold

After gold was discovered in California, tales spread of an Oregon stream pebbled with gold nuggets. According to legend, children traveling with a wagon train in 1845 filled a blue bucket with the stones, then later tossed them aside.

In October, 1861, prospectors searching for the mythical Blue Bucket Mine discovered gold in Griffin Gulch, a few miles south of present-day Baker. Within a few months the rush began, as gold became the prime force in settling eastern Oregon. Mining towns—including Auburn, Sumpter, Bourne, Granite, Malheur City, and Sparta—mushroomed near the claims.

More than a century ago, gold spurred the settlement of the region. Escalating prices of the precious metal periodically focus attention on the mining district. You'll occasionally see weekend prospectors camped beside tumbling creeks.

Baker, eastern Oregon's first "boom town"

Baker City, "Queen City of the Mines," became an important freight and stagecoach center, serving the miners who combed the creeks and gullies of the Blue and Wallowa mountains. Prospectors, gamblers, and camp followers mingled with ranchers, cowboys, and sheepherders in the local dance halls and saloons or sauntered along the town sidewalks.

Business is still prospering in Baker, though today the economy is based on timber, livestock, and tourism. Hub of several highways, Baker is the gateway to forested recreation lands, ghost towns, and the Snake River country. You'll find information about the region's mining history and recreational activities at the Baker County Chamber of Commerce, located at the Baker city center exit from I-84. The Oregon Trail Regional Museum is located at Grove and Campbell streets.

Unlike many mining towns, Baker was built to endure. Its commercial district contains many historic structures built of locally quarried gray volcanic stone; this district was granted National Historic Site status in 1979. Among the city's distinctive buildings is the square, three-story Baker County Courthouse at 3rd and Court streets, built in 1908 of local stone and surmounted by a clock tower. Baker's historic downtown district is lively during the Miners' Jubilee in late July.

Samples of local gold—including dust, ore, and the famous 80.4-ounce "Armstrong" nugget—are displayed in the lobby of the U.S. National Bank, 2000 Main Street.

The Powder River flows through Baker's pleasant city park, a green oasis where families can picnic and relax.

Along U.S. 30

At Haines, about 10 miles northwest of Baker on the old highway, the Eastern Oregon Museum features local family articles from the Oregon Trail era. Located four blocks east of Main Street, the museum is open daily from April through October. Its varied displays include reconstructed kitchen and parlor rooms with models in typical costumes, horse- and steam-powered equipment, and an 1880s railway depot.

Pine-covered mountains

The cool, fragrant pine woods and quiet meadows of the Blue Mountains and Elkhorn Ridge provide a pleasant contrast to the warm, dry ranch land and cultivated fields of northeastern Oregon.

Picnickers, campers, anglers, hikers, hunters, and water sports enthusiasts linger beside mountain lakes and valley reservoirs. Remnants of old mining camps and logging towns invite exploration, and visitors can ride on a historic narrow-gauge railway.

Unity Reservoir. Southwest from Baker, motorists follow the Burnt River canyon to meet U.S. Highway 26 north of Unity. Campers and picnickers stop at Unity Lake State Park, 37 miles southwest of Baker, where they can also enjoy lake boating, swimming, and fishing.

Phillips Reservoir. Modern tent and trailer campsites are located at popular Union Creek Campground, 17 miles southwest of Baker bordering Phillips Reservoir, on the Powder River behind Mason Dam. A boat ramp, a swimming area, and lakeside trails await visitors.

Sumpter Valley. Once the crossroads of mining trails, Sumpter boomed when the Sumpter Valley Railroad arrived in 1896 and ore veins were opened in the Blue Mountains. The narrow-gauge rail network extended from Baker as far west as Prairie City. Later, giant mining dredges tore up the valley; one is still near Sumpter, mired in gravel. Today the Sumpter Valley is a wildlife haven, a

45-mile zigzag chain of shoestring ponds alive with shore birds, migratory waterfowl, and small animals such as beaver and muskrat.

On weekends and holidays from late May through September you can board the Stump Dodger, a restored narrow-gauge steam train operated by the Sumpter Valley Railroad, for a 5-mile ride through the valley's wildlife area. Trips depart hourly from 11 A.M. to 5 P.M. from Baker County's Dredge Depot Park, west of Phillips Reservoir. You can picnic here, and explore nature trails that lead into the wildlife area.

Residents of Sumpter welcome visitors in early July to the annual Sumpter Valley Days celebration. It includes an old-time fiddlers' contest, ax throwing competition, black powder shoot, arts and crafts fair, marathon race, and a variety of food and entertainment.

Elkhorn Drive.   A 106-mile road—the Elkhorn Drive—loops west of Baker through scenic and historic Wallowa-Whitman National Forest. For a booklet describing the self-guided loop trip, stop at the Baker County Chamber of Commerce office or at the Baker Ranger Station on U.S. 30. The route winds through the Sumpter Valley past mining towns and pioneer logging camps, then curves north from Granite near several mines, the eastern border of North Fork John Day Wilderness, and Anthony Lakes Recreation Area. Take along a picnic lunch and beverage —and a gold pan if you want to try a bit of prospecting.

North Fork John Day Wilderness.   The rugged gorge of the North Fork John Day River gives its name to this 121,800-acre wilderness in the Greenhorn Mountains of Umatilla National Forest. This region was a busy gold and silver mining area in the latter half of the 19th century, and old mining structures, ditches, building foundations, and other traces of mining days are still visible. About $10 million in gold and silver were mined here. The area also includes about 6,000 acres of the Vinegar Hill-Indian Rock Scenic Area.

More than 130 miles of trails lace the area, including three National Recreation Trails (Elkhorn, North Fork John Day, and Winom Creek). Rocky Mountain elk and mule deer roam here, and fishing is good in the North Fork John Day and its tributary streams. For trail and recreation information, contact Umatilla National Forest offices in Pendleton or Ukiah.

Elkhorn Crest Trail.   Winding at elevations about 7,000 feet, this scenic trail commands the sharp, high mountain ridge between the Baker and Sumpter valleys. It offers magnificent views of mountain lakes, glaciated valleys, the route of the old Oregon Trail, and the Wallowa Mountains. In summer, the best approach is through Anthony Lakes.

Ghost towns of the golden past

The discovery of gold in Griffin Gulch in 1861 lured thousands of miners east from the Willamette Valley and north from California. In the early months of 1862, eastern Oregon was aflame with gold fever. New prospectors arrived daily; boom towns sprang up around each strike.

Another surge of activity came in the 1880s and '90s with the arrival of the railroads. Spur lines penetrated the mountain valleys, and logging and mining camps dotted the hillsides. Later, dredges chewed away at the river beds, leaving mounds of waste gravel in their wake.

When the gold dwindled, the camps declined. Weather-beaten buildings, abandoned mine shafts, and crumbling foundations attest to heavy winter snows, fire, and the passage of time.

New dwellings have been built amid the weathered structures, but enough remains to provide intriguing glimpses of bygone days. Tremendous increases in the price of gold have focused new attention on prospecting and mining in the gold country.

State 7 leads southwest from Baker into the historic Sumpter Valley mining district, and the Austin-Sumpter cutoff offers a scenic short cut between Baker and U.S. 26. Most roads to old mining areas and other remote sites are graded gravel and dirt; inquire locally about road conditions if you plan to explore off the paved roads. A Forest Service map (which can be purchased in Baker) is helpful in identifying back roads.

Visitors should secure permission before exploring mining areas; mines are all located on mining claims, many of which are "patented" private lands. It is unsafe to enter tunnels or shafts, because the timbers shoring them may be rotten.

Auburn.   Seven miles south of Baker on State 7, a graded road leads 6 miles west to the site of Auburn. In 1862 it was the metropolis of the mining district and the first seat of Baker County. At its peak, Auburn had a population of 5,000 and was the second largest town in the state. But by 1868 the richest diggings were worked out, and most of the miners had moved on. Today few signs remain.

Sumpter.   In 1862 several ex-Confederate soldiers found gold in the gravel beds of the Powder River, but the mining camp did not boom until the Sumpter Valley railroad arrived in 1896. In Sumpter's heyday, the business district—including numerous saloons—stretched 7 blocks up a steep hill; the town even had an opera house where fancy-dress balls were held.

Nearly $16 million in gold was extracted here by placer and deep mining. Gold dredges left great piles of boulders and gravel in the valley, and ore smelters discarded large piles of black slag. In 1917 a fire erased most of the town, leaving only brick walls and foundations to mark the old settlement. In recent years, many vacation and retirement homes have been built here.

Bourne. From Sumpter you can make a 7-mile side trip up Cracker Creek to the site of Bourne, center of one of Oregon's most productive hard-rock mining areas. Known in the 1870s as the boisterous mining camp of Cracker, in later years Bourne was notorious for many wildcat mining schemes devised to fleece gullible Eastern investors.

In 1937 a cloudburst diverted the creek, and a wall of water swept down the town's main street. Foundations and a few buildings remain, scattered amid newer vacation homes. Some of the old mines are being reopened.

Whitney. Though surrounded by mining camps, Whitney was a logging town. Located about 9 miles south of Sumpter, Whitney was built in a large meadow near the North Fork of the Burnt River. Weathered residences are scattered along the main street, and the deserted sawmill stands beside a log pond. Occasionally you'll see signs of the old narrow-gauge railroad, which transported logs, lumber, and supplies to towns along its route.

Bonanza. From Whitney the 7-mile route to Bonanza heads northwest through meadows, along the river, and up Geiser Creek through pine forests. The mining camp grew up around the rich Bonanza mine. An aerial tram transported gold ore in buckets from the mine to stamp mills nearer town. Once one of the district's richest mines, Bonanza today contains tumble-down buildings, the ruins of a stamp ore mill, and part of the old mine.

Greenhorn. Seven miles west of Bonanza (up some steep stretches on the dirt road) is Greenhorn, christened when two young men fresh from the East struck a rich vein of gold. Summer homes are being built, but little remains to mark the mining era.

Granite. Forest Road 73 continues west past McCully Fork Campground, but an all-weather road continues west to Granite. The old mining town sits on the hill east of the road junction; many weathered buildings survive amid the town's occupied dwellings. In contrast to most mining camps, Granite made its money on trading, distributing, and shipping rather than on miners' vices. But when the mines were worked out, the town shriveled.

From Granite, roads continue west up Congo Gulch to the Fremont Powerhouse and north to mines along Granite Creek.

Fremont Powerhouse. About 8 miles west of Granite, near the crest of the mountains, you can visit the Fremont Powerhouse, built in 1908 to provide electrical power for the mines and nearby towns.

Water was transported to the powerhouse through wood and steel pipelines from Olive Lake, about 8 miles west. Original equipment, used until the plant closed in 1967, includes antique machinery and a blue Florentine marble instrument panel.

Along Granite Creek. As you travel north from Granite, you can see rock walls in the stream bottom made by Chinese miners nearly 100 years ago. They built the walls by hand, moving large boulders to work the gravel and sand underneath.

About 3 miles north of Granite the road passes the Cougar-Independence Mine, one of several mines in the region being rehabilitated. Mining engineers are tunneling into the mountains to reach a mineral vein several hundred feet under the older mines. The Buffalo Mine, 2 miles farther north, also is being reopened.

Evidence of hydraulic gold mining can be seen along the North Fork of the John Day River. Water sprayed under high pressure through giant nozzles washed gravel down banks and through sluice troughs.

The western slope. If you take State 7 across the Blue Mountains from Sumpter to Austin, you can detour to more old mining camps near the Middle Fork of the John Day River.

Austin, 3 miles north of U.S. 26, was a supply depot for many mining camps and a terminus of the narrow-gauge railroad from Sumpter. A few old buildings remain.

From Bates an enjoyable route follows the river through Malheur National Forest to Galena and Susanville, where mines were worked beginning in the early 1860s. The riverside route also cuts through a large cattle ranch before intersecting State Highway 395 north of Long Creek.

Year-round recreation at Anthony Lakes

Twenty-eight miles northwest of Baker by way of North Powder, the Anthony Lakes present a cool retreat on warm summer days. Motorists climb by good road to the larger lakes—Anthony, Grande Ronde, and Mud—located above the 7,000-foot level. Several smaller lakes beyond the road are accessible only by trails.

Shady Forest Service campgrounds are located at Anthony and Grande Ronde lakes; the camps usually remain open through the autumn hunting season. At the small lakeside resort, summer visitors can obtain meals, food supplies, and rowboat rentals.

Anglers toss their lines in the quiet lake waters. Summer visitors can swim or pick berries. Hikers and horseback riders enjoy a network of maintained trails.

In winter the skiers take over. Powder snow, rugged scenery, and informal hospitality draw winter sports fans to Anthony Lakes Ski Area, less than an hour's drive west of Baker and La Grande. High elevation and dry snows provide good skiing from November to May.

Anthony Lakes Ski Area offers more than 300 acres of skiable terrain. Lifts ascend from 7,100 feet to near 8,000 feet, making Anthony Lakes one of the Northwest's highest ski areas. A double chair and Poma lifts transport skiers to packed slopes and untracked powder snow. You'll find cross-country and snowmobile routes as well. The area has a day lodge and ski shop.

SOUTHEASTERN CORNER

Search for surprises in a spacious, sun-drenched land

Oregon's sprawling, sparsely settled southeastern corner remains the state's least-known region. Yet it promises surprises for those who venture to explore green mountain meadows and vividly colored gulches, challenge the white water of the Owyhee River, fish in rock-rimmed reservoirs, go rockhounding or search for Indian artifacts, or stalk the wild birds and game that inhabit this rugged country. Here, large ranches still stretch across range lands on which, a century ago, cattle barons grazed immense herds.

Because relatively few highways penetrate this vast, silent country, you must sometimes venture off paved roads to discover its special attractions. Passenger cars can safely navigate most of the improved roads, but the primitive routes are best probed by sturdy four-wheel-drive vehicles. Inquire locally before setting out on unpaved roads; be sure your car is in good working order, and carry drinking water.

South to Klamath County

U.S. Highway 97 cuts south through Klamath County's scattered pine forests toward the California border.

About 30 miles north of Klamath Falls, Collier Memorial State Park and Logging Museum offers a pleasant break in a satiety of pine and sagebrush countryside. Families enjoy the inviting green lawn and children's play area beside the Williamson River. Fly fishers head up Spring Creek. West of the highway, visitors see machinery and equipment used by early loggers, marvel at cross sections of enormous logs cut from Oregon forests, and

peer into various rustic cabins built and furnished by trappers, miners, loggers, and homesteaders.

As U.S. 97 nears Klamath Falls, it skims the eastern shore of Upper Klamath Lake, one of several large, shallow lakes and marshes lying astride the Oregon–California border. White pelicans, western grebes, night herons, and other waterfowl often sojourn here. Each year millions of birds funnel through the Klamath Basin on their spring and autumn migrations (see page 121).

Oregon's largest natural lake, Upper Klamath becomes a boating and sailing center in summer. Sports enthusiasts fish for big rainbows in spring-fed tributary creeks and, in autumn, come here for duck and goose hunting. Two canoe trails wind through the fresh-water marsh north of Pelican Bay on the northwest shore of Upper Klamath Lake; all other areas are closed to protect nesting wildlife.

You can pick up a map and information at the U.S. Forest Service district office in Klamath Falls or from the U.S. Fish & Wildlife Service at Klamath Basin National Wildlife Refuge headquarters in Tulelake, California.

Historic Klamath Falls

Settlement of the Klamath country was slowed by conflicts between local Indian tribes and homesteaders, culminating in the Modoc Indian War, 1872–73. In the late 1860s, settlers chose the spot where the mile-long Link River tumbled into Lake Ewauna. From this lake—where you may see pelicans—the Klamath River flows across northern California to the Pacific.

After rail lines linked the town to Weed (in 1909) and Eugene (in the mid-1920s), Klamath Falls grew rapidly

Buffalo may not roam southeastern Oregon, but cattle still do. After the roundup, it's branding time on century-old Alvord Ranch at foot of lofty, snow-crested Steens Mountain.

to become the marketing and distribution center for south-central Oregon's livestock, lumber, and agricultural products.

Reminiscent of this era is the turn-of-the-century Baldwin Hotel Museum at 31 Main Street, a State and National Historic Landmark. Victorian craftsmanship is evident in the leaded stained-glass panel above the entrance and in hand-beveled doors and banisters. The museum is open Tuesday through Saturday from 11 to 5.

Klamath Falls sits on a geothermal "hot seat," atop a subterranean reservoir of high-pressure steam and hot water that was used a century ago by Klamath Indians to cook their food and soothe sore limbs. Several hundred businesses and families located in the "hot springs belt" use geothermal energy to provide clean, inexpensive heat and hot water for their homes, offices, schools, county museum, and community hospital. Hot-water coils beneath the pavement melt snow from city streets.

In late May, Klamath Falls hosts Pow Wow Days, featuring a parade, all-Indian rodeo, and Indian dances.

Klamath County Museum. Exhibits detail the history of the Klamath Basin and its people, geology, and wildlife. A fine display features the Modoc Indian War. Located east of the business district at 1451 Main Street, the museum is open from 9 A.M. to 5 P.M. Tuesday through Saturday, 1 to 5 Sunday. In summer, a restored trolley car makes free loop trips from the museum through the business district.

Indian artifacts and western art. On the west side of the Link River, a splendid museum combines regional Indian crafts and artifacts with art and sculpture by some 300 western artists. The Favell Museum of Western Art and Indian Artifacts, at 125 West Main Street near the bridge, is open Monday through Saturday from 9:30 to 5:30.

Exhibits display artifacts from tribes of the Columbia River Basin and nomadic Plains Indians, woodcarvings from Northwest coastal tribes, pottery and stonework crafted by Southwest Indians, and pre-Columbian artifacts from Mexico. Other displays include arrowhead collections, stone and bone tools, baskets, and beadwork. Paintings, sculpture, and woodcarvings by contemporary western artists are featured in the museum's gallery.

Lakeside parks. Klamath Falls has a pair of pleasant parks overlooking its local lakes. At the foot of Main Street near Lake Ewauna, Veterans Memorial Park has picnic tables and an old locomotive.

Moore Park borders Upper Klamath Lake at the northwestern city limits; drive north to town and take Nevada Avenue west across the river to Lakeshore Drive and the park. The large natural area includes picnic tables, sports and play areas, a nature trail, and a marina. You may spy eagles and hawks resting in the trees.

Riverside nature trail. A ¾-mile trail along the Link River lets you combine birdwatching with a glimpse of history. Beginning just behind the Favell Museum parking lot near West Main Street, the trail follows an old roadbed along the river's south bank. Indians once camped here, near the falls that cascaded into Lake Ewauna. Thickets provide cover for small birds and pheasants; wild geese, ducks, and other migrating waterfowl use the river as a resting place.

Agricultural valleys

Southeast of Klamath Falls, the Lost River meanders through some of the Klamath Basin's most productive agricultural valleys. Potatoes, barley, and oats are raised here, along with livestock.

Families can picnic and fish at Stevenson County Park on the Lost River, 11 miles east of Klamath Falls. From State Highway 140, roads branch southeast from Olene to the Poe Valley and from Dairy toward Bonanza and the Langell Valley. State Highway 39 follows the river southeast to Merrill, site of the Klamath Basin Potato Festival in October. Malin's showplace is Malin Park, with picnic tables and a swimming pool.

Across the Plateau

Three main routes cross southeastern Oregon's broad and lonely plateau, connecting U.S. Highways 97 and 395. U.S. Highway 20 heads southeast from Bend toward Burns. State Highway 31 follows a route traveled by John Charles Fremont and Kit Carson in 1843. The Winnemucca to the Sea Highway (State 140) parallels the state's southern border.

Eastward to Burns

U.S. 20 offers few diversions as it cuts southeast from Bend across the high plateau toward Burns. You drive almost without interruption through miles and miles of sagebrush plateau. Now and then a country road branches off into lonely grazing lands, and occasionally a butte rises abruptly from the plateau.

SOUTH-CENTRAL OREGON

In summer it's a long, hot trip. Temperatures may reach 100° in the shade—and there's little shade. You can plan ahead, though, to take advantage of roadside rest areas at Brothers Oasis, 43 miles east of Bend; at Sagehen, 16 miles west of Burns; and at Buchanan Springs, 24 miles east of Burns.

The Fremont Highway

State 31 cuts diagonally across Lake County's semiarid high plateau from La Pine on U.S. 97 to Valley Falls on U.S. 395. Probably the most interesting of the roads across the high desert, it was named in honor of John C. Fremont. As a 30-year-old Army lieutenant, he brought his party of explorers—including scout Kit Carson—over much of this route in the winter of 1843.

Scenery varies from corridors of ponderosa pine to high rocky passes offering sweeping views of distant valleys. Yellow daisies speckle the sagebrush-covered hills in late spring, and the lakes—which recede in summer—are surrounded by meadows. State rest areas are located near the turnoff to Fort Rock and near the community of Summer Lake. You can detour to picnic at Fort Rock State Monument or to camp in Fremont National Forest.

Remnants of ancient volcanos and prehistoric lakes mark this sparsely settled land. Side roads from U.S. 20 lead to unusual geologic sites. Fossils and Indian artifacts lurk here, but the gathering of archeological materials (including fossils and arrowheads) on Federal lands is prohibited unless authorized by a Federal permit.

A pair of explosion craters—Big Hole and Hole-in-the-Ground—hollowed by volcanic forces punctures the plateau about 20 miles southeast of La Pine.

Fort Rock State Monument features a remnant of an ancient volcano, a gigantic crescent of rock rimming a natural desert amphitheater. Artifacts found here indicate that prehistoric hunters inhabited one of the caves near the rock's base, which once bordered an ancient lake.

Another side road leads toward Table Rock, a 5,630-foot butte with a great view, and on to the isolated desert retirement settlement of Christmas Valley. Primitive roads continue to Fossil Lake, site of outstanding fossil discoveries a century ago, and to the drifting sand dunes that envelop the ancient pines of Lost Forest.

Southeast of the community of Silver Lake are several shallow lakes and marshes, all that remains of prehistoric landlocked lakes that once filled these valleys. In autumn and winter, hunters seek migratory waterfowl and upland game birds in marsh lands near the highway.

Largest community along this route is Paisley, which originated in the 1870s as a stockman's town and still serves Lake County ranchers. About 10 miles south, ancient beach markings on the hills indicate former shorelines of Lake Chewaucan, which covered this country in Pleistocene times.

Into Fremont National Forest

Logging roads provide access to the pine forests and inviting lakes and streams of Fremont National Forest. By June the roads are passable for automobiles. Except during autumn hunting season, you'll probably have the

BIRDWATCHING ON THE PACIFIC FLYWAY

One of the greatest congregations of migratory waterfowl known on earth takes place each spring and autumn as millions of birds move along the Pacific Flyway, funneling into lakes and marshes along the Oregon–California border where they make a major stopover on their migration. Their flight range stretches from north of the Arctic Circle to south of the Mexican border.

Within a 50-mile radius of Klamath Falls, six national wildlife refuges host these varied throngs. Many other birds stop at the lakes and marsh lands of Malheur National Wildlife Refuge, about 30 miles south of Burns.

You'll see birds in any season, but spring and autumn are the liveliest times, when canvasback ducks, whistling swans, pintails, mallards, Canada geese, sandhill cranes, and snowgeese stop on their route. Shorebirds include dowitchers and avocets. Among resident birds to watch for are trumpeter swans, blue herons, owls, hawks, white pelicans, golden eagles, prairie falcons, chukars, quail, ravens, grebes, and egrets. Hundreds of bald eagles winter in the Klamath Basin from December through February. Mammals in the area include mule deer, pronghorn antelope, beaver, coyotes, rabbits, and porcupines.

Each refuge provides a slightly different habitat. You can obtain refuge maps and leaflets describing local birds and mammals at the Klamath Basin refuge headquarters at Tulelake (just south of the Oregon–California border) and at Malheur National Wildlife Refuge headquarters on the south shore of Malheur Lake.

Peak activity occurs from mid-March through June and in October and November. In spring, birds show off their beautiful mating plumage; many birds nest in the marshes. In autumn, skeins of ducks and geese approach in long wavering Vs as they prepare to land, and pheasants whir out from the high roadside grass as you pass.

Bring your binoculars, and borrow extra ones if you can so that more than one party member can watch at a time. If you own a camera with a telephoto lens, use it to obtain close-up photographs. Wear layers of warm clothing and a windbreaker; to avoid alarming the birds, keep colors dull (khaki or straw hues) and avoid flapping belts or scarves. Other items to bring: light rain gear, mosquito repellant, sunglasses, lunch, and drinking water.

Sunset silhouettes Mount McLoughlin and flock of geese coming in for landing on Upper Klamath Lake. National wildlife refuge lies on far side of lake.

Boaters challenge Owyhee River Gorge. Navigable only in spring, river's countless rapids restrict sport to expert oarhandlers.

mile-high campgrounds and fishing lakes almost to yourself. For recreation information stop at a Forest Service ranger station in Lakeview, Silver Lake, Paisley, or Bly.

Near the Silver Lake Ranger Station, forest roads climb south into the northern part of Fremont National Forest to campgrounds beside Silver Creek and Thompson Reservoir, a favorite trout fishing spot. Southwest of Paisley are pine-rimmed Campbell and Deadhorse lakes (no motorboats). More campgrounds are located along the Chewaucan River and Dairy Creek roads. You'll find other popular recreation areas—Dog Lake, Cottonwood Meadows, and Lofton and Drews reservoirs—west of Lakeview.

Deep in the national forest is Gearhart Mountain Wilderness. Rugged, rocky hiking is in store for those who set out to climb 8,634-foot Gearhart Mountain. It's a steady, uphill climb to the top of the rough, glaciated peak. Canyons and ridges radiate from the mountaintop.

Winnemucca to the Sea Highway

Paralleling Oregon's southern border is the Winnemucca to the Sea Highway, a 494-mile road linking major north-south routes and cutting across a rather empty piece of the West. From Crescent City, California, U.S. Highway 199 winds northeast to Grants Pass; travelers continue on Interstate Highway 5 to Medford, then take State 140 through Klamath Falls and Lakeview to Winnemucca, Nevada. More than 300 miles of the route are in Oregon.

From Klamath Falls east to Lakeview the road climbs gradually, crossing three passes above 5,000 feet. About 60 miles east of Klamath Falls, the Sprague River offers good sites to picnic, swim, and fish. Hunters and fishers turn south at Bly to reach the Gerber Reservoir area. The loneliest part of the journey is the 207-mile stretch from Lakeview to Winnemucca across barren high desert, occasionally blessed by unexpected streams and water holes.

Beneath the Abert Rim

In this land of cloudless skies and expansive horizons, oceans of sage and rabbitbrush stretch toward upthrust rimrock buttes and colorful rolling mountains. Often you'll see jackrabbits and coyotes; occasionally an antelope races across a dry lake bed. From Riley on U.S. 20, lonely U.S. 395 veers southwest toward Lakeview.

The small oasis of Wagontire offers a place for travel-weary families to stretch cramped legs. A state rest area is located south of dry Alkali Lake, 61 miles north of Lakeview; its grass provides a refreshing contrast to the gray sage desert. You'll find picnic tables and primitive campsites at Chandler State Wayside south of Valley Falls.

For nearly 20 miles, the highway follows the base of the 30-mile-long Abert Rim, a massive fault scarp looming 2,000 feet above Lake Abert and the Crooked Creek Valley. Looking up, you can see layers of superimposed lava. Shallow Lake Abert is the brackish remnant of an ancient lake; its former shorelines are plainly visible high above the current level.

Hang gliding enthusiasts come to the north and south areas of Abert Rim for routine downwind runs of 22 miles; thermal activity is best during the summer months. Other gliding sites are located in the Warner Mountains. Inquire at the Forest Service or BLM office in Lakeview for more details.

South of Valley Falls, the country softens as sage and alkali flats give way to grazing land, pine trees, and prosperous ranches. Near Lakeview the highway passes "Old Perpetual," Oregon's only continuously spouting geyser; it spurts a 60-foot column of 200° water into the air at 20-second intervals.

Lakeview's western hospitality

Hub and county seat of vast Lake County, Lakeview serves as the marketing and shipping center for some of the state's largest cattle ranches. Mature trees planted by early settlers add a pleasing touch to the town's highway approaches.

Travelers who enjoy the color and excitement of rodeos will find good ones here; a junior rodeo is presented in June, and a major amateur rodeo draws outside contestants during Labor Day weekend as part of the Lake County Fair.

Relics of pioneer days are displayed at the Schminck Museum at 128 South E Street; the museum is open Monday through Saturday afternoons from February through November.

Native plants and wildlife can be seen along Lakeview's nature trail, which begins in the park at Center and D streets.

Lake County's pine-covered ridges and wide-open spaces delight those who come here to fish and hunt. Rockhounds search nearby for agates, petrified wood, jasper, and thundereggs. Water sports enthusiasts head south for 30-mile-long Goose Lake on the Oregon-California border; the shallow lake supports lake trout and is a rest stop for wild Canadian honkers and other migrating waterfowl. Skiers enjoy the powdery slopes at small Warner Valley Ski Area 10 miles northeast of Lakeview off State 140. Many miles of cross-country and marked snowmobile trails are within easy access of Lakeview.

Warner Valley & a wildlife refuge

Northeast of Lakeview, the lush Warner Valley contains several large ranches and a long chain of lakes and marshes—a magnet for waterfowl hunters. Surrounded by large ranches, the little hamlet of Plush serves local ranchers and sports enthusiasts. Anglers head for Hart Lake or nearby Honey Creek. Hunters come here not only for waterfowl, but also for deer, antelope, and game birds. Rockhounds can hunt for sunstones north of Plush.

From the Warner Valley at elevation 4,500 feet, a graded gravel road climbs steeply, winding to the top of Hart Mountain's massive volcanic ridge at 8,065 feet.

Atop the plateau is the Hart Mountain National Antelope Refuge, established in 1936 to protect pronghorn antelope and the more than 300 other wildlife species here. Stop at refuge headquarters for information on road conditions and leaflets describing the area's varied wildlife. Mule deer, antelope, and many smaller mammals browse the plateau, bighorn sheep roam the crags, and migratory waterfowl and upland game birds nest and feed in the Warner Valley.

Cattle Country

The paved highways of southeastern Oregon cut through the heart of range land where the cattle frontier made its last stand. In the mid-19th century, tales of the region's well-watered valleys and grass-covered hills attracted hardy pioneer stockmen—among them John Devine, Henry Miller, and Pete French—who became legendary figures.

Today cowboys still herd white-faced cows on the lonely ranges of Harney and Malheur counties. Small communities such as Drewsey and Diamond are often Saturday night gathering spots for local cowboys. Isolated private ranches remain, but large corporations hold most of the land. Ranching is big business here.

Harney County's population is centered in Burns, the county seat, and neighboring Hines, where a modern lumber mill dominates the community. Local events include Steens Mountain Days in August and the Harney County Fair and Rodeo in early September.

Indian and pioneer artifacts are displayed at the Harney County Historical Museum, 18 West D Street in Burns, from June through September (closed Sundays and Mondays). Burns stands in the center of good fishing and hunting country. Nearby mountain streams yield rainbow trout, and in late summer and fall the county abounds with hunters.

On a side trip south from Burns on State Highway 205 you'll cross Malheur Lake, now Oregon's largest inland body of water. In recent years the lake's size has increased dramatically as unusually large amounts of rain and snowmelt have collected in the closed basin, causing several modest lakes to merge into one large lake. (Three miles of railroad are currently under water, and lake expansion also has brought ecological changes to the fish and bird populations.) Malheur National Wildlife Refuge (see page 121) offers a fascinating look at migratory waterfowl and local wildlife.

From State 205, a side road leads east to Diamond Craters, a small isolated volcanic field.

Frenchglen, a bit of the Old West

Continue south on paved State 205 through the Blitzen Valley to Frenchglen, a hamlet 60 miles south of Burns near the southern end of Malheur National Wildlife Refuge. The settlement is named for Pete French, one of the region's cattle kings. (His round barn, used to break and train horses, is located east of the refuge.)

Reminiscent of a western movie set, Frenchglen has a handful of buildings including a general store and the eight-room Frenchglen Hotel, now protected as a state historic wayside.

Dramatic Steens Mountain

Dominating the Harney plain is Steens Mountain, a giant geologic fault block. Rising high above the sagebrush and sandy grasslands, it stretches some 30 miles north and south and resembles a massive bulge in the earth's crust.

Steens Mountain Summit Road. From Frenchglen, a loop road climbs from the desert valley into cool, aspen-bordered meadows watered by trout-filled streams. Antelope and mule deer roam the western slopes, cattle graze in the high valleys, and game birds rustle in the brush. Remnants of old homesteads stand within sight of the road, and scenic view points overlook deep glacial canyons, stream-fed lakes, and dry, alkali Alvord Lake.

You can explore this country independently or join one of the all-day tours by 12-passenger van operated by Steens Mountain Tours, P.O. Box 351, Burns, OR 97720. Camping facilities are available at Frenchglen or at unimproved BLM sites along the loop road (for information and a map, stop at the BLM office in Burns). Usually the road is free of snow from mid-July through October, but sudden summer storms may make travel temporarily hazardous.

Along the eastern face. A well-maintained gravel road provides access to a handful of remote ranches lying against the sheer eastern side of Steens Mountain. The community of Fields clusters around its general store and one-room schoolhouse; at the turn of the century, it was a prosperous stage and freight station, where mule-drawn wagon trains loaded with borax from the nearby Alvord Valley departed for the railroad shipping point at Winnemucca, Nevada.

Mann and Juniper lakes offer excellent rainbow and cutthroat trout fishing. Mule deer, antelope, and bighorn sheep roam the eastern face of the Steens, and chukar and quail are common in the canyons.

Desert hiking trail. A 130-mile hiking route through Harney County is part of the Oregon state recreational trails system and of the proposed national desert hiking trail. Elevation ranges from 4,000 to more than 9,000 feet.

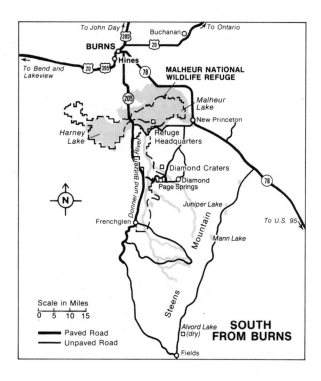

Hikers follow game trails and sheepherders' paths, cross alpine meadows, skirt shallow lakes and marshes, traverse sage-covered plateaus and juniper forest, and pass volcanic craters and lava caves. Some sections are relatively easy to hike; others are difficult and isolated. The trail cuts north from Denio, Nevada, through the Pueblo Mountains to Fields, Oregon, then crosses the Alvord Desert and climbs the east side of Steens Mountain. After descending to the Blitzen River Valley, the trail continues to Frenchglen and the Page Springs Campground, then passes east of the Malheur National Wildlife Refuge and on to Diamond Craters.

Guides for each of the trail's five sections can be purchased from the Desert Trail Association, P.O. Box 589, Burns, OR 97220. More information is available from the BLM office in Burns.

Eastward toward Idaho

Once a tedious 2-day journey by stagecoach over parched hills, the 114 miles between Burns and Vale can be covered today in about 2 hours. Only a few intersecting roads—and still fewer settlements—interrupt the highway as it winds across the plateau.

About 18 miles east of Buchanan Springs, a paved road branches 3 miles north to Drewsey. In the 1880s, this was a lively stagecoach stop called Gouge Eye. Today only a few dozen people remain, and the community's old-fashioned buildings mirror another era.

As you cross into Malheur County, adjust your watch ahead 1 hour to Mountain Standard Time.

With fewer than 100 people, Juntura is the largest community between Burns and Vale. Take a look at the town's quaint railroad depot. The north and south forks of the Malheur River merge at Juntura. Anglers follow gravel roads along the river's north fork to trout-stocked Beulah Reservoir or south to Warm Springs Reservoir. Tall Lombardy poplars mark ranches in small valleys.

At Harper a paved road leads the lonely 12 miles north to the ghost town of Westfall.

Green farm lands

The change from sagebrush-covered hillsides to irrigated farm lands near Vale comes as a surprise. Water, impounded in reservoirs on the Malheur and Owyhee rivers, is diverted by canals to irrigate vast fields of alfalfa, wheat, potatoes, onions, sugar beets, corn, mint, and other crops. Lakes formed behind the region's dams are popular for fishing, boating, and water-skiing.

Vale, the Malheur County seat, and its larger neighbors, Ontario and Nyssa, are the regional trading and population centers, with several converging roads. In addition to supporting a diversified agriculture, Malheur County leads Oregon's beef production and has a major dairy industry as well. Ranchers sell livestock at weekly auctions in Vale.

Tree-shaded community parks in both towns provide recreation centers for residents and rest stops for visitors. Treasure Valley Community College in Ontario arranges most local cultural activities and offers a variety of special-interest and vocational programs.

Vale hosts several rodeos and special Fourth of July festivities. Ontario's Japanese-American community celebrates an Obon Festival in July, and in mid-August county residents gather in Ontario for Malheur County Fair activities.

Oregon's Desert Corner

From the irrigated crop lands in northern Malheur County, paved roads lead south toward the rugged desert, a land of solitude where wild horses still roam free. The Owyhee River flows northward, cutting a spectacular canyon through red rock country before broadening into Lake Owyhee.

This is prime rockhounding country. In early June collectors from all over the United States gather in Nyssa for the 5-day Thunderegg Days celebration. Local rockhounds lead field trips in search of thundereggs, agate, petrified wood, and picture jasper.

For information on backcountry road conditions and river expedition operators, contact the BLM office in Vale.

Boating on the Owyhee

Keystone of the massive Owyhee irrigation project is Owyhee Dam, 33 miles southwest of Nyssa. Bordered by rainbow-colored cliffs, Lake Owyhee is a desert oasis.

Accommodations, supplies, and boat and houseboat rentals are available at the lakeside resort. You can arrange to explore some of the lake's rugged side canyons, at their most spectacular in spring. Lake Owyhee State Park, on the eastern shore, has camping and picnicking sites and a boat ramp. Anglers pull in crappie, bass, trout, and catfish.

One of the least-known river runs in the West is the trip down the Owyhee, navigable only in spring, through an awesome gorge in Oregon's remote southeastern corner. Most boat trips begin near Rome, on U.S. Highway 95, and end near Lake Owyhee. The 5-day excursion covers more than 50 miles.

Scenery along the river is spectacular. The Owyhee flows—sometimes gliding quietly, sometimes tumbling in white water rapids—between the sheer walls of a 1,000-foot chasm. Rock spires, balanced rocks, and multicolored geological formations attest to eons of wind and water erosion. Occasional slopes along the river are verdant with grass and bright with wildflowers. You may glimpse deer, coyotes, wild horses, beavers, or otters. Wild ducks and geese nest along the river; a golden eagle may soar overhead. Petroglyphs in the canyon's rock walls mark ancient Indian camps.

Canyon country

Relatively few Oregonians and visitors explore the stark yet colorful canyon country a few miles west of the Idaho border. In May, except in especially dry years, the hillsides and valleys of this canyon region are bright with wildflowers—yellow arrowleaf balsamroot, pink phlox, bright red Indian paintbrush, white serviceberry, and purplish blue camas.

Rockhounds come here seeking prime rock specimens—thundereggs, petrified wood, jasper, and agates. Succor Creek Canyon is the main hunting ground for thundereggs, one of the most distinctive and sought-after stones. Knobby and round, these agate-filled nodules reveal beautiful designs when cut and polished.

Other good rockhounding areas are Leslie Gulch Canyon, Painted Canyon, and Dry Creek. Agates and petrified wood have been found north of Jordan Valley. The BLM district office in Vale and the Ontario and Nyssa chambers of commerce issue maps marking the region's popular rockhounding areas.

Succor Creek Canyon. About 8 miles south of Adrian, an improved gravel road branches off State Highway 201. From rolling hills and sagebrush plains you enter Succor Creek Canyon, whose rocky walls rise steeply toward brilliant blue sky. Eagles nest in overhanging rocks.

The road was once a stagecoach route. One station, now marked only by several rose bushes and trees, was located near the site of Succor Creek State Recreation Area. Campsites, picnic tables, and drinking water are available here. Another stage station was at Rockville, 16 miles farther up the canyon. The stage road continued south from Jordan Valley to San Francisco.

On hot summer days, the canyon's cool beauty is reason enough for a detour. On its way north to join the Snake River, Succor Creek has sliced well into the multicolored canyon walls. Though the scenic all-weather road is lightly traveled, you will usually find someone poking

about—hunting for thundereggs, taking photographs, painting, or even fishing—though fishing is usually wasted effort.

Leslie Gulch. Approximately 7 miles south of Succor Creek Canyon, another improved gravel road branches westward, winding about 14 miles through rugged mountains down to the southeastern shore of Lake Owyhee. Wild horses and bighorn sheep still roam there.

The final 10 miles of the road are the most spectacular: in subdued light or bright sunshine the volcanic tuff cliffs become a palette of changing colors—soft lavenders, beiges, grays, vivid reds, umber, and gold. Some formations gleam as if polished. Though the canyon has not been extensively explored, Indian writings and artifacts have been found. Down at the lake's edge, you can fish or launch small boats.

Basques settle the Jordan Valley

About 1890, Basques settled in Oregon's Jordan Valley and other communities near the Oregon-Idaho border. From their homes in the Spanish and French Pyrenees, they brought their own cultural traditions—a unique language, lively music and folk dances, regional foods, and the sport of *pelota*, a game similar to handball. Some of the newcomers became sheepmen; others worked as stonemasons, miners, merchants, or hotel keepers.

Many second and third-generation Basques still live in the region, and they congregate occasionally for folk dancing in winter, at the Jordan Valley rodeo in mid-May, and for the Basque picnic in Boise, Idaho, in late July. Many are members of the Basque Center in Boise, which carries on Basque dancing, language, and traditions.

For many years local Basques played pelota on the handhewn stone *frontone* (ball court) in the town of Jordan Valley; the court has now been deeded to the Oregon Historical Society. Nostalgia fans will enjoy a stop at the drug store in Jordan Valley, where antique bottles and other old items are displayed amid modern merchandise.

Near Jordan Valley, side roads branch to several unusual geologic sites. Get detailed directions in town before you set out; perhaps you can arrange to tour the region with a local driver-guide.

About 8 miles north of Jordan Valley, an unpaved road leads west from U.S. 95 along Cow Creek. Eleven miles from the highway the road forks. The left route goes south to Cow Lakes, formed when lava blocked the flow of the creek. You'll find a primitive BLM campground and boat camp at Cow Lakes, where bullhead catfish, bass, and crappies are abundant. The right branch continues northwest to Jordan Craters, a dark and intriguing lava field where several small volcanic cones surround a larger one. Five miles beyond the craters, a pasture gate crosses the county road on the brink of Owyhee Canyon, where you look down on a chaos of buttes and canyons.

Southwest of Jordan Valley at Rome, an unpaved road heads north from U.S. 95 about 3 miles to the Walls (or Pillars) of Rome. Mile-long walls of eroded lake sediments form the vertical sides of a dry tributary canyon of the Owyhee River. From nearly every angle the scene resembles a lost city of antiquity. From the road you walk about 100 yards to the base of the cliffs.

Sunset Proof-of-Purchase
ISBN 0-376-06616-4

Photographers

Ray Atkeson: 7 bottom, 43 top and bottom left, 59 top, 114 top, 119, 122. **Jon Brenneis:** 98 top. **Bob/Virginia Brunner:** 51 bottom left. **Willard Clay:** 46 bottom left. **Ed Cooper:** 38, 43 bottom right. **Frances Cox:** 46 bottom left. **Ed Cooper:** 38, 43 bottom right. **Frances Cox:** 46 bottom left. **David Falconer:** 15 right, 23 bottom, 67 bottom left, back cover. **Philip Hyde:** 91 top. **Hank Kranzler:** 78. **Russell Lamb:** 2, 7 top left, 10, 18 top left, 35 bottom, 51 top, 86, 91 bottom, 94 top, 98 bottom left, 103, 114 bottom. **Hal Lauritzen:** 15 bottom, 23 top, 46 top, 51 bottom right, 62 top. **Luther Linkhart:** 106. **William D. McKinney:** 7 top right, 26, 31 top, 94 bottom. **Don Normark:** 75 top and bottom right. **Oregon State Tourism Division:** 18 top right, 67 bottom right, 70, 98 bottom right, 111, **Norman A. Plate:** 54. **Ted Streshinsky:** 62 bottom. **Steve Terrill:** 18 bottom, 31 bottom, 59 bottom, 83. **Michael S. Thompson:** 15 top left, 62 bottom, 67 top, 75 bottom left. **Paul Wheeler:** 35 top. **Doug Wilson:** 46 bottom right.